Equality and Opportunity

Egalitarians have traditionally been suspicious of equality of opportunity. But the past twenty-five years or so have seen a sea-change in egalitarian thinking about that concept. 'Luck egalitarians' such as G. A. Cohen, Richard Arneson, and John Roemer have paved a new way of thinking about equality of opportunity, and infused it with radical egalitarian content. In this book, Shlomi Segall brings together these developments in egalitarian theory and offers a comprehensive account of 'radical equality of opportunity'.

Radical equality of opportunity (EOp) differs from more traditional conceptions on several dimensions. Most notably, while other accounts of equality of opportunity strive to neutralize legal and/or socio-economic obstacles to one's opportunity-set, the radical account also seeks to remove natural ones. Radical EOp, then, aims at neutralizing all obstacles that lie outside individuals' control. This has far-reaching implications, and the book is devoted to exploring and defending them.

The book touches on four main themes. First, it locates the ideal of radical EOp within egalitarian distributive justice. Segall advances three claims in particular: that we ought to be concerned with equality in individual holdings (rather than merely social relations); that we ought to be bothered, as egalitarians, with unequal outcomes, and never equal ones; and that we ought to be concerned with disadvantages the absolute (rather than relative) badness of which the agent could not have controlled. Second, the book applies the concept of radical equality of opportunity to office and hiring. It demonstrates that radical EOp yields an attractive account both with regard to justice in the allocation of jobs on the one hand, and discrimination, on the other. Third, the book offers an account of radical EOp in education and upbringing. Segall tries to defend there the rather radical implications of the account, namely that it may hold children responsible for their choices, and that it places quite demanding requirements on parents. Finally, the book develops an account of radical equality of opportunity for health, to rival Norman Daniels's Rawlsian account. The proposed account is distinguished in the parity that it creates between social and natural causes of ill health.

Equality and Opportunity

Shlomi Segall

OXFORD
UNIVERSITY PRESS

OXFORD
UNIVERSITY PRESS

Great Clarendon Street, Oxford, OX2 6DP,
United Kingdom

Oxford University Press is a department of the University of Oxford.
It furthers the University's objective of excellence in research, scholarship,
and education by publishing worldwide. Oxford is a registered trade mark of
Oxford University Press in the UK and in certain other countries

First published 2013
First published in paperback 2015

Published in the United States of America by Oxford University Press
198 Madison Avenue, New York, NY 10016, United States of America

British Library Cataloguing in Publication Data

Data available

Library of Congress Cataloging in Publication Data

Data available

ISBN 978–0–19–966181–7 (Hbk.)
ISBN 978–0–19–871366–1 (Pbk.)

For Timka

Preface

I have been thinking about equality of opportunity for a while now, in fact for longer than I have realized. I did not always know I was thinking of equality of opportunity because like many other students of egalitarianism, I have been discouraged from doing so. Equality of opportunity, my Oxford training in political philosophy has taught me, is the ugly, right-wing, sister of equality. But gradually, while working on luck egalitarian justice, and with the help of the work of Dick Arneson, Jerry Cohen, and John Roemer, I have come to realize the centrality of equality of opportunity to egalitarian thought. More specifically, I came to appreciate the important role, and the attractive implications of equality of opportunity within a leftist (some say, socialist), radical, luck-sensitive account of egalitarian justice.

One of the first venues in which I tested these ideas was a seminar (of the same name as this book) that I gave at my university. My first thanks, then, go to my students. I should also like to thank participants in the Jerusalem Political Philosophy Seminar, the Law and Philosophy Seminar (both at the Hebrew University); the *Brocher Summer Academy in Measurement and Ethical Evaluation of Health Inequalities* in Geneva; the *Priority-Setting in Health Care* workshop at the Karolinska Institute, Stockholm; the Philosophy Department Seminar at McGill; the participants of the *Frontiers of Political Philosophy* workshop in Campinho, Portugal; the *Workshop on Justice in Hiring* in the Université Catholique de Louvain; and the conference on *Justice, Luck, and Responsibility in Health Care* at the Katholieke Universiteit Leuven, where I have presented some of the ideas in this book.

I am fortunate to be part of a community of political philosophers, and this book has benefited immensely from generous feedback from members of that community. I am grateful to Avner de-Shalit, David Enoch, Axel Gosseries, Alon Harel, Dan Hausman, Iwao Hirose, Piki Ish-Shalom, Niklas Juth, Carl Knight, Ori Lev, Andrew Mason, Roberto Merrill,

Iddo Porat, Adina Preda, Efrat Ram-Tiktin, Orsolya Reich, Yonathan Reshef, Ram Rivlin, Daniel Sabbagh, Christian Schemmel, Re'em Segev, Adam Swift, and Nicholas Vrousalis for helpful comments and suggestions. I am especially indebted to Gustaf Arrhenius, Dani Attas, Nir Eyal, Kasper-Lippert-Rasmussen, Daniel Schwartz, Zofia Stemplowska, and Kristin Voigt who read and commented on most or all of the manuscript. The late Jerry Cohen has provided hand-written, barely legible, extremely useful feedback on a predecessor of Chapter 3, but his influence and inspiration presides over the entire manuscript.

Some of the chapters in the book make use of previously published material, and I am thankful to the editors of these journals and volumes for allowing me to draw on it. Chapter 2 draws on 'Why Egalitarians Should Not Care about Equality', *Ethical Theory and Moral Practice* 15 (4) (2012), 326–34. Chapters 4 and 5 build on 'What's So Bad about Discrimination?' *Utilitas* 24 (1) (2012), 82–100; and 'Should the Best Qualified Be Appointed?' *The Journal of Moral Philosophy* 9 (1) (2012), 31–54. Chapter 7 is a revised version of 'If you're a Luck Egalitarian, How Come you Read Bedtime Stories to Your Children?' *Critical Review of International Social and Political Philosophy* 14 (1) (2011), 23–40. Chapter 9 has a predecessor in Yvonne Dennier, Chris Gastmans, and Antoon Vandevelde (eds), *Justice, Luck, and Responsibility in Health Care* (Dordrecht: Springer, 2013), 43–54.

Financial support for this project was provided by the Israeli Science Foundation (Grant no. 436/08). I am grateful to Michal Ben Noah, Tani Frank, and Daphna Perry for their invaluable assistance in researching material for the book. I am also grateful to Peter Momtchiloff, my editor at OUP, for his encouragement and support from the very first moment the idea for the book was pitched to him, and for bringing this idea to fruition. Last, but not least, I want to thank my family for their unconditional support.

Jerusalem, February 2013

Contents

Introduction

Although we now think of it as an essential component of egalitarian justice, for a long time, equality of opportunity was actually thought to be antithetical to the egalitarian ideal. Equality of opportunity, John Rawls wrote, 'means an equal chance to leave the less fortunate behind in the personal quest for influence and social position'.[1] John Schaar similarly wrote: 'Equality of opportunity is really a demand for an equal right and opportunity to become unequal'.[2] But the concept of equality of opportunity has been undergoing a quiet revolution in the past twenty years or so.[3] The work of 'luck egalitarians' such as Richard Arneson, G. A. Cohen, and John Roemer has pioneered a new way of thinking about equality of opportunity, and has infused it with a content that is radically egalitarian. This book is an attempt to provide a comprehensive defence of this new, radical ideal of equality of opportunity.

Radical equality of opportunity (which Cohen sometimes referred to also as 'socialist equality of opportunity')[4] concerns, in a nutshell, the neutralization of bad brute luck. Exploring that ideal is the focus of Part I. This, essentially luck egalitarian, understanding of equality of opportunity (I shall use 'radical' and 'luck egalitarian' interchangeably throughout the book) yields, I want to argue, some attractive implications for social policy, three major areas of which (corresponding to the three latter parts of the book) shall be explored here: hiring, upbringing, and health. These parts of the book are not merely an application of the theory, but are also designed to flesh out some important theoretical aspects of the very concept of

[1] John Rawls, *A Theory of Justice* (Oxford: Oxford University Press, 1971), pp. 106–107.

[2] John Schaar, 'Equality of Opportunity and Beyond', in J. Roland Pennock and J. W. Chapman (eds), *Nomos IX: Equality* (New York: Atherton Press, 1967), p. 238. Cited in Lesley A. Jacobs, *Pursuing Equal Opportunities: The Theory and Practice of Egalitarian Justice* (Cambridge: Cambridge University Press, 2004), p. 48. For a similar view see Peter Singer, *Practical Ethics*, 2nd edition (Cambridge: Cambridge University Press, 1993), p. 39.

[3] For a good review of this process see Andrew Mason, 'Equality of Opportunity, Old and New', *Ethics* 111 (2001), 760–81.

[4] G. A. Cohen, *Why Not Socialism?* (Princeton, NJ and Oxford: Princeton University Press, 2009), p. 17. See also John E. Roemer, 'Jerry Cohen's Why Not Socialism: Some Thoughts', *The Journal of Ethics* 14 (2010), 255–62.

radical equality of opportunity. The part dealing with hiring focuses the discussion on the relation between equality of opportunity and the key concept of discrimination. The third part, concerning education and the family, unpacks the tension between the demands of radical equality of opportunity on the one hand, and the constraints posed by children's moral agency, parental partiality, and familial intimacy, on the other. The fourth and final part, concerning health, highlights, for the most part, the divide between social and natural impediments to equality of opportunity.

This book is about luck egalitarian equality of opportunity, but it does not presume to touch on all things luck egalitarian. There are several topical points of debate among luck egalitarians, and ones that divide luck egalitarians and their (mainly Rawlsian or Relational) critics which this book does not touch on (at least not directly). It is worth pointing these out, if only to get them out of the way. For example, a major sticking point between luck egalitarians concerns the currency of egalitarian justice. On the one hand, Cohen, Arneson, and Roemer prefer the currency of opportunity for welfare (or 'access to advantage', a mixture of welfare and resources, in Cohen's case). On the other hand, Ronald Dworkin, perhaps the father of luck egalitarianism (although he himself rejected the mantle), explicitly endorses the rival currency of resources. For what it is worth, I side with the welfarist camp here, but the book does not engage in that debate. I would like to think that my discussion here can be relevant whichever answer one provides for the 'equality of what' debate. Another pertinent point of debate between luck egalitarians and their critics with which this book does not engage directly concerns the expansion of egalitarian justice beyond the basic structure of society. Although I do address (in Chapter 7) issues of (parental) personal conduct (which typically fall outside the basic structure of society), I do not address the other important topic pertaining to the scope of justice, namely global justice (I only touch on that briefly in Chapter 9). That topic has become in recent years a much-explored source of debate between the typically cosmopolitan luck egalitarians and the typically anti-cosmopolitan Rawlsians.[5] Nevertheless, this book is not about that debate. Finally, an important debate among luck egalitarians, as well as between them and their rivals, concerns the concept of responsibility. When can it be said that a person is responsible

[5] For a recent in-between view, see Kok-Chor Tan, *Justice, Institutions, and Luck: The Site, Ground, and Scope of Equality* (Oxford: Oxford University Press, 2012).

for the consequences of her actions? Although I touch on that question in Chapter 6 (when discussing whether children can be held responsible), for the most part I try, as much as I can, to steer clear of it here. My discussion of radical equality of opportunity assumes, without argument, that we may sometimes hold individuals accountable for certain consequences. That is a loaded assumption to be sure, but since I have nothing interesting to say about it here, I simply bracket it for the sake of argument.

I. Radical Equality of Opportunity

What is radical equality of opportunity? To get a grip on the concept it would be useful (indeed imperative) to contrast it with the two more traditional ideals of equality of opportunity (henceforth EOp), namely, formal and substantive (or 'fair') EOp. *Formal* EOp obtains when there are no legal or otherwise institutional barriers to individuals' ability to pursue careers and other competitive positions (university admission, say). Apartheid and an entrenched caste system, for example, are clear breaches of formal EOp. Since formal EOp essentially boils down to a non-discrimination requirement, it is (almost) never contested. However, most of us do not think that non-discrimination satisfies the concern for EOp. Left liberals recognize that entrenched socio-economic inequalities spell, in effect, unequal access to such positions. To pursue a genuinely equal starting point in the race for careers, the playing field, as it were, must be levelled. Equality at the point of entry will not, then, suffice to guarantee real, *substantive* EOp. This insight was most prominently recognized in Rawls's theory of justice, where his ideal of 'fair equality of opportunity' supplements the formal requirement of 'careers open to talent' with the substantive requirement of providing a 'fair background'.[6] The requirement of fair background can be pursued either early (say, through inheritance tax and publicly subsidized education) or later in life (say, through affirmative action).[7]

---

[6] See Rawls, *A Theory of Justice*, §14, 17. I say that substantive EOp supplements Formal EOp. But of course it is sometimes suggested that the two may clash, namely when the former gives rise to affirmative action, which some see as violating the requirements of formal EOp by actually being discriminatory. In Chapter 5 I shall argue that affirmative action, properly understood, cannot be discriminatory.

[7] Although Rawls himself, I should say, was rather ambiguous about affirmative action. Specifically, he believed it necessary in the interim period, but saw it as incompatible with his 'fair equality of opportunity' in the long term. See Robert S. Taylor, 'Rawlsian Affirmative Action', *Ethics* 119 (2009), 476–506.

Radical EOp incorporates the requirements of formal and substantive EOp, but pushes the ideal of EOp much further. It does so in (at least) three respects. These concern its currency, subject matter, and scope. Consider, first, the issue of *currency*. While substantive EOp seeks to level the playing field by neutralizing socio-economic inequalities, radical EOp supplements that requirement by neutralizing also inequalities that are owed to individuals' natural attributes (their 'natural endowment' as Dworkin put it).[8] The ideal thus holds that individuals should not be disadvantaged by their (inferior) natural endowment (where endowment would encompass both native talent and physical handicap).[9] It follows that while substantive EOp sees the requirements of 'fair background' as concerning fair socio-economic circumstances, on the radical understanding, fair background consists also of an equal starting point with regard to innate talent and health. A second respect in which radical EOp expands the traditional understandings of EOp concerns its *subject matter*. Formal EOp is concerned with avoiding discrimination with regard to benefits and goods allocated by formal and legal institutions. The substantive ideal expands EOp to cover all careers (in the form of jobs and higher education), even when those lie outside the public sector. The radical account, in contrast, extends EOp to other goods, such as health (to be distinguished from health *care*),[10] income, and indeed welfare more generally.[11] On the radical account, then, there is no apparent limit to the type of goods to which EOp applies. While the second distinguishing feature of radical EOp extends its subject matter, a third feature expands its spatial *scope*. The two more traditional accounts of EOp are restricted, more or less, to the public sphere. (Formal EOp is restricted to the formal and legal institutions, whereas substantive EOp encompasses also civil society, as it were.) On these accounts, one does not undermine EOp (or discriminates) if one favours individuals of one's own race in one's choices of who to rent one's

---

[8] Ronald Dworkin, *Sovereign Virtue: The Theory and Practice of Equality* (Cambridge, MA: Harvard University Press, 2000), p. 89.

[9] This, obviously, does not reduce radical equality of opportunity to equality of outcome, for it allows for individuals' lots to differ according to their effort. See John E. Roemer, 'Defending Equality of Opportunity', *The Monist* 86 (2003), p. 272. Cf. Janet Radcliffe Richards, 'Equality of Opportunity', *Ratio* 10 (1997), p. 254.

[10] See for example, John E. Roemer, *Equality of Opportunity* (Cambridge, MA and London: Harvard University Press, 1998), ch. 8.

[11] See Richard J. Arneson, 'Equality of Opportunity for Welfare', *Philosophical Studies* 56 (1989), 77–93.

apartment to, who to invite over for a dinner party, not to mention who to marry. Equally, for a university to charge foreign students a higher tuition fee (than what it would charge domestic students) is no breach of EOp for the champion of formal and substantive EOp. These more traditional (and minimal) accounts thus locate EOp somewhere between the global and the private sphere. The radical ideal extends EOp both upwards and downwards, as it were. It expands it, on the one hand, to the so-called private sphere (as I discuss in Chapter 7), and, on the other hand, to the global sphere. To illustrate, the fact that a baby girl born in Japan can expect a life of almost double (86) the length of a boy born in Malawi (44)[12] is (among other moral failures) a breach of equality of opportunity on the radical reading. (I touch on this in the final chapter.)

I have contrasted radical EOp with the two more traditional accounts of EOp, namely formal and substantive EOp. But there is actually a fourth type of EOp which is arguably even more radical than 'radical EOp'. I refer, of course, to EOp by lottery, which is sometimes referred to as *total* EOp.[13] Now, total EOp may seem more radical than radical EOp and as such perhaps more desirable (at least for luck egalitarians).[14] But it is easy to see that this is not the case. If radical EOp neutralizes all obstacles to equality apart from choice, total EOp neutralizes also the impact of choice (hence, 'total'). But it does so, obviously, by allowing luck to affect outcomes. It is for that reason that radical EOp is distinctly more attractive: it decrees that individuals' well-being should depend as little as possible on arbitrary factors, such as luck. Radical EOp would thus not appeal to lotteries (at least not as engines of justice).

The distinction between radical and total EOp is rather straightforward (one sees luck as hindrance to justice, the other as its very engine), and yet confusing the two, we shall see in various places along the book, accounts for more than a few objections to luck egalitarian EOp. Just to give a taste of that, consider the following. In his much-cited book, James Fishkin notes that equality of opportunity cannot be our sole moral concern (something which I do not dispute). For if it was, we should have

---

[12] WHO Health Report 2011. <http://www.who.int/whosis/whostat/2011/en/index.html>. The figures are for life expectancy at birth for 2009.

[13] Barbara Goodwin, *Justice by Lottery* (Exeter: Imprint, 2005).

[14] Peter Stone seems to hold that view. *The Luck of the Draw: The Role of Lotteries in Decision Making* (New York: Oxford University Press, 2011), p. 114.

been content with a lottery that swapped around newly born babies. Fishkin objects to a policy of this sort (I do too!) on the plausible grounds that it violates the autonomy of the family.[15] But one need not invoke the external (to fairness) consideration of familial autonomy in order to reject baby lotteries. Radical EOp allows us to see why such a lottery is undesirable (also) for reasons of egalitarian justice itself. Such a lottery would be wrong, says the radical egalitarian, because it allows avoidable differential luck to affect people's lives.[16]

The point just made helps bring out one final unique feature of radical EOp that I should like to stress. Substantive EOp has traditionally been associated with the notion of *equal chances*. On that (Rawlsian) reading, equality of opportunity obtains when equally talented individuals have equal chances to receive a certain position. Correspondingly, substantive EOp would judge an act of hiring (say) to have entailed no discrimination when it is ascertained that all equally talented applicants had, ex post, equal chances to obtain the job. Radical EOp, in contrast, does not necessitate a comparative assessment of chances (something which is problematic in itself).[17] Since it is concerned with eliminating the differential impact of un-chosen factors, radical EOp may be said to apply when individuals' outcomes are judged to be a matter of equal *choice*. EOp obtains between two individuals, then, when their relative (and potentially unequal) bundles of goods are the product of an identical amount of choice (or effort). The radical conception, in other words, moves EOp *from chance to choice*. This may have some welcome by-products for the application of EOp to social policy, and we shall note some of these in Chapter 8, among others.

Let me end this section by trying to summarize the ideal that this book attempts to defend:

Radical Equality of Opportunity: It is unjust for one to be worse-off, over her lifetime, compared to another, with respect to what ultimately matters to persons (e.g. welfare), to the extent that she is not responsible for being at that absolute level (of the said ultimate good). This ideal holds across political borders, across families and within them, and at all ages. It follows that: (1) justice requires neutralizing

[15] James Fishkin, *Justice, Equal Opportunity, and the Family* (New Haven, CN: Yale University Press, 1984), p. 57. For a more recent account to the same effect see Harry Brighouse and Adam Swift, 'Parents' Rights and the Value of the Family', *Ethics* 177 (2006), 80–108.

[16] See also Richard J. Arneson, 'Luck and Equality', *The Aristotelian Society Supplementary Volume* 75 (2001), p. 81.

[17] See Matt Cavanagh, *Against Equality of Opportunity* (Oxford: Oxford University Press, 2002), pp. 122ff.

all obstacles for which the agent is not responsible, that is, both social and natural; (2) the allocation of less-than-ultimate goods (such as jobs or university slots) is just when it offsets the said unjust inequalities in overall (e.g. in welfare) inequalities.

This ideal entails several contentious features, the argument for which the reader might want to look out for. These include, among others, the claim that unfairness requires outcomes (e.g. the distribution of welfare) inequalities (and never equalities); that the idea investigates one's responsibility for her absolute (rather than relative) level (of welfare, say); and that it applies at all (and I do mean *all*) ages.

II. Plan of the Book

The first three chapters aim to break down the concept of radical equality of opportunity and to identify its proper place within distributive justice (or fairness, I use these interchangeably). The first chapter looks at *equality* itself; the second narrows the focus to equality of *outcomes*; and the third further still to equality of *opportunities* (or, correspondingly, *risks*).

Chapter 1 begins the defence of radical EOp by taking a step back and asking why we ought to be concerned with equality to begin with. Even more specifically, it asks whether the object of equality should be individual holdings of some material good, as luck egalitarians hold, or, in contrast, some social or political relationship, as relational egalitarians hold. The latter typically claim that the quest to equalize some individual material good (be it welfare, resources, capabilities, or other) is misguided (and even counterproductive). The first step in defending radical EOp as part of a theory of egalitarian distributive justice is to defend the luck egalitarian 'materialist' view against this 'relational' view. The argument employed in defence of the materialist position places an emphasis on the demands of *second-person justification*. This is rather surprising because second-person justification is normally held as a hallmark of relational egalitarianism. Nevertheless, I argue that any material inequality, however mundane, calls for a justification. Many, perhaps most, inequalities may actually be justified. But all inequalities (if they are, to begin with, inequalities) are in need of justification.

Given that this book is an attempt to celebrate the ideal of (radical) equality of opportunity it may seem surprising that two of the first three chapters of the book are devoted to actually delimiting the place of EOp within egalitarian justice. Although EOp is often what fairness requires, I claim in Chapter 2 that it is outcomes, and not opportunities, that egalitarians should ultimately care about. More importantly, I argue that egalitarians should be bothered only by unequal outcomes. This may seem trivial, but two controversial conclusions nevertheless follow. First, the suggestion that egalitarians should be bothered only by unequal outcomes implies that they should never be bothered by equal ones, no matter how these came about. And second, I claim that egalitarians are troubled by unequal opportunities only in so far as these lead to unequal outcomes. Defending the first claim is the subject of Chapter 2, whereas defending the second claim is the subject of Chapter 3.

Chapter 3, then, seeks to further narrow our concern with EOp. It starts off from the typical luck egalitarian assertion that a disadvantaged (i.e. unequal) outcome that is traced to the agent's choice is not unjust. Luck egalitarians have in the past decade or so pondered the resulting inequality between lucky and unlucky agents who have taken identical risky decisions (e.g. smokers). That inequality is unjust, some luck egalitarians say, since it is owed to sheer luck rather than choice. (Within the luck egalitarian family those who hold this position are sometimes known as 'Choice egalitarians' or 'All-luck egalitarians'.) But what have curiously received very little attention are inequalities (between lucky and unlucky risk-takers) that could be traced to an initial inequality in ex ante risks. This is well exemplified in the case of smoking. It seems unfair, on the luck egalitarian view, for two smokers to face unequal risks (for contracting a smoking-related disease) when these are due to some difference in their genetic propensity to contract a smoking-related disease. I argue, perhaps contra widespread intuition, that this is not the case. Egalitarian justice, the chapter tries to show, need not pursue equal opportunity to do 'wrong' (i.e. act imprudently), as it were.

Chapters 2 and 3 thus seek to limit the scope of our concern as egalitarians in general, and with equality of opportunity in particular: we should be concerned only with unequal outcomes, and among those, only in those that resulted from unequal opportunities pursuant to prudent conduct.

*   *   *

Careers are usually the first thing that comes to mind when equality of opportunity is invoked. Predictably, there is no shortage of literature (both legal and philosophical) on discrimination and equal opportunity in hiring. Still, understanding equal opportunities along the radical lines may well provide a fresh and attractive perspective on the well-trodden notions of discrimination and meritocracy. The aim of the second part of the book, then, is to present a radical account of EOp in hiring. Chapter 4 begins that defence by first arguing against a prevalent meritocratic view, according to which individuals have a claim to the jobs for which they are best qualified. It then spells out the alternative, luck egalitarian account of justice in hiring. Chapter 5 then addresses a major objection to that account, namely that luck egalitarian justice in hiring may condone discrimination.

The argument proceeds as follows. Chapter 4 puts forward an account that has three components: *non-meritocracy* (individuals do not have a special claim to the jobs for which they are the best qualified), *monism* (jobs have no special status within a theory of justice), and *non-discrimination*. A major objection to this account of justice in hiring is that its three components are in conflict. In particular, the requirements of non-meritocracy and monism on the one hand, may clash with that of non-discrimination, on the other. Chapter 5 attempts to meet that challenge. I argue there that when discrimination is bad (or wrongful) it is so for one and only one reason, namely when and because it exacerbates inequality of opportunity for welfare.[18] The latter, then, is a necessary condition for discrimination. This claim is more controversial than it may initially seem, and I defend it from rival accounts of discrimination (e.g. that the badness of discrimination is rooted in disrespect, prejudice, or desert). I also address some familiar types of discrimination which do not seem, at least not initially, to entail inequality of opportunity (e.g. segregation). If the argument is sound, it will follow that the ideal of radical equality of opportunity in hiring cannot, by definition, lead to discrimination.

* * *

The family's deleterious impact on equality of opportunity has been noted already by Plato. Given the rich and extensive literature on this topic, my inquiry aims only at two quite specific questions that are of particular interest for the exploration of radical EOp. Chapter 6 provides an account of radical EOp in basic education. It looks, rather narrowly, at the requirements of justice for the allocation of educational resources in the classroom. Chapter 7 looks at the tension between EOp and parental prerogative. Recall that one of the distinguishing features of radical EOp is its spatial extension into so-called private spheres. My claim in Chapter 7

---

[18] Or for whatever the ultimate currency of justice is (e.g. resources).

is a defence of such an expansion. But Chapter 6 also stretches the spatial and thematic contours of EOp to its limits, in a way, since it argues, controversially, for applying the *responsibility*-sensitive account of EOp also to children.

Chapter 6, then, argues that *radical* EOp helps us escape the various objections to EOp in education. But it achieves that feat in a rather controversial way, namely by applying EOp to minors. The chapter argues that while we have (obvious) good reasons to resist holding people responsible for decisions they have made as minors, there is no justice-based reason to refrain from doing so. John Roemer's famous 'pragmatic guide for egalitarians' may help realize this. Namely, we may identify a mean standard of conduct for children of a certain age (say with regard to spending time doing homework), and hold accountable (for their failure to do so) anyone falling below that mean. This would allow us to pursue equality of opportunity even between children. Controversial as this may sound, the suggestion has attractive implications for the ideal of EOp in education.

Chapter 7 takes on the clash between EOp and legitimate parental partiality. The sort of radical egalitarian stance that luck egalitarians bring into discussions of EOp force them, some critics say, into some unsavoury conclusions with regard to the family. Since the conception of EOp espoused by luck egalitarians is all-encompassing (rather than being merely 'political'), it would seem to entail severe restrictions on parents' interaction with their children. For example, radical EOp prohibits parents who are affluent and educated from reading bedtime stories to their children, inasmuch as doing so would bestow an advantage. In reply, I show that it *is* intuitive to think of egalitarian justice as being concerned with what better-off parents are allowed or not allowed to do in their interactions with their children. But at the same time, a fuller set of (what Cohen called) rules of regulations may exempt such EOp-upsetting interactions when they are valuable for other important reasons (such as familial intimacy). A parent–child interaction could only be justified, however, after trading off the impact on EOp with the indispensability of the action for a fundamental family relationship. Inequality-generating parental care is *not* a-priori just.

*　*　*

Finally, what does the radical conception of EOp have to say about health? I answer that question in two steps: first, developing and defending an account of radical EOp for health, and second, teasing out an important implication of the latter, namely pursuing affirmative action in health.

Equality of opportunity has been central to thinking of justice in health at least ever since Norman Daniels's pioneering work in that field almost thirty years ago. Daniels's fundamental principle is that of 'health as a means to fair equality of opportunity'. In Chapter 8 I review some decisive objections to that principle, and then defend the alternative, radical application of EOp to the sphere of health. That principle, 'equality of opportunity for health', says that it is unfair for one individual to be worse off, health-wise, compared to another, if this is so due to reasons that are beyond her control. I then defend that principle from two particular objections. These say that EOp for health is false because, first, EOp is suitable for regulating only competitive goods, something which health is patently not (or ought not to be). And second, that EOp for health purports to regulate both social and natural inequalities in access to health, but that this is incoherent. It is allegedly incoherent for the simple reason that there is no such phenomenon as natural inequalities (for there are only, allegedly, social inequalities).

In Chapter 9 I take the principle of EOp for health one step further and introduce the idea of affirmative action in health. We often think of affirmative action in employment and higher education as something that follows from the substantive (and also radical, for that matter) version of EOp. The chapter introduces a similar move with regard to health. I argue, contra Daniels, that affirmative action in health does *not* entail prioritizing patients whose medical condition is the consequence of socially unjust (say, racist) policies. We must not, I claim, prefer those patients to equally needy (worse-off) patients whose condition is the result of mere natural bad luck. Instead, what affirmative action in health entails, I suggest, is prioritizing patients who are ex ante worse-off health-wise (whether this is owed to social *or* natural causes). This suggestion is more controversial than it may initially seem, since it implies, among other things, giving priority to men over women (inasmuch as the former have inferior life expectancy). After defending these conclusions, I end the chapter by discussing the implications of affirmative action in health to the global sphere.

*   *   *

This book seeks to provide a radical account of equality of opportunity, a concept that is increasingly gaining prominence in recent thinking of justice. It examines and unpacks our intuitions with regard to discrimination, educational opportunities, and the disparity in life-expectancy between individuals and groups. If successful, the book will have established radical equality of opportunity as an essential component of egalitarian justice, and as an attractive guide to justice in major areas of social policy.

PART I

Radical Equality of Opportunity

1

Why Equality?

My aim in the next three chapters is to delimit the scope of our concern with equality of opportunity. The present chapter seeks to establish that in as much as we care about equality, it is an egalitarian distribution of some individual good (be it some material good or a state of being), and not merely some social relations, that we ought to strive for. Chapter 2 will then seek to show that once we have identified the object of our material concern, it is only unequal distributions of that currency that we ought to rectify, never equal ones. Chapter 3 will then argue that of those unequal distributions, it is only those that individuals could not have reasonably avoided that are of concern to egalitarian justice.

* * *

Why should we be concerned with equality of personal holdings? That question has become a major point of contention between luck egalitarians and their critics. The former maintain that something that individuals have access to (be it welfare, resources, capabilities, opportunity for welfare, or access to advantage)[1] must be equalized (or maximinized, I bracket here the question of the pattern of distribution). 'Social' or 'Relational' egalitarians, in contrast, claim that this quest is misguided. Egalitarian justice should focus, instead, on the requirements of citizenship itself or, alternatively, on the good of some other social relationship. It is that political relationship that ought to be the object of egalitarian justice, according to Relational Egalitarians, not some individual holding.[2] While Relational Egalitarianism

---

[1] Amartya Sen has famously argued that an answer to the question 'equality of what' already yields an answer to the question 'why equality'. [See *Inequality Reexamined* (Oxford: Clarendon Press, 1992), p. 12.] Here, however, I shall try and treat the latter independently of the former.

[2] Samuel Scheffler writes: '...equality is not, at the most fundamental level, a distributive ideal. It is, instead, an ideal of social and political relations.... it tries to identify the distributive

(henceforth RE)[3] does have important implications with regard to the distribution of particular goods (in as much as this would serve to reduce inequality of relations and the possibility of oppression and domination), it is not an equal distribution (of some personal holding) as such, these philosophers claim, that is the end of equality. The justice of any given state of affairs is judged, then, not by assessing the distribution of the holdings of some good in question, but rather by assessing the quality, as it were, of the relevant socio-political relations.[4]

This debate between RE and Luck Egalitarians (LE) seems to be at an impasse.[5] Luck egalitarians often try and put the point across that while the requirements of equal citizenship are no doubt tremendously important, they do not, by any means, exhaust what egalitarian justice, pure and simple, requires.[6] RE, for their part, typically retort that they do not see the point

principles that are appropriate to a society of equals', *Equality and Tradition: Questions of Value in Moral and Political Theory* (Oxford: Oxford University Press, 2010), p. 7. Also—'Equality, as it is more commonly understood, is not, in the first instance, a distributive ideal, and its aim is not to compensate for misfortune. It is, instead, a moral ideal governing the relations in which people stand to one another' (p. 191). Other relational manifestations can be found in: Elizabeth Anderson, 'What is the Point of Equality?' *Ethics* 109 (1999), 287–337; 'How Should Egalitarians Cope with Market Risks?' *Theoretical Inquiries in Law* 9 (2008), pp. 239–70; David Miller, 'Equality and Justice', in Andrew Mason (ed.), *Ideals of Equality* (Oxford: Blackwell, 1998); Richard Norman, 'The Social Basis of Equality', in that same volume.

   [3] I juxtapose 'Relational' and 'Luck' egalitarians, but one should note that the two are not mutually exclusive. In principle, a luck egalitarian may hold that justice requires neutralizing only the impact of differential brute luck on holdings that affect relationships. So it is possible, at least in principle, to be both a relational and a luck egalitarian. Thomas Nagel and Kok-Chor Tan come, perhaps, the closest to such a position. See Thomas Nagel, 'The Problem with Global Justice', *Philosophy and Public Affairs* 33 (2005), 113–47; Kok-Chor Tan, 'A Defence of Luck Egalitarianism', *The Journal of Philosophy* 105 (2008), 665–90. The position is coherent, I acknowledge, but not necessarily attractive. Christian Schemmel, for example, has shown that Tan's hybrid position makes luck egalitarianism a pale alternative to Anderson's and Scheffler's 'Democratic Equality'. See his 'Luck Egalitarianism as Democratic Reciprocity? A Response to Tan', *The Journal of Philosophy* 109 (2012), 435–48.

   [4] Zofia Stemplowska has a good summary of the differences between the two approaches in 'Responsibility and Respect: Reconciling Two Egalitarian Visions', in Carl Knight and Zofia Stemplowska (eds), *Responsibility and Distributive Justice* (Oxford: Oxford University Press, 2011), pp. 115–35.

   [5] A fact that has been recognized by philosophers in both camps. See Elizabeth Anderson, 'The Fundamental Disagreement between Luck Egalitarians and Relational Egalitarians', *Canadian Journal of Philosophy* 36 (2010), 1–23; Stemplowska, 'Responsibility and Respect', p. 115.

   [6] Alternatively, it has been noted that equality of some social relation is important not because of some 'holistic features of the social compact' but rather because of the personal good that goes with these equal, oppression-free, social relations. Marc Fleurbaey, *Fairness, Responsibility, and Welfare* (Oxford: Oxford University Press, 2008), p. 245.

(indeed, they see fault)[7] in pursuing justice beyond those requirements of ensuring equal citizenship and ending oppression and domination. Why should we care about an inequality of income that might exist between the fabulously rich (Bill Gates and Warren Buffet, say)?[8] Or, why should it be any concern of justice that Mozart is more talented than Salieri?[9]

This chapter is an attempt to answer that question. But I want to note how my focus here differs slightly from other prevalent inquiries into the 'why equality' question. There are at least three related questions which are *not* of concern to me here. First, some philosophers have taken the 'why equality' question to mean: what is it about our common humanity that requires treating individuals as morally equal.[10] That is not my concern here. Rather, my inquiry begins, so to speak, only once we have established who is morally equal, and by virtue of what. Once that question is settled, I ask, what does treating these agents equally mean. Second, it is worth repeating that I do not ask, at least not directly, why we should equalize some good, as opposed to prioritize its distribution to the worse-off, or provide some sufficient level of it.[11] I ask, rather: in as much as we strive for equality of something, why should that something be individuals' holdings (of some good) and not merely some social relation? ('Holdings' should be interpreted here in the widest possible manner, namely the possession both of external material goods, but also internal ones, such as talents, cheerful dispositions, and indeed welfare.) Third and finally, my inquiry is deontic rather than telic. That is, I do not ask, at least not

---

[7] Relational egalitarians claim not only that the luck egalitarian quest for justice is superfluous, but also that it is actually harmful, for example because it requires gathering much information on individuals, thus trampling on their privacy. Luck egalitarians have addressed already these particular claims and I shall not tackle them again here. See my 'In Solidarity with the Imprudent: A Defence of Luck Egalitarianism', *Social Theory and Practice* 33 (2007), 177–98.

[8] Roger Crisp, 'Equality, Priority, and Compassion', *Ethics* 113 (2003), p. 755.

[9] Anderson, 'The Fundamental Disagreement between Luck Egalitarians and Relational Egalitarians', pp. 8–9.

[10] Or as Thomas Nagel puts it: 'What it is in each of us that must be given equal weight'. 'Equality', in his *Mortal Questions* (Cambridge: Cambridge University Press, 1979), p. 112. See also, Ian Carter, 'Respect and the Basis of Equality', *Ethics* 121 (2011), 538–71.

[11] Although it is probably the case that an answer to the question I ask here will determine also the question of pattern. If you happen to think that inequalities in *all* holdings are morally suspect then you are unlikely to think that striving for some level of sufficiency would satisfy what justice requires. Cf. Joseph Raz, *The Morality of Freedom* (Oxford: Oxford University Press, 1986), ch. 9; Harry Frankfurt, 'Equality as a Moral Ideal', *Ethics* 98 (1987), 21–43.

directly, 'why is inequality bad',[12] nor do I ask, correspondingly, 'why is equality good'. I ask, rather, why we must strive for equality, independently of any good-making features it may have. And I ask, correspondingly, why inequality is problematic, and why we ought to curb it, independently of any badness that it might harbour.

The outlines of the specific question I ask are hopefully clearer by now. My aim is to show that the luck egalitarian interpretation of the ideal of equality as requiring the equalization of some personal holding is not 'arbitrary, pointless, and fetishistic'.[13] To meet that charge I employ a rather simple idea (but one whose power to adjudicate between LE and RE has not been fully explored, I think). My suggestion is to look at the requirements of *second-person justification*. The claim is very simple: we owe justification for our advantaged holdings. Some advantages cannot, at the end of the day, be justified, but others can. Some advantages will turn out to be not unjust, whereas others will turn out to be unjust but still (all things considered) excusable. But what all advantages, with no exception, nevertheless call for is a justification. For this reason, all inequalities in holdings (and not merely in relations), should be treated as morally suspect. Crucially, the requirement to justify one's advantage should be compelling for all egalitarians, whether luck- or relational- ones.

I. Disadvantage and Justification

Relational egalitarians claim that in advocating equality between Buffet and Gates and between Mozart and Salieri luck egalitarians betray their misunderstanding of the point of equality. Moreover, these critics also claim, perhaps not unjustly, that the luck egalitarian 'idea that justice requires the equal distribution of *something* is often simply taken for granted as the starting point of discussion'.[14] I hope to commit no such

[12] See for example, Thomas Scanlon, 'The Diversity of Objections to Inequality', in his *The Difficulty of Tolerance: Essays in Political Philosophy* (Cambridge: Cambridge University Press, 2003), pp. 202–18; David Miller, 'Arguments for Equality', *Midwest Studies in Philosophy* 7 (1982), 73–87; Martin O'Neill, 'What Should Egalitarians Believe?' *Philosophy and Public Affairs* 36 (2008), 119–56; Daniel M. Hausman and Matt Waldren, 'Egalitarianism Reconsidered', *Journal of Moral Philosophy* 8 (2011), 567–86.

[13] Scheffler, *Equality and Tradition*, p. 192.

[14] Scheffler, *Equality and Tradition*, p.187. Scheffler may have a point. Cohen, for example, begins his seminal paper on the currency of egalitarian justice by stating that he takes '*for granted* that there is something which justice requires people to have equal amounts of' ['On the Currency of Egalitarian Justice', *Ethics* 99 (1989), p. 906, emphasis added].

sin here, and claim, in response to RE, that the reason why there is a pro tanto requirement to equalize some individual material good is that all advantages, however minute or mundane, must be justified. To the RE's exclaim of 'what is the problem with these inequalities', the luck egalitarian should reply, I suggest, that *any* advantage is morally suspect, and thus must be justified. This gives us a pro tanto reason to equalize *all* holdings. My claim, then, is that we owe justification for any advantage we might possess. To start making sense of this claim I need to explain, first, what I mean by 'justification', second, what I mean by 'advantage' (and 'disadvantage'), and third, to whom that justification is owed.

First, then, by a justification (for an advantage) I mean *a bona fide attempt to provide reasons for why an advantage should not be neutralized.* So when I say that there is a duty to provide a justification I will always mean a duty to provide a *bona fide* justification (as opposed, say, to a sham of a justification). Now, a bona fide justification might, of course, be persuasive and it might not. For the purposes of our discussion here, what is important is that the advantaged person makes a bona fide attempt to provide a justification, and less so whether the justification is ultimately successful. Still, it is worth noting that if a justification is persuasive it will succeed in establishing one of two things. At its best the justification will explain why the advantage is not an unjust one (say, on the luck egalitarian reading, if it fully tracks choice).[15] Less successfully, it will establish that while the advantage is indeed unjust it is nevertheless one that is morally permissible, all things considered (say, if the alternative, equal distribution ends up being worse for all involved).[16] In other words, a justification may show an inequality to be *just* (or not unjust), or it may prove it to be (merely) *justified* (or excused).

Let me, next, say something about 'advantage'. That term refers, simply, to having more of a good and less of a bad.[17] 'Disadvantage', in other words, concerns the relative holding of benefits and burdens. This should be obvious since we are dealing here with equality and not with identity. Tracey having a

---

[15] To put this in Cohen's terms, genuine choice 'excuses' inequality. 'On the Currency of Egalitarian Justice', p. 951.

[16] For a recent formulation of the claim that Rawls's difference principle is indeed such a case of justified injustice, see Thomas Christiano, *The Constitution of Equality: Democratic Authority and its Limits* (Oxford: Oxford University Press, 2008), p. 23.

[17] For a rich account of the concept of disadvantage see Jonathan Wolff and Avner de-Shalit, *Disadvantage* (Oxford: Oxford University Press, 2007). The focus of that book is the multi-dimensionality of disadvantage, which is something I leave aside here.

six-letter name and Grace having a five-letter name makes them different in that respect, but not (necessarily) unequal. This seems rather obvious to me, but unfortunately it is a point in need of stressing. For, critics sometime saddle luck egalitarianism with the implausible view of treating differences and inequalities as one and the same.[18] But this is a caricature. Rather, inequality to begin with obtains with regards to something that *matters*.[19] Now, we may ask, of course, what turns a difference into a disadvantage. There is no easy answer, but the task is not insurmountable. An envy test such as suggested by Ronald Dworkin, for example, may serve to establish that a certain discrepancy constitutes not only a difference but also an inequality.[20] If Jones is shorter than Smith it does not automatically follow that he is also worse-off than him. But if both Jones and Smith prefer to have Smith's height then this indicates, as well as constitutes, that they are unequal with regard to the good of height. Inequality in talent or in genetic makeup is therefore nothing like 'inequality' in freckles, grains of sand, or length of one's surname.[21]

It does follow, however, from my description of disadvantage (and inequality) that it may pertain to the most mundane and negligible goods. If my office is three paces closer to the coffee machine than yours is then,

---

[18] Christiano refers to the length of surname as an example of an inequality that does not matter morally. (*The Constitution of Equality*, p. 34.) Jospeh Raz similarly writes: 'There is no reason to care about inequalities in the distribution of grains of sand..', *The Morality of Freedom*, p. 235. But I think it is a mistake to treat these as inequalities to begin with. Cohen's approach on that matter makes much more sense. One person having more freckles than another constitutes '(in itself) neither an equality nor an inequality'. *On the Currency of Egalitarian Justice, And Other Essays in Political Philosophy* (Princeton and Oxford: Princeton University Press, 2011), p. 117.

[19] Here is a useful test: if it does not matter to the utilitarian that there are more rather than less grains of sand or letters in one's surname then, similarly, it does not matter to the egalitarian that some people have more of these compared to others.

[20] See Ronald Dworkin, *Sovereign Virtue: The Theory and Practice of Equality* (Cambridge, MA: Harvard University Press, 2000), pp. 67–8.

[21] I should perhaps mention that RE are typically suspicious of envy tests (such as Dworkin's). They object partly because they think that the concern of egalitarian justice lies elsewhere, but partly also because they think it manifests 'the ethics of envy'. [See Anderson, 'The Fundamental Disagreement between Luck Egalitarians and Relational Egalitarians', p. 8.] ['To even offer one's envy as a reason to the envied to satisfy one's desire is profoundly disrespectful', Anderson, 'What is the Point of Equality?' p. 307.] But this takes the 'envy' in 'envy test' too literally. Luck egalitarians may (and should) reply that the motives of the agents in question are irrelevant to an external assessment of the state of affairs. So, to use Anderson's example, Salieri's envy in Mozart is, indeed, used as a litmus test for the fact of inequality between them. But what matters is not the attitude of the participants in that thought experiment, but rather the judgement of the external assessor. What motivates (luck) egalitarians, as Temkin puts it, is fairness, not envy. 'Egalitarianism Defended', *Ethics* 113 (2003), p. 769.

it follows, that there is an inequality between us in terms of access to caffeine.[22] You might not be troubled much by this inequality, nor, do we think, should society be required to intervene in order to rectify it. But this does not preclude that an unjust inequality nevertheless obtains between us. Other things being equal, the unequal access to coffee represents an incidence of (local) injustice. Of course, we are surrounded by countless inequalities, and even though they are by default unjust, many of them do not deserve our practical concern. They are simply too mundane. Perhaps more importantly, these small and mundane inequalities might even out in the grand scheme of things, and thus warrant no attention. Still, none of this precludes characterizing a state of affairs as an inequality; as an unjust inequality; and as not requiring intervention, all things considered. Simply put: we have other things to worry about in life besides rectifying all injustices. [Think how many times a day your children cry 'not fair!' (and not always unjustifiably) and go unanswered because it is the large picture that as parents we should be concerned with.]

I have said what I mean by 'justification' and what I mean by 'disadvantage'. Let me now say something about the *duty* to justify a disadvantage. This is important because even if RE accept my account regarding what constitutes disadvantage (or inequality) they are yet to be convinced that these 'inequalities' matter. What is the problem with 'inequalities' in height, distance from coffee machines, musical talent, and even income when it obtains between the fabulously rich?[23] The 'problem', begins the luck egalitarian, is that these inequalities are potentially morally arbitrary.[24] And, morally arbitrary advantages call, at the very least, for a justification. You have the right to ask me why is it right that my office should be closer to the coffee machine, and I have a duty to provide you with a bona fide answer. This duty, note, is not (or not necessarily) a duty of justice, but may be a prior and more basic moral duty. Jones may ask Smith why is it right that he should be shorter than him, and Smith is under a duty to provide him with an answer. Likewise, Warren Buffet must explain to Bill Gates why he should have more money, and Mozart must provide Salieri a justification for his superior musical talent. And, to venture even further, I have a duty to justify to a fourteenth-century Inca peasant (not

---

[22] Larry Temkin gives as a similar example the inequality between his two incredibly fortunate daughters, where the only relevant difference between them is that one finds a 20$ bill once a week, and the other does not. 'Egalitarianism Defended', p. 774.

[23] Dan Hausman, Personal communication.

[24] See also Temkin, 'Egalitarianisn Defended'.

to mention a contemporary Nigerian one)[25] my superior life expectancy and wellbeing.[26] We owe other persons—present, past, and future ones—a justification for our superior holdings.[27]

What is the source of one's duty to justify one's superior holding? Its source, I want to say, goes beyond the need to justify a morally arbitrary state of affairs. For, if it were merely the latter, the presence of a justification, whether provided by the advantaged or by someone else, would have sufficed in alleviating it. Instead, my claim is stronger: superior holdings are not just morally suspicious but actually prompt an interpersonal duty of justification. We may think of the source of this duty as one which follows from our common membership in a justificatory community.[28] One may get a fuller understanding of the nature of that duty by thinking of the implications of breaching it. G. A. Cohen writes (in, admittedly, a slightly narrower context):

What if the agents are actually asked to justify their stance and, for one reason or another, they refuse to do so? Then the argument in question does not necessarily fail the test [the test of interpersonal justification, SS], for it might be that they could justify their stance. But if their reason for refusing to justify it is that they do not think

---

[25]   Philippe Van Parijs, 'Talking to Stanley: What Do We Need for Global Justice to Make Sense', <http://www.uclouvain.be/cps/ucl/doc/etes/documents/Van_Parijs_-_Oxford_1.pdf>.

[26]   See Derek Parfit, 'Equality or Priority?' *The Lindley Lectures* (Lawrence: Kansas, 1991), p. 7; 'Equality and Priority', *Ratio* 10 (1997), p. 214; Hausman and Wladren, 'Rethinking Egalitarianism'; O'Neill, 'What Should Egalitarians Believe?', p. 134. Some may say that irremediable inequalities are not unjust. But I think this is false. Even irremediable inequalities can be compensated. And even when they cannot be compensated it is still useful (not to mention correct) to know that they are unjust, for circumstances may always change. It is even intelligible, I would argue, to depict the inequality in life expectancy and general welfare that exists between myself and a fourteenth-century Inca as unjust. Fanciful as this may seem, it is worthwhile knowing that if we could travel in time we would thereby be compelled to transfer resources to that individual. The RE may say: 'what's the point of that? I am happy to assess this potential injustice once time-travel becomes an option. Until then, please leave me alone.' To that the LE replies: 'Fine, but I gather from your response that you have no objection to me taking the trouble to assess the potential injustice between us and those who lived in the past. You are not prepared to undertake this futile exercise yourself, but you have no (good) objection to others undertaking it.'

[27]   Do I also owe justification of my superior life expectancy to my cat? That question, vexing as it is, is not peculiar to the point I am making here, but to any distributive theory, be it egalitarian, prioritarian, sufficientarian, or utilitarian. See for example, Peter Vallentyne, 'Of Mice and Men: Equality and Animals', in Nils Holtug and Kasper Lippert-Rasmussen (eds), *Egalitarianism: New Essays on the Nature and Value of Equality* (Oxford: Clarendon Press, 2007), 211–37. I therefore allow myself to remain agnostic with regard to it.

[28]   G. A. Cohen, 'Incentives, Inequality, and Community', *The Tanner Lectures on Human Values* 13 (1992), p. 282. See also his, 'Casting the First Stone: Who Can, and Who Can't Condemn the Terrorists', *Royal Institute of Philosophy Supplement* 58 (2006), 113–36.

themselves accountable to their interrogators, that they do not think that they need to provide justification, then they are forswearing community with the rest of us in respect of the policy issue in question. They are asking us to treat them like a set of Martians in the light of whose predictable aggressive, or even benign, behaviour it is wise for us to take certain steps, but whom we should not expect to engage in justificatory dialogue.[29]

To fail to engage in a justificatory dialogue, in other words, is to cast oneself as a Martian; it is to exclude oneself from membership in humankind as a moral community. Notice that this interpersonal test (for assessing the morality of superior holdings) is something that relational egalitarians, given their emphasis on the role of relationships in egalitarianism,[30] should feel compelled by.[31]

II. Justifying Disadvantages

We have a duty to justify our superior personal holdings. A state of affairs that lacks justification, either for its being brought into being, or for the failure to rectify it, is morally suspect. If Jim's answer to Jill regarding why should his office be closer to the coffee machine is 'just so', or 'tough luck', then he has failed in his duty of justification to her. Suppose he instead says something like: 'True, I am closer to the coffee machine, but you are closer to the kitchenette. In the larger scheme of things, the inequalities between us even out'. Or suppose he says: 'I drink more coffee than you, Jill. I make twice as many trips to the coffee machine. I need it more'. Or suppose he says: 'you, Jill, had the first choice of office. How can you complain now about being further away from the coffee machine?' In these cases, I maintain, he *has* met his duty to provide a (bona fide) justification. Now, that does not, of course, mean that any of these justifications is ultimately successful. But that, as I said, is besides the point for the purpose of the fundamental duty to provide a justification.

---

[29] Cohen, 'Incentive, Inequality, and Community', p. 282.

[30] I say 'egalitarian' because RE may already hold that we owe justification also to *non-members*. For example, RE need not deny that we owe a justification to a would-be immigrant for keeping her out of our political community. But this, notice, is not an egalitarian (or equality-inspired) justification. I am grateful to Christian Schemmel for pointing this out to me.

[31] Anderson imputes to luck egalitarians a 'third-person conception of justification'. In this kind of justification, she says, 'the identity of the person making the argument and the identity of her audience are irrelevant for the justification' ('The Fundamental Disagreement', pp. 2–3). My account, if successful, shows that this is not correct.

There are two other types of responses that Jim may provide Jill which are worth mentioning. First, Jim may say that he had no hand in allocating offices; it was their boss's decision. And second, Jim may say that no matter how the office allocation came about, there is nothing now that he can do about it. (Suppose Jill and he are forbidden by their boss from swapping offices or re-locating the espresso machine.) These are also good, bona fide replies (whether or not they are ultimately persuasive). The point I want to stress here, though, is that neither of these reasons *pre-empt* Jim's duty to justify his caffeine-access advantage. One has a duty to justify *any* advantage one might enjoy, independently of whether one is responsible for it, and independently of whether one is in a position to rectify it. These latter concerns will pertain to the particular justification one is able to provide; they are irrelevant for the very duty to provide them.

Agents, then, owe justifications for advantages they have even if they had no control in coming to have them. Gifts are, of course, a primary example. If a large bequest from my parents leads to my being better-off than you, then this leads to an advantage that is in need of a justification. This is a duty that left-liberals will readily recognize. But the inequality generated by gifts goes much further, of course. If Julia bestows the gift of her love on you rather than me, this entitles me to a justification, or so my position compels me to say. This may look (more than) a little curious.[32] But notice two things. First, the justification is owed by you, the advantaged, not by Julia, the benefactor. It is not, then, that lovers should be egalitarians in their choice of objects of affection. Rather, it is that the advantaged owe something, at the very least a justification, to the disadvantaged. And second, the justification owed pertains to your advantaged level of welfare all-things-considered, and not for the particular benefit of being the recipient of another person's affection. It is unfair for me to be unlucky in love *as well as* in a whole range of goods.

Inequalities (once they have been established as inequalities, as opposed to mere differences) are in need of justification, we said. Return now to Anderson's Mozart and Salieri example. Anderson writes that she cannot see in what way the inequality in talent between them can be unfair.[33] Imagining the dialogue between the two may

---

[32] 'To be the object of another's romantic desire may be crucial to a person's happiness. Yet no one owes such desire to the person who longs to be its object. That person suffers unhappiness, not injustice'. Anderson, 'The Fundamental Disagreement', p. 6.

[33] Anderson, 'The Fundamental Disagreement', p. 8.

prove helpful.[34] When Salieri asks his interlocutor to justify his superior talent, Mozart may reply that, indeed, he cannot think of a good reason why he should have superior talent (who can?).[35] But he may add that while this particular inequality between the two of them is indeed unjust, no compensation [or rectification, either by levelling down (crushing one of his fingers) or genetic enhancement (to Salieri)] is called for since Salieri has won more money, influence, and even prestige (in their life time, that is). So things (their welfare, resources, capabilities, or what have you) are perhaps evened out (or even, perhaps, work to Salieri's overall advantage). Whether or not this hypothetical reply by Mozart is actually sound is debatable, but what is relevant here, I said, is that he is under a duty to make a bona fide attempt to justify the fact of his superior talent.

Exchanges of the sort I invite imagining might harbour some difficulties for my argument. Suppose that Gates presses Buffet regarding his (negligibly) superior wealth, and that the latter replies as follows: 'Who are you to talk? You are much better-off than (Richard) Branson'. Does this *tu quoque* response constitute a bona fide justification on Buffet's behalf? Has he met his duty to justify his superior holding? In following Cohen's account of a justificatory dialogue, it may seem that I am committed to answering in the affirmative. (Cohen famously denied the duty of the terrorist to justify her actions to a terrorism victim who, through his acts of oppression, brought about the need for the terrorist's use of violence.)[36] But the case before us is different in an important way. Buffet has no recourse to the *tu quoque* justification because he himself also stands in a relation of advantage to Branson (that is, in addition to his advantage over Gates). By getting rid of his excess wealth, and distributing it to Gates *and* Branson, the inequality between the latter two may well be neutralized. Nothing resembling this option is available to the terrorist/freedom-fighter in his relation to his oppressor.

---

[34] As Anderson also does (p. 9).

[35] Even Rawls wrote: '...we do not deserve (in the sense of moral desert) our place in the distribution of native endowment. This statement is meant as a moral truism. *Who would deny it?*' John Rawls, *Justice as Fairness: A Restatement* (Cambridge, MA: The Belknap Press of Harvard University Press, 2001), p. 74 (emphasis added).

[36] 'Casting the First Stone', p. 122.

III. Does Equality (also) require Justification?

Unequal distributions, then, call for a justification. But shouldn't the same hold also for *equal* ones? If unequal distributions require a justification because they are morally arbitrary, then so is the case, potentially, with equal ones. After all, equalities can also be arbitrary. Think of equally endowed individuals who are showered with equal amounts of manna-from-heaven.[37] If arbitrariness in and of itself was the problem then the choice to leave this equal distribution undisturbed would have called for a justification. This can pose a problem for my account. But I think there is a simple way out. The reason equality does *not*, after all, require justification, is that since no one is better-off than anyone else, there is nobody who is under a duty to justify herself. Nor, perhaps more importantly, is there anyone who is in a position to demand a justification: everyone, after all, is equal.[38]

But isn't this reply itself arbitrary? Why should equality enjoy the privileged status of a moral default? Why may I only demand from you a justification for your advantaged position? Why am I not entitled to ask, in some relevant contexts, why it is right that you should be equal to me? As a matter of historical fact, we may note, individuals have pressed precisely such a demand. Take two obvious examples: following reforms in nineteenth-century Britain, the landed aristocracy may well have pressed a claim that men of no financial means justify why they should have equal voting rights to them. Similarly, male factory workers in 1950s Britain may well have demanded to know why it is right that female employees should receive the same pay cheque. There is nothing unusual, therefore, in a demand to justify one's equal holding. But there is nevertheless an important difference here. In the case of equality it seems right that the

---

[37] Susan L. Hurley, *Justice, Luck, and Knowledge* (Cambridge, MA and London: Harvard University Press, 2003), pp. 151–2.

[38] Which is why I do not find Arneson's claim about the alleged symmetry between luck-induced inequalities and luck-induced equalities to be convincing. [Richard J. Arneson, 'Justice is Not Equality', *Ratio* 21 (2008), p. 388.] More on that alleged symmetry in the next chapter. Now, Christian Schemmel asks: 'why is it only advantaged holdings that one must be called to justify, why not also one's lack of kindness (or any other virtue)?' The previous paragraph provides an answer: The duty in question is not some general duty to justify one's moral character. The duty is to justify one's advantages. The comparative element lies at the heart of the duty canvassed here. (Which is not to deny that there might be other, different moral requirements to answer for one's lack of kindness.)

burden of proof should lie with the person laying the charge.[39] It is plausible to think that to the question 'why should you have equal voting power as me', or 'why do you get the same pay-cheque as me', the proper reply should be 'why the hell not?!' And it is then the task of the challenger to provide reasons (e.g. 'because you work only half as hard as me', 'because you are not a head of a family', etc.). [I personally think there are no such good reasons (see the next chapter), but that, as I said, is beside the point here.] There is therefore an asymmetry between justifying inequality and justifying equality. There is, as Bruce Ackerman says, 'a significant conversational burden upon the opponents of initial equality'.[40] Notice that this asymmetry between justifying equalities and inequalities does not treat equality as some privileged and arbitrary default (contrary to Scheffler's claim). My account successfully explains why: under equality, there is simply no one who is in a position to demand a justification.

Let me say one more thing about justifying equalities (as opposed to inequalities). Notice that my claim that equality requires no justification pertains only to a moral, *inter*personal duty to provide a justification. Matters might be different if we switch to a more fundamental self-regarding duty concerning personal holdings. That is, I want to allow for the possibility that we may be under a more fundamental ethical duty to justify *to ourselves* both our advantaged, but also our equal, position to others.[41] It may be instructive, for example, to ask oneself if it is right for one to have equal (not to mention, more) welfare as Mother Teresa or Aung Sun Suu Kyi. This possibility

---

[39] As Isaiah Berlin writes: 'If I have a cake, and there are ten persons among whom I wish to divide it, then if I give exactly one-tenth to each, this will not...call for justification; whereas if I depart from this principle of equal division I am expected to produce a special reason.' Isaiah Berlin, 'Equality', *Proceedings of the Aristotelian Society* 56 (1956), p. 305. Cited in William E. O'Brian, 'Equality in Law and Philosophy', *Inquiry* 53 (2010), p. 266. Bruce Ackerman equally envisages the following dialogue: 'Since I am at least as good as you are, I should get at least as much of the stuff we both desire—at least until you give me some neutral reason for getting more.' *Social Justice in the Liberal State* (New Haven: Yale University Press, 1980), p. 58.

[40] Ackerman, *Social Justice in the Liberal State*, p. 58.

[41] We each have a duty, Ronald Dworkin has argued, to live our lives purposefully. We must therefore each give account to ourselves about the way we lead our lives. *Justice for Hedgehogs* (Cambridge, MA, and London: The Belknap Press of Harvard University Press, 2011), esp. ch. 9. (See also *Sovereign Virtue*, p. 324.) The duty to justify our actions to ourselves follows from what Dworkin identifies as the principle of self-respect (namely, taking one's own life seriously), and the principle of authenticity (namely, the responsibility to create a life through a coherent narrative that one can endorse). See Dworkin, *Justice for Hedgehogs*, pp. 203–4.

is merely something I want to register here, but since the duty of justification that I discuss is an interpersonal one I shall leave this self-regarding duty aside.

Suppose the RE is convinced by all that I have said so far (it is difficult to see how she wouldn't be). Still, she might mount the following objection. I am willing to accept, she begins, that envy tests can identify disadvantages (albeit in some technical rather than moral sense). And I am even willing to accept that these advantaged positions may call for some interpersonal justification. What I deny, she says, is that any of this makes a jolt of difference to justice. For consider: you yourself (the luck egalitarian) admit that unjustified advantaged positions give us only a pro tanto consideration of justice. The inability to justify Mozart's superior talent gives us, *even on the LE account*, only a pro tanto reason to rectify the state of affairs. It does not give us an all-things-considered reason to act on Salieri's behalf. Thus, your story about justifying disadvantaged positions tells us nothing that we need to know about justice. Let me make a general and a particular point in reply. The general point is a familiar one. The luck egalitarian is wholly un-persuaded by the claim that pro tanto reasons are irrelevant for justice. Consider just one example: although lotteries are without doubt the correct way to allocate a kidney between two equally deserving patients (and with equal prospects of benefit), we may nevertheless think that the resulting (inevitable) inequality is unjust.[42] There is a pro tanto reason to think that the loser in the lottery is unfairly disadvantaged (she is worse-off, namely kidney-less, and through no fault of her own). It would be insane, of course, to refrain from the lottery (and allow the kidney to go to waste) merely on that score. And still, it is useful (never mind true) to note that there is a pro tanto injustice here. For one thing, it allows us to know what to do with the next available resource (be it another kidney, or perhaps, some opera tickets) when it next comes along.[43]

---

[42] John Broome, 'Selecting People Randomly', *Ethics* 95 (1984), p. 45. In another place Broome writes: 'By holding a lottery, each can be given an equal chance of getting the good. This is not a perfect fairness, but it meets the requirement of fairness to some extent.' 'Fairness', *Proceedings of the Aristotelian Society* 91 (1990), p. 98.

[43] Or consider Cohen's example about doctors who are trained at the great expense of the non-American taxpayer, and who then go to ply their trade in California. We may and should deplore them on grounds of justice, but that does not mean we should restrict their freedom of movement ('On the Currency of Egalitarian Justice', p. 239). If you think (as I do) that it is useful to know whether or not these individuals' actions are deplorable from the point of view of justice, even while resolving to do nothing (at least by way of legal means) about it, then it follows that pro tanto concerns of justice do matter. See also Michael Otsuka, 'Equality, Ambition, and Insurance', *Proceedings of the Aristotelian Society* 78 (2004), p. 166.

My other, particular point of response is this. I said that the ambition of this chapter is rather limited to begin with. I have no illusions that, accepting my argument so far, RE would change their view about the nature of justice. My goal here is more modest than that. It is to convince the RE that *if* they ever happened to care about pro tanto reasons of justice, they must then concede that *all* arbitrary disadvantaged positions, including, say, in genetic endowment, should then be a concern for justice. And if so, the burden of proof is on the RE to show why pro tanto injustices do not matter.

IV. Levelling Down and Other Implications

The duty to justify all advantages explains why egalitarians are exercised by inequalities in all holdings, and not merely by inequalities in (some particular) relations. That is perhaps the most important (for my purposes at least) implication of the 'interpersonal justification' account provided here. But it might not be the only one. Allow me to sketch out a few others. One implication follows from the very last point made, concerning whether or not equalities must also be justified (when they are arbitrary). I earlier said that my inquiry into 'why equality' is independent of any good-making features of equality (or bad-making features of inequality). The deontic requirement which I defended here, namely to justify arbitrary advantages, remains agnostic with regards to the goodness of equality. This is important because it means that my account is compatible with the view that *in*equality can also be good (for example when, due to some incentivizing effect, it improves everyone's absolute position). To put this differently: even if a particular equal distribution is not good (whether instrumentally or, less plausibly, intrinsically), and even if inequality is, for some reason, good, my account would require that they be justified nevertheless.[44] In justifying such an inequality, the fact that it happens to be instrumentally good (say, in improving the lot of the worse-off) will indeed be registered. That good-making feature, I said, will determine whether that particular distribution is rendered not unjust to begin with, or unjust yet permissible all things considered. The important point here

---

[44] I therefore do not take a stand here on the view that inequality as such is not a bad thing. For such a view see for example Hausman and Waldren, 'Egalitarianism Reconsidered'.

is that the account's agnosticism with regard to the goodness of equality is consistent with the requirement to justify *all* arbitrary advantages.

Here is a related (and potentially, a second attractive) implication of my account. Much debate among egalitarians concerns the question of whether equality is valuable in itself, or whether it is some other related value that is motivating our concern for equality. Such other value, it has been suggested, might be the concern for the absolute position of the worse-off (prioritarianism),[45] the concern with alleviating misery which we might associate with the position of the worse-off (sufficientarianism),[46] or some quasi-utilitarian concern for welfare.[47] If my account is convincing, then, it would succeed in explaining why we should worry about inequality *as such*, independently of any other value (or disvalue) that it might be associated with. It is inequality itself—not misery; not aggregate welfare; nor the absolute position of the worse-off—that is suspect. Notice that if anything, it is the RE position that might be vulnerable to the objection that its alleged concern for equality is parasitic on some other principle. RE's concern for equality is better explained in terms of community, prevention of oppression and stigma, and concern for democracy. The charge that equality as a value is redundant *might* be true for the RE position; it cannot be true of the position endorsed here.[48]

A third implication concerns the levelling down objection. The objection says that a commitment to equality leads to levelling down, whereby everyone is made worse-off, and that that is an implausible outcome. Some

---

[45] Derek Parfit, 'Equality or Priority'; Arneson, 'Justice is Not Equality'.

[46] Miller, 'Arguments for Equality'; Harry Frankfurt, 'Equality as a Moral Ideal', in Louis P. Pojman and Robert Westermoreland (eds), *Equality: Selected Readings* (New York and Oxford: Oxford University Press, 1997), p. 268.

[47] Raz, *The Morality of Freedom*, pp. 239–40; Christiano, *The Constitution of Equality*, ch. 1.

[48] Consider a variant of the sufficientarian complaint against egalitarianism. Sufficientarians sometimes reason that if there were a maximal level of wellbeing for individuals then an inequality that obtains above that level would be unproblematic. What possible reason could we have to care about inequality of that kind? One strategy in replying to this objection is to challenge the factual premiss on which it is based. Namely, one may claim that there is no limit to human happiness and welfare. Almost any technological innovation we can think of improves our wellbeing, no matter how minutely. (This is Christiano's response: *The Constitution of Equality*, pp. 28–30.) But I don't think this answers the principled point in question. My account provides a different (and better, I think) reply. If improvements above a certain maximal threshold truly do not matter to human welfare then, on my account, differences in them would not, to begin with, constitute inequalities (recall the envy test).

philosophers have responded to that objection by arguing that there is nothing bad, nor anything requiring a justification, in an inequality when the only alternative distributive patterns to it are those in which no one would be better-off. If inequality does not violate, what is sometimes called, 'the principle of personal good' (or 'the person-affecting view') then it cannot possibly be morally troublesome. Thomas Christiano, for example, has argued that the principle of equality need not (and should not) lead to levelling down once it is understood as grounded in a concern for wellbeing.[49] My account sidesteps both the objection and that particular reply to it. It holds, first, that inequalities obtain, to begin with, with respect to something which matters to individuals. Moving from an equal distribution to an unequal Pareto-superior one may make me better-off but it makes me, at the same time, potentially envious of you. The unequal distribution, by definition, makes a difference to the parties. And second, once a distribution has been identified as an inequality (*because* the parties do care about it, indicated by the fact that it makes one of them envious), it calls for a justification, *whether or not* there is a preferable alternative to it.[50] *Any* inequality, therefore, calls for a justification. The fact that a particular inequality happens to improve everyone's lot might show that it is justified all things considered, or even (not my view) that it is not unjust to begin with. But it nevertheless must be justified, and as such it should be of concern to egalitarians.

A fourth and final noteworthy feature of the justificatory account of equality is that it dovetails with some other components of the luck egalitarian credo. Some luck egalitarians (present author included) hold that some inequalities are not bad *at all*. Inequalities that are the result of choice say, the inequality of welfare between yourself and a justly convicted criminal—are not bad at all. There may be all sorts of regrettable aspects to the story of the rightly convicted criminal, but a concern for *equality*—for the *relative* holdings between the two of you—says the

---

[49] He also claims that since his 'principle of equality is partly grounded in a concern for the well-being of each person' it therefore sees levelling down as actually defeating the purpose of equality (and is therefore not vulnerable to it). *The Constitution of Equality*, pp. 37–8.

[50] Notice that levelling down is not only what justice requires, but it is also sometimes that which is required all things considered. In other words, levelling down is not always counterintuitive. This might be the case, for example, with regard to a hypothetical inequality between mortals and immortals (see also Temkin, 'Egalitarianism Defended', p. 781), or between ordinary humans and fabulously enhanced super-humans. See my *Health, Luck, and Justice* (Princeton, NJ: Princeton University Press, 2010), pp. 133–5.

luck egalitarian, is not one of them.[51] If you happen to share that intuition, then, the account offered here successfully explains it. Our concern is with inequalities that are morally arbitrary. If an inequality is purely a result of choice then it ceases to be arbitrary, and as such it is not bad *whatsoever*. Again, it is the fact of inequality, as opposed, say, to the absolute position of the (justly) worse-off person, which is not bad, and importantly, not bad at all.

Conclusion

One should not exaggerate the strength, nor the weakness, of the case made in this chapter. In one way, the case for egalitarianism that I have put forward here is a rather weak one. It says that *in the absence of reasons to the contrary* it is morally wrong to deviate from an equal distribution of holdings. But I have said very little, in this chapter, about the nature of the reasons which may excuse unequal distribution. Indeed, the case as put here is compatible with the view that any reason, however weak, may be sufficient to justify deviations from equality.[52] The case made here is weak in an additional way. I started this chapter by mentioning the impasse between luck egalitarians and their RE critics. I have no illusion, of course, to having breeched it. But I do happen to think that RE ought to feel forced to concede that we do have a duty to justify holdings. Failing that, they must concede, at the very minimum, the claim that luck egalitarians *do* have an account of why the ideal of equality spells out a (prima facie) requirement to equalize individual holdings (and not merely relations). I mentioned that critics portray the luck egalitarian requirement of equalizing individual holdings as 'arbitrary, pointless, and fetishistic—no more compelling than a preference for any other distributive pattern.'[53] My argument sought to meet that challenge. The prima facie requirement to equalize holdings is anything but arbitrary. Luck egalitarianism explains

---

[51]   Temkin, 'Egalitarianism Defended', p. 767.

[52]   Arneson similarly writes: 'At one extreme, one might hold that if one knows nothing at all about a number of persons and one has to allocate goods among them somehow, since there is no basis for treating anyone asymmetrically, a respectful policy is to divide the goods equally across the persons. This *very weak* presumption gives way once any reason at all appears to give more goods to some rather than others.' Arneson, 'Justice is not Equality', p. 384 (emphasis added).

[53]   Scheffler, *Equality and Tradition*, p. 192.

how tackling arbitrary advantages requires the justification of all inequalities. It is that interpersonal requirement which lies, I suggest, at the heart
of the luck egalitarian interpretation of the egalitarian ideal. Rather than
being pointless, curbing morally arbitrary inequalities in holdings is the
very point of equality. If my argument has been persuasive, then, at the
very least it would imply that it is not for LE to explain why justice is so
comprehensive and radical; it is rather for RE to explain why certain disadvantages do not matter for justice. They may well be right, but they nevertheless owe us an explanation.

2

Equality of Outcome

Departures from equality, including from equality in opportunities, must be justified. Still, our ultimate concern, I said in the introduction, should be outcomes, not opportunities.[1] More specifically, it is *only* unequal outcomes that should bother us, I want to argue in this chapter, never equal ones.

I should quickly qualify this. My claim is not that egalitarians may never find equality, or the move towards equality, troubling, for whatever reason. Consider (to invoke an often-used example) the suggestion that we ought to gouge out the eyes of the sighted in the name of equality with the blind. It is unlikely that anyone, including egalitarians, would opt for this particular equal distribution. But the repugnance of this equal distribution (of sight, or the lack thereof) stems from reasons *other than* ones of distributive justice. Indeed, if there is any reason to even begin contemplating such a gruesome suggestion it is precisely *for* reasons of distributive justice. And conversely, the reason sane people (and I include most of my fellow egalitarians in that category) would reject it, all things considered, is precisely for reasons *other than* egalitarian distributive justice (such as a utilitarian consideration for more rather than less human welfare). In short, when I claim that egalitarians should not be bothered by equality, I mean that egalitarians *qua egalitarians* should not be bothered by it, or, in other words, that equality should never bother us *for reasons of justice*.

---

[1] Already this position is controversial. Richard Arneson, whose conception of equality of opportunity I largely follow, writes: '...the duty of the just state is to provide a fair share of opportunity to each citizen, not to guarantee the attainment of a particular pattern of outcomes' [Richard J. Arneson, 'Liberalism, Distributive Subjectivism and Equal Opportunity for Welfare', *Philosophy and Public Affairs* 19 (1990), p. 176]. But we shall see that that statement is compatible with the view that it is still outcomes, rather than opportunities, which is the ultimate concern for egalitarians.

But this formulation of the claim is still in need of qualification. Suppose a car thief and a murderer each gets a six-month jail term. This equality would probably strike many people as unjust.[2] But the reason we feel that way might be owed to something that is peculiar to *retributive* justice.[3] To be precise, then, the claim I want to defend is that equalities can never be unjust for reasons of egalitarian *distributive* justice.

Saying that equality is never worrisome and that only inequalities matter is perhaps not very interesting before one specifies what these inequalities consist of. Doing so, notice, does not require a definitive answer to the famous 'equality of what' question. The equalities and inequalities with which I am concerned here, I want to repeat, are of whatever it is we think matters most. My own favoured answer is 'welfare', but the discussion in this book may equally hold for other potential currencies of egalitarian justice, such as resources or functionings.[4] Henceforth, when I speak of 'outcome equality' I shall refer to equality of that which is of ultimate interest. Notice, though, that one type of currency which this understanding of outcome-equality excludes, and which is of obvious interest to us here, is opportunities. For, whatever we might think of opportunities (for any X) as a currency of egalitarian justice, it does not seem plausible to think of them as of *ultimate* interest to the recipient. In as much as a rational agent has an interest in an opportunity for X, it is surely because she might ultimately have an interest in X itself.[5]

---

[2] Thomas Hurka, 'Desert: Individualistic and Holistic', in Serena Olsaretti (ed.), *Desert and Justice* (Oxford: Oxford University Press, 2003), p. 53; Richard J. Arneson, 'Desert and Equality', in Nils Holtug and Kasper Lippert-Rasmussen (eds), *Egalitarianism: New Essays on the Nature and Value of Equality* (Oxford: Oxford University Press, 2007), p. 283.

[3] There might be several other things going on here, including the concern for legitimate expectations, but that need not detain us.

[4] I say 'functionings' rather than 'capabilities' because the latter already contains in it an element of opportunity. See my discussion of opportunities in the next few sentences.

[5] There may be an interesting distinction here between opportunities and 'freedoms'. (I am grateful to an anonymous referee for pointing this out to me.) It might be true of freedoms that individuals value them independently of their subject. We may care more about the freedom to vote than the actual vote itself. This is manifested in the denial of such freedom. We may be interested in the freedom to burn the national flag even when we have no intention of ever doing so. There are two points to note here, though. One, what is true for liberties might not be true for opportunities more narrowly understood. Second, I do not deny that the denial of the freedom for X might be more important than the denial of X itself. But even then, it is still the case that X in itself matters. Any value in having a freedom for X is necessarily dependent on the value of X. For a somewhat similar account see G. A. Cohen, 'Freedom and Money', *On the Currency of Egalitarian Justice: And Other Essays in Political Philosophy* (Princeton and Oxford: Princeton University Press, 2011), 166–99.

We may understand egalitarian justice, I want to suggest, then, as being concerned solely with outcome inequalities. It is a rather modest claim, I should say. I do not presume to *refute* here the view that egalitarians may condemn equalities as unjust. Rather, I aspire to put forward an egalitarian account according to which equalities are never unjust, and show that this account is coherent, plausible, and attractive.[6] A (not necessarily the only) formulation of egalitarian justice that captures that understanding is the view that *it is unjust when and because one person is worse-off than another through no fault of her own.* This view, noticeably, is agnostic with respect to whether it is just that one is as well-off as another (e.g. when she does not deserve to be). If I am right, and equality can never be unjust, then undeserved (in whatever sense of the term, I elaborate on this in Section III) equalities cannot be considered unjust.

The formulation of egalitarian justice that I just invoked, it is obvious, can be characterized as a luck egalitarian one, but it is by no means the only formulation endorsed by luck egalitarians. Indeed, despite the extensive inquiry into the nature of luck egalitarianism (henceforth LE) in recent years, the question of whether equalities can ever be unjust seems to be curiously under-explored. As I show in Section I, leading luck egalitarians pay little attention to the issue of unjust equalities, and when they do, they appear not to speak in one voice. I begin to examine this very question, in Section II, by employing two rival interpretations of egalitarianism: what we may call *the responsibility view*, which may condemn equalities as unjust (when they reflect unequal levels of personal responsibility or prudence); and, what we may call *the non-responsibility view*, which does not. In Section III I tease out the implications of these two views, in the hope of establishing that the latter is at least as plausible as the former. In Section IV I examine and rebut some residual objections to the claim that equality is never unjust. I conclude that, at the very least, egalitarian distributive justice can be formulated in a way that condemns only (certain) inequalities. One particular advantage of the non-responsibility view over the standard formulation of LE is that it seems to escape Susan

---

[6] Richard Arneson writes that a luck egalitarian can hold both that it is bad that one is worse off than another through no fault of her own, *and* that it is bad that one is as well off as another through no merit of her own ['Justice is Not Equality', *Ratio* 21 (2008), p. 386, for example]. The claim of this is chapter is not that a luck egalitarian cannot hold the latter view, but rather that she shouldn't.

Hurley's distinct critique of luck egalitarianism. I show this in an appendix at the end of this chapter.

I. Unjust Equalities

Some may consider the question I pose in this chapter to be rather trivial. To be an egalitarian, it might be thought, is to be disturbed by inequalities.[7] An egalitarian is someone who believes that inequality is, at least sometimes, bad, and that, at least on those occasions, it ought to be curbed. It is thus trivial that egalitarian justice is undisturbed by equalities. But the picture is obviously more complex than that. For example, on a certain interpretation of John Rawls's Difference Principle (DP), equality may indeed be unjust. Consider two possible distributions A:(2, 2) and B:(4, 3). The DP can be interpreted as saying that it is not only *permissible* to move from A to B, but that it would actually be *unjust* not to do so. The equal distribution (2, 2) is here rendered unjust by the availability of a Pareto superior alternative. Luck egalitarians, however, do not find this claim particularly persuasive, and it is not difficult to see why. We may allow that the Pareto optimal distribution (4, 3) is preferable all things considered; and it is also possible to see how some Rawlsians may arrive (mistakenly) at the conclusion that moving from A to B is *not unjust*; but it is something else entirely to say that for the parties to stay at A rather than move to B is, in any way, *unjust*.[8] But I shall say no more in this chapter about that type of argument for unjust equality, mainly because others (G. A. Cohen in particular) have done so already,[9] and I have nothing to add in that respect.

Whatever the truth is regarding the injustice of Pareto-inferior (and hence allegedly unjust) equalities, we can already see that the question of

---

[7] Of course, there is a brand of egalitarianism, namely Prioritarianism, according to which we need not be disturbed *even* (or also) with *in*equalities. As mentioned in the previous chapter, Derek Parfit has famously questioned whether we ought to be concerned with achieving equality or rather with improving the position of the worse off person [*Equality or Priority?* (Lawrence, KS: University of Kansas Press, 1995)]. But in difference to Parfit, my inquiry here is not concerned with whether equality has any value, but rather with whether it can ever be unjust.

[8] As Thomas Christiano wrongly, I think, seems to suggest. 'A Foundation for Egalitarianism', in Nils Holtug and Kasper Lippert-Rasmussen, *Egalitarianism: New Essays on the Nature and Value of Equality* (Oxford: Oxford University Press, 2007), p. 42.

[9] G. A. Cohen, *Rescuing Justice and Equality* (Cambridge, MA, and London: Harvard University Press, 2008), ch. 2.

whether egalitarians may consider equalities to be unjust is not so trivial as it may initially seem. This is even more so the case when we take on board non-Rawlsian views of egalitarian justice.[10] Whereas for Rawlsians, as we just saw, equalities may be unjust for reasons of Pareto improvement, for non-Rawlsians, and primarily luck egalitarians, they are potentially unjust for reasons of personal responsibility (or prudence).[11] Given how extensive the literature on luck egalitarianism is, it is curious that those philosophers have paid little attention to the issue of unjust equalities. Richard Arneson in his seminal paper, for example, does not address the question explicitly, but his ideal of equality of opportunity for welfare does seem to suggest that the focus is on opportunities rather than on outcomes. 'Equal opportunity for welfare obtains among persons when all of them face equivalent decision trees'.[12] Since two individuals may end up equally situated as a result of two unequal opportunity sets, it follows that outcome equality, according to Arneson, can be unjust.[13] Cohen similarly writes that 'the primary egalitarian impulse is to extinguish the influence *on distribution* of both exploitation and brute luck'.[14] Thus, he allows that egalitarianism may be concerned with extinguishing the effect of brute luck from both inequalities *and* equalities. At one place he says so rather

---

[10] The next two paragraphs elaborate a discussion I started in *Health, Luck, and Justice* (Princeton, NJ: Princeton University Press, 2010), p. 15. In his review of that book, Marc Fleurbaey notes that my argument that equality can never be unjust is the only one in the book which he could not understand ['Review of Shlomi Segall's "Health, Luck, and Justice"', *Utilitas* 22 (2010), p. 504. For a similar worry see Kristi A. Olson, 'Review of Jennifer Prah Ruger's "Health and Social Justice" and Shlomi Segall's "Health, Luck, and Justice"', *Perspectives on Politics* (2012), p. 491]. I hope this chapter will do a better job of explaining it.

[11] Although it is worth pointing out that at some point Rawls also seems to endorse the view that equalities can be unjust for reasons of personal responsibility. He writes, for example, that in a just society, any equality of welfare between those who cultivated expensive tastes and those who have prudently kept their tastes cheap would be unfair. John Rawls, 'Social Unity and Primary Goods', in his *Collected Papers* (Cambridge, MA: Harvard University Press, 1999), pp. 369–70.

[12] Richard J. Arneson, 'Equality and Equal Opportunity for Welfare', in L. P. Pojman and R. Westmoreland (eds), *Equality: Selected Readings* (New York, Oxford: Oxford University Press, 1997), p. 234. See also his 'Liberalism, Distributive Subjectivism and Equal Opportunity for Welfare', p. 178.

[13] The same view is held by Kasper Lippert-Rasmussen, another notable luck egalitarian. He writes that '... *inequality* that reflects differential exercises of responsibility is *less bad* than inequality (and *equality*) that does not reflect differential exercises of responsibility'. 'Egalitarianism, Option Luck, and Responsibility', *Ethics* 111 (2001), p. 549 (my emphasis).

[14] G. A. Cohen, 'On the Currency of Egalitarian Justice', *Ethics* 99 (1989), p. 908 (emphasis added). Similarly, he writes that 'the fundamental egalitarian aim is to extinguish the influence of brute luck *on distribution*' (p. 931, emphasis added).

explicitly: 'People's advantages are unjustly unequal (or equal) when the inequality (or equality) reflects unequal access to advantage, as opposed to patterns of choice against a background of equality of access.'[15]

In a later piece (his response to Susan Hurley) Cohen appears rather explicit and unequivocal on the possibility of unjust equalities. 'So, in deference to fairness, the relevant egalitarian says that she's against inequalities in the absence of appropriately differential responsibility (just as, she now realizes, she is also against equalities in the presence of appropriately differential responsibility).'[16] Moreover, Cohen acknowledges here the curious silence on unjust equalities in the luck egalitarian literature. The passage is worth quoting at length:

> Since there is a-symmetry in the luck egalitarian's attitude to plain, ordinary equality and plain, ordinary inequality—both are bad if and only if they are in disaccord with choice—it might seem that it is not luck but *equality* that plays no role in specifying luck egalitarianism. Why, indeed, is unjust inequality, rather than unjust equality, salient in statements of luck egalitarianism and in luck egalitarian sentiment? For several reasons. First, there is an historical reason: huge inequalities cried out for rectification at the bar of justice, given what was known about their origin. Nothing similar was true of any equalities. Second, there remains in contemporary society typically much more offensive inequality than offensive equality: there are reasons for objecting more strongly to the corporate welfare bum than to the able-bodied plain welfare bum who gets as much as the working stiff does.[17]

Cohen seems to say here that although as a matter of practical concern, inequalities are in need of more urgent rectification than equalities (when both are owed to luck), as a matter of principle, equalities can be as unjust as inequalities (when both are the product of differential luck).[18]

I want, then, to try and defend here the rival view, according to which equalities, even if owed to differential luck, are of no concern to justice.[19] If

---

[15] 'On the Currency of Egalitarian Justice', p. 920.

[16] G. A. Cohen, 'Luck and Equality: A Reply to Hurley', *Philosophy and Phenomenological Research* 72 (2) (2006), p. 444 (original emphasis).

[17] 'Luck and Equality', p. 444 (original emphasis).

[18] In his penultimate book, it is worth noting, Cohen seems to revert back to characterizing luck egalitarianism as concerned only with inequalities: '... what has been called luck egalitarianism, which is the view that identifies distributive justice with an allocation which extinguishes *inequalities* that are due to luck rather than to choice'. *Rescuing Justice and Equality*, p. 300 (emphasis added).

[19] One way of characterizing the debate is as that between those, like Cohen, who think that luck egalitarianism treats equalities and inequalities symmetrically, and my position which treats them asymmetrically. See also Carl Knight, 'Inequality, Avoidability, and Healthcare: On Shlomi Segall "Health, Luck, and Justice"', *Iyyun: The Jerusalem Philosophical Quarterly* 60 (2011), p. 74.

true, it would follow that we should only strive for equality of opportunity when doing so contributes to curbing inequality of outcome. To put this differently, we should only be concerned with *in*equality of opportunity when it leads to inequality of outcome. Notice that I leave aside the question of what pattern of distribution one ought to adopt in rectifying unjust inequalities (be it strict equality, priority, or sufficiency). Here, I simply try to identify what it is that ought to be the object of concern for egalitarians, without specifying what it is that they recommend doing about it.[20]

II. Two (Luck Egalitarian) Views about Responsibility

I have already mentioned that the reason why egalitarians (and luck egalitarians in particular) may think that equalities can be unjust is, probably, that they are bothered by the moral arbitrariness of brute luck. Hence the luck egalitarian view that 'the fundamental egalitarian aim is to extinguish the influence of brute luck on distribution'.[21] Since an equal distribution can also be the result of brute luck, it follows that a concern for the moral arbitrariness of brute luck may lead us to judge equality to be unjust. But it is doubtful, as Susan Hurley has already demonstrated, that this is a plausible egalitarian position.[22] Suppose, for example, that a group of individuals is showered with equal amounts of manna-from-heaven. Presumably, no egalitarian would consider it a requirement of justice to extinguish the impact of brute luck in that case. It does not, therefore, seem plausible for egalitarians to oppose a distribution (including an equal one) simply for being a product of luck. If (luck) egalitarians hold that equalities could be unjust, it is probably because these equalities are the product of *differential* brute luck and not simply the product of luck as such.[23]

---

[20] I acknowledge, nevertheless, that there is probably a strong link between what pattern one finds to be objectionable and what pattern one would advocate as a remedy.

[21] Cohen, 'On the Currency of Egalitarian Justice', p. 931.

[22] S. L. Hurley, *Justice, Luck, and Knowledge* (Cambridge, MA: Harvard University Press, 2004), pp. 151–2. I shall discuss Hurley's critique of luck egalitarianism in more detail in the appendix to this chapter.

[23] See also Peter Vallentyne, 'Hurley on Justice and Responsibility', *Philosophy and Phenomenological Research* 72 (2006), p. 436; Kasper Lippert-Rasmussen, 'Hurley on Egalitarianism and the Luck-Neutralizing Aim', *Politics, Philosophy, and Economics* 4 (2005), p. 254.

The (revised) question before us, then, is whether equalities that are owed to differential brute luck ought to be considered unjust. I want to argue that the answer to that question should be in the negative. (Or, more precisely, that it is possible to answer that question negatively and still provide a coherent and attractive account of egalitarian justice.) To facilitate that argument, I want to employ a distinction (introduced by Christopher Lake)[24] between two alternative egalitarian views of the relation between luck (or its converse, responsibility) and equality. The first view, call it *the responsibility view* of egalitarianism, says that it is unjust for one's relative lot to be determined by factors which are beyond one's control. According to the alternative view, call it the *non-responsibility view*,[25] it is unjust for one's lot to be worse than another's through no fault of one's own. The two views accordingly differ with regard to what they see as the point of egalitarian justice. While the responsibility view is geared toward extinguishing the impact of differential (brute)[26] luck,

---

[24] Christopher Lake, *Equality and Responsibility* (Oxford: Oxford University Press, 2001), p. 12.

[25] Lake, *Equality and Responsibilty*, p. 91. The view may also fall under what Holtug and Lippert-Rasmussen have termed 'responsibility-agnostic egalitarianism'. See their, 'An Introduction to Contemporary Egalitarianism', in their *Egalitarianism: New Essays on the Nature and Value of Equality* (Oxford: Oxford University Press, 2007), p. 20. Samuel Scheffler, in his critique of luck egalitarianism, also offers a distinction which closely mirrors the one employed here. Scheffler distinguishes 'defensive' from 'affirmative' arguments for luck egalitarianism, which somewhat correspond with that between the non-responsibility view and the responsibility view (respectively). See his *Equality and Tradition: Questions of Value in Moral and Political Theory* (Oxford: Oxford University Press, 2010), pp. 212–13. Finally, Elizabeth Anderson, in her critique distinguishes 'desert-catering luck egalitarianism' from 'responsibility-catering luck egalitarianism', which correspond, perhaps with the responsibility and the non-responsibility views. 'How Should Egalitarians Cope with Market Risks?' *Theoretical Inquiries in Law* 9 (2008), p. 240.

[26] I put 'brute' in parenthesis because (as we shall see in more detail in the next chapter) some egalitarians hold the view that all differential luck ought to be neutralized, that is, both brute *and* option luck. See Marc Fleurbaey, 'Egalitarian Opportunities', *Law and Philosophy* 20 (2001): 499–530, esp. pp. 513–22; 'Equal Opportunity or Equal Social Outcome', *Economics and Philosophy* 11 (1995): 25–55; *Fairness, Responsibility, and Welfare* (Oxford: Oxford University Press, 2008); Lippert-Rasmussen, 'Egalitarianism, Option Luck, and Responsibility'; 'Hurley on Egalitarianism and the Luck-Neutralizing Aim', p. 259; Nicholas Barry, 'Reassessing Luck Egalitarianism', *The Journal of Politics* 70 (2008): 136–50; Alexander Cappelen and Bertil Tungodden, 'A Liberal Egalitarian Paradox', *Economics and Philosophy* 22 (2006): 393–408, p. 394; 'Relocating the Responsibility Cut: Should More Responsibility Imply Less Redistribution?' *Politics, Philosophy, & Economics* 5 (2006): 353–62. I find this view to be implausible (see my *Health, Luck, and Justice*, ch. 3), but that debate is irrelevant for the purposes of this chapter, so I shall set it aside here and will revisit it in the next chapter.

the non-responsibility view sees the point of egalitarian distributive justice as extinguishing *disadvantages* that are owed to brute luck. Here is a formulation of how the two views assess the justice or injustice of any given distribution:

- *The Responsibility View*: it is unjust for one to be worse-off than others through no fault of one's own, and it is also unjust that one is equally well-off as others while being comparably less responsible.[27]
- *The Non-Responsibility View*: it is unjust for one to be worse-off than others through no fault of one's own.[28]

Notice that the term 'non-responsibility' is suitable here because while the responsibility view is concerned with rewarding individuals for what they *are* responsible for, the non-responsibility view is concerned, instead, with ridding individuals of bad outcomes for which they are *not* responsible.[29] The difference between the two views can be further captured in the following, not quite precise but rather illustrative, way. The responsibility view, in a sense, says that *the absence of responsibility* triggers a concern with equality (or, more accurately, egalitarian distributive justice). The non-responsibility view, in contrast, says that *the absence of equality* triggers the interest in responsibility.

Now, it is easy to see that the responsibility view may lead to the conclusion that equalities can be unjust (when they do not reflect equal levels of responsibility), whereas the non-responsibility view negates such a possibility (for it talks only about 'being worse-off'). My aim in the rest of this

---

[27] Note that I resist formulating the second half of the principle to read: 'it is unjust that one is equally well off as others through no choice of one's own'. That formulation would have implied that there is something unjust in a scenario in which a person is equal to everyone else despite that person having no choice or say about her situation. I am grateful to Kasper Lippert-Rasmussen for pointing this out to me.

[28] I shall further qualify this principle in the next chapter.

[29] Here is an example of the responsibility view, as advocated by John Roemer: 'Let me state clearly that the moral premiss of the EOp view is that rewards should be sensitive only to the autonomous efforts of individuals.... Thus, strictly speaking, the EOp view is not one whose fundamental primitive is equality: deservingness is fundamental, together with the normative thesis that justified inequality tracks deservingness', 'Defending Equality of Opportunity', *The Monist* 86 (2003), p. 279. And here is a manifestation of the non-responsibility view, as put forward by Nagel: 'What seems bad is not that people should be unequal in advantages or disadvantages generally, but that they should be unequal in the advantages or disadvantages for which they are not responsible'. *Equality and Partiality* (Oxford: Oxford University Press, 1991), p. 71.

chapter, then, is to argue that the non-responsibility view can be defended as a no less (compared to the dominant responsibility view) plausible understanding of egalitarianism. To stress: I do not presume to offer here a refutation of the responsibility view. Rather, I only wish to defend the non-responsibility view—and consequently the view that only inequalities are objectionable—as an (at least) equally valid account of egalitarian justice. To do so I shall examine several hypothetical cases, each allegedly demonstrating the implausibility of the non-responsibility view. I hope to show that none of them succeeds.[30]

III. Is the Non-Responsibility View Counterintuitive?

In fleshing out the differences between the responsibility view and the non-responsibility view, I want to draw attention, in particular, to two dimensions along which these views, or any other egalitarian formulation for that matter, may differ. Call these the dimension of undeserved equalities and the dimension of causality. The former concerns our primary preoccupation here, namely, whether an egalitarian view judges undeserved equalities to be just or not. The latter dimension asks whether egalitarian justice judges a certain distribution as just or unjust when it is simply correlated with a certain pattern of deservingness or, whether it must be causally derived from that deservingness to qualify as just (or unjust).[31] These distinctions, I hope, shall become clearer as we proceed, but for now let us note that there are, prima facie, four distinct positions here (of which only two will concern us),[32] which we may summarize in Table 2.1.

---

[30] Carl Knight elegantly poses the following challenge to me. 'From the luck egalitarian side it can be asked: if we should neutralize brute luck when it results in inequalities, why shouldn't we neutralize it when it results in equalities? From the outcome egalitarian side it can be asked: if we think that equality is important enough that we should allow brute luck-created equalities to stand, why should we let option luck-created inequalities stand?' 'Inequality, Avoidability, and Healthcare', p. 77. The rest of this chapter is, in a way, an attempt to answer this question.

[31] See also Richard J. Arneson, 'Egalitarianism and Responsibility', *The Journal of Ethics* 3 (1999), pp. 230–1.

[32] I am grateful to Kasper Lippert-Rasmussen for helping me clarify this.

Table 2.1 Deserved and undeserved equalities

	Undeserved equalities can be unjust	Undeserved equalities are not unjust
Deservingness matters only when causally related to distribution		The non-responsibility view
Deservingness matters whether or not causally related to distribution	The responsibility view	

I have placed the responsibility and non-responsibility views in what I take to be the appropriate cells. (My choice of cells shall become apparent as we proceed.) In the discussion to follow I shall elaborate on this typology, and argue that, on both dimensions, the non-responsibility view is (at the very least) no less attractive than the responsibility view. If so, the view that egalitarian justice may not condemn equalities, no matter how undeserved, would appear as least as plausible as the rival view.

To see this, consider the following example, fashioned after Peter Vallentyne.[33] Imagine, as egalitarians often do, a desert island. On this island, the leisure of lying about in the sun for a whole day gives one 5 units of welfare, whereas a tasty fish gives one 20 units of welfare. Going out fishing, let us assume, counts as work rather than leisure. (Work has no negative utility, but unlike leisure has no positive utility either.) Prudence and Lazy are two survivors on this island. While Lazy lies on the beach, Prudence goes fishing and returns with a fish which she then proceeds to grill and enjoy on her own. Their respective levels of welfare are now 5 for Lazy (hungry but rested), and 20 for Prudence. The two views of egalitarianism agree that there is nothing unjust about this outcome inequality (call it A). Imagine now that a nice coconut, worth 15 units, rolls up to Lazy who, recall, is simply lying there.[34] This turn of events generates a

---

[33] Peter Vallentyne, 'Brute Luck Equality and Desert', in Serena Olsaretti (ed.), *Desert and Justice* (Oxford: Oxford University Press, 2003), 169–85, p. 176. The following discussion is an elaboration of an example I discussed in *Health, Luck, and Justice*, pp. 17–18.

[34] Of course, the story may be structured a little differently to say that Lazy has in fact taken a gamble that a coconut will roll to her. (Marc Fleurbaey has alerted me to this.) But I assume, as in Vallentyne's equivalent example, that the coconut was pure good *brute* luck. I shall consider a slight variation on this later on.

new distribution (B), whereby both Lazy and Prudence have 20. Is there anything unjust about the new distribution (B)? The responsibility view tells us that there clearly is. The two individuals' equal level of welfare does not reflect their unequal levels of effort. Justice, then, requires that Lazy transfer half of the coconut (or some equivalent of it) to Prudence, to the effect that *in*equality is restored. The resulting distribution is C: (27.5, 12.5). The non-responsibility view, in contrast, entails no such conclusion. It denies that there is anything unjust about equality, including the equality that now obtains between Prudence and Lazy.[35]

Let us summarize the different scenarios of our two desert island survivors so far discussed:

A: Prudence's hard earned reward + no brute luck to Lazy   20, 5
B: Prudence's hard earned reward + good brute luck to Lazy   20, 20
C: Prudence's hard earned reward + splitting up the spoils of good brute luck   27.5, 12.5

The responsibility view says that justice requires moving from B to C, whereas the non-responsibility view denies that doing so is a requirement of justice.

Now, a critic of the non-responsibility view might say the following. Suppose, she may say, that we reversed the story a little, and suppose that the coconut rolled up to Prudence rather than Lazy. This is represented as B*, whereby Prudence gets 35 and Lazy gets 5:

B*: Prudence's hard earned reward + good brute luck to Prudence   35, 5

There is no dispute between the two views on what egalitarian justice recommends here. Given that the coconut was a matter of brute luck,

---

[35] I should say that, for what it's worth, the view I put forward here seems to be more consistent with the luck egalitarian reading of Rawls. Rawls, of course, was no luck egalitarian, but luck egalitarianism is sometimes read as 'taking Rawlsian justice to its logical conclusion'. [See Will Kymlicka, *Contemporary Political Philosophy* (Oxford: Oxford University Press, 2002), p. 72. Cf. Samuel Scheffler, 'What is Egalitarianism?' *Philosophy and Public Affairs* 31 (2003), 5–39.] Namely, Rawls is held as one of the first egalitarians to recognize the moral arbitrariness of factors for which we are not responsible, such as talents. [See *A Theory of Justice* (Oxford: Oxford University Press, 1999), for example, p. 63.] In a way, Rawls's theory of justice can be read as the twin ideas of making justice independent of both morally arbitrary factors such as luck and, on the other hand, of the ideal of desert. (See Hurley, *Justice, Luck, and Knowledge*, p. 134 on this.) A luck egalitarian who wishes to implement this twin Rawlsian ideal should endorse the non-responsibility view, rather than a formulation that enjoins egalitarianism with desert. Later, I shall point out how the responsibility view may be seen as undertaking precisely the latter.

egalitarians would say that B* is unjust. Since Prudence's new reward is an un-deserved one, she should, at the very least, split it with Lazy. [This would give rise, again, to C (27.5, 12.5).] The relevant point for us here is this. If brute luck rewards must be shared under B* then, to be consistent, so must they under B. The coconut, being a matter of good brute luck, ought to be split up, *no matter who it rolls up to*, the critic might say.[36] Thus, if the coconut rolled up to Lazy, justice would require splitting it up between him and Prudence [again, giving rise to (27.5, 12.5)]. This may show the responsibility view to be the more intuitive of the two. But notice, in reply, that under B* Lazy is now even more disadvantaged than Prudence (compared to his situation in A), and crucially, that additional widening of the gap between them is due to no fault of his (there was nothing that Prudence did [nothing which Lazy didn't] to lure the coconut to roll onto her).[37] It follows that, at the very least, Prudence must transfer half of the coconut to Lazy [giving rise to (27.5, 12.5)]. Thus, reversing the story of Lazy and Prudence does not show that an equality that may exist between them is unjust.

The critic may suggest a different reversal of the story. Suppose, as in our original story that Prudence goes fishing, being aware of the very slight chance of coming home empty-handed, and Lazy lies on the beach. But in this scenario, Prudence is indeed rather unlucky and (against the great odds) ends up empty handed, while lucky Lazy yields a coconut. We have now state of affairs D (0, 20), in Lazy's favour. Since Prudence is worse-off now, and (by hypothesis) through no fault of her own, egalitarians are unanimous in (at the very least) recommending splitting the coconut between them, giving rise to E (7.5, 12.5). However, this state of affairs is not the end of the story. Towards the end of the day, while the sun is almost down, a fish gets caught in Prudence's hook. So from E we now arrive again at C (27.5, 12.5). Prudence's new gain is entirely a matter of effort and on any luck egalitarian account it does not need to be shared. So far, nothing is controversial. But now the question is this: if C is *not unjust* here (as I concede), then how is it that my formulation told, in the previous scenario discussed, against switching to the exact same state of affairs? Surely, this shows an inconsistency in my position. In our initial example my formulation told against making Lazy split the coconut with Prudence. And yet here my formulation

---

[36] This objection was put to me by Kristin Voigt.

[37] The fact that Lazy is worse-off through no fault of his own now is obvious, among other things, from the fact that even if he would have made the effort of trying to catch a fish, and were successful (as much as Prudence was in doing the same), his level of welfare would still fall below that of Prudence.

requires that she do precisely that. And still the only difference between the two stories concerns the *timing* of the arrival of the coconut (namely, before or after Prudence has caught her well-earned fish). Surely, this is arbitrary, the critic might say. Can outcomes be judged just or unjust simply on the basis of the order in which the sequence of events has unfolded? Notice, in reply, that the non-responsibility view does *not* rule C to be unjust, neither in the original scenario, nor in the present one. It simply judges that inequality to be neither unjust, nor required by justice. Hence, despite the objection, there is no inconsistency between allowing it to stand here, and not recommending moving to it, earlier.

Consider a final version of the story: Lazy here has no coconut and Prudence hooks up a nice fish, giving rise, as before, to A (20, 5). Prudence is busy cutting up the fish in preparation for cooking it, when all of a sudden a tidal wave comes along and sweeps away most of her well-earned fish. (The wave, let us assume, is an extraordinary and unexpected event.) Things are now reversed, let us suppose, to F (5, 5). Isn't this equality unjust? The responsibility view clearly says that it is. The new, equal distribution, does not track the unequal levels of prudence (or effort) exercised by the two. The non-responsibility view, on the other hand, is compelled to say that here again nothing is amiss (for the simple reason that there is no inequality). Does this not reflect badly on the non-responsibility view? Shouldn't Prudence be compensated for her bad brute luck? After all, she is now worse-off than she previously was and through no fault of her own. Notice, first, that even if we did happen to think that Prudence is owed compensation we would still need to figure out how to fund it. In our two person story this compensation would inevitably have to be taken from Lazy, and this would give rise to a fresh inequality, something which even proponents of the responsibility view may balk at. After all, the tidal wave was not Lazy's fault.[38] But suppose we leave that worry aside. (We may suppose, for example, that Prudence and Lazy have in the past set aside some joint emergency compensation fund especially for such scenarios.) In that case, ought not Prudence be compensated and brought back to her pre- bad-brute-luck level (20)? The answer, according to the

---

[38] But what if it was? Suppose Lazy did, somehow, start the tidal wave. The resulting situation would then, I concede, be unjust. But notice that even here, the injustice is not the property of the *equal* distribution between Lazy and Prudence. Rather, the injustice resides in the harm caused by Lazy to Prudence, independently of the equality which the harm (through the tidal wave) brings about. If the wave harmed Prudence while retaining her advantage over Lazy, we would still consider the latter to be at fault. Equality has nothing to do with it.

non-responsibility view, is of course still 'no', and this might be thought of as counterintuitive. We may observe how the non-responsibility view leads to this outcome. It does so because it conditions injustice on some individuals being worse-off *than others*; it does not speak of a state of affairs as being unjust when some are merely worse-off than *they themselves were* (or could have been). And there is a good reason to formulate egalitarianism in a way that insists on an interpersonal aspect and not just on an *intra*personal[39] one.[40] (I shall discuss this aspect in more detail in the next chapter.) The reason is that the principle we are after is one that seeks to capture the concern with *egalitarian* distributive justice. The starting point is equality, namely the property of relative holdings *between* individuals. It is not, in contrast, a principle of *redress*.[41] Thus, when some are worse-off than they were (or could otherwise have been) and through no fault of their own, this might be regrettable for all sorts of reasons, but not for ones of egalitarian distributive justice.

Here is one other difference between the two views of egalitarian justice under consideration, and one which allegedly shows the responsibility view to be the superior one. Consider the case of Smith and Jones, as recounted by Arneson.[42] Smith is extremely imprudent, repeatedly playing Russian roulette but somehow managing to come out unharmed. On one occasion though, he suffers a terrible unrelated brute luck (his house is destroyed by a hurricane). Jones, on the other hand, is extremely prudent in everything she does. On one occasion, however, she does something foolish (forgets to put out a candle) and ends up burning down her house.[43] The story, it might be suggested, reflects more favourably on the responsibility view. In

---

[39] Alternatively referred to as the 'counterfactual' reading of the luck-neutralizing approach.

[40] See Hurley, *Justice, Luck, and Knowledge*, p. 156. Notice that I am *not* saying that the responsibility view *is* committed to this intrapersonal view of egalitarianism. I am only saying that it is committed to the view that the equal distribution here should be upset and a fresh inequality generated. By invoking the intrapersonal view I merely seek to establish that refraining from doing so, as the non-responsibility view recommends, is *not* counter-intuitive.

[41] Lake correctly writes: 'In interpreting the egalitarian intuition, egalitarians must decide whether the target of their concern is equality or whether it is compensation.' Lake, *Equality and Responsibilty*, p. 103. Since this is something that luck egalitarians are not always careful about, it is hardly surprising that Rawlsian critics sometimes confuse luck egalitarianism with that ideal of redress (see for example, Samuel Scheffler, *Equality and Tradition*, p. 194), an ideal that Rawls happened to explicitly reject. See *Theory of Justice*, pp. 100–1.

[42] Arneson, 'Luck and Equality', *Proceedings of the Aristotelian Society*, Supplement 75 (2001), p. 85.

[43] See also Arneson, 'Egalitarianism and Repsonsibility', p. 230; 'Justice is Not Equality', p. 389.

as much as it seeks to match individuals' levels of welfare to their level of prudence, the responsibility view would tell us to restore the (generally) prudent Jones to something close to her previous level of welfare,[44] and allow us to leave the (generally) reckless Smith to his destitution (or something slightly above it).[45] In contrast, the non-responsibility view would seek to compensate the reckless Smith (because the particular disadvantage he suffered was not casually related to his imprudence) but permit leaving prudent Jones uncompensated (because the particular disadvantage she suffered *was* a result of her imprudence).[46] Some may find this highly counterintuitive.[47] The reason the non-responsibility view leads to this allegedly counterintuitive outcome here is owed to the view it takes on causality (the vertical dimension in Table 2.1 above). It says that it is bad if some are worse-off than others *through* no fault of their own. For one's disadvantage to count as unjust, on the non-responsibility view, it (the disadvantage) must be *causally related* to one's imprudence. One's *general* (or 'global' [as opposed to 'local'])[48] imprudence, and the absence of a direct correlation between one's imprudence and the resulting disadvantage, does not justify leaving her worse-off. (And conversely, one's general prudence does not make it a requirement of justice to alleviate her disadvantage when the latter is causally related to a particular act of imprudence.) Smith's being generally reckless with his life has nothing to do with his particular disadvantage (his house being destroyed by a hurricane), and thus does not excuse it. (I use 'excuse' in the same sense used by Cohen in a similar context.)[49] In contrast, the responsibility view, perhaps owing

---

[44] I say 'close' because there is no requirement, even on the responsibility view, to restore her to the exact same level of welfare since she was indeed less than perfectly prudent. So perhaps we ought to help her rebuild the house but not pay for the burned curtains, say.

[45] Again, given that he wasn't reckless on this one occasion.

[46] This is only true, of course, in so far as there is some *in*equality somewhere in the society, such as between Smith and Roberts (who has been prudent, as well as lucky, throughout), say. If the society in question is made up only of Smith and Jones, and if now there is equality between them, no compensation would be owed to Smith, on my view.

[47] Or so, at least, Arneson and Temkin seem to think. Arneson, 'Luck and Equality', p. 85; Larry Temkin, 'Justice, Equality, Fairness, Desert, Rights, Free Will, Responsibility, and Luck', in Carl Knight and Zofia Stemplowska (eds), *Distributive Justice and Responsibility* (Oxford: Oxford University Press, 2011), p. 242.

[48] Temkin, 'Justice, Equality, Fairness, Desert, Rights, Free Will, Responsibility, and Luck', p. 243.

[49] '...genuine choice excuses otherwise unacceptable inequalities'. 'On the Currency of Egalitarian Justice', p. 951.

to its strong affinity to the ideal of desert, does not insist on such causality.[50] It may seek, rather, to match one's overall welfare with one's *overall prudence*.[51] Again, some readers' intuitions may rebel against the implications of the non-responsibility view here, and side with the responsibility account in condemning this equality. But upon reflection, the sense of counterintuition here may not seem all that warranted. Much as we might be infuriated by Smith's general reckless behaviour, we must admit that the disadvantage represented by his destroyed house is not his fault, and thus ought to be neutralized.[52] And, equally, much as we value and admire Jones's lifestyle, we must admit that the disadvantage brought about by her one-time-only reckless conduct was avoidable and is thus not a concern for distributive justice. If our intuitions still rebel against this outcome then this may simply indicate that we value considerations of desert in our overall moral judgement of how good or bad, *all things considered*, a state of affairs is. But we should be mindful not to infer from that a judgement on the *fairness* of the state of affairs in question. In sum, despite some initial sense of counter-intuition, the insistence in the non-responsibility view on a causal link between one's conduct and one's disadvantage is a correct one, and one that properly distinguishes it from the desert-like responsibility view.[53]

---

[50] See also Holtug and Lippert-Rasmussen, 'An Introduction to Contemporary Egalitarianism', p. 19.

[51] It is also worth noting that a principle that is concerned with matching individuals' comparative welfare to their comparative responsibility would find it difficult to stick to a local rather than a global account. For it is not obvious why we ought to restrict such a principle to local events given that the rationale is to reward individuals for their prudence. The non-responsibility view, it is easy to see, forswears any such rationale, and is thus not committed to a 'global' account of responsibility. That is why, I believe, the responsibility view belongs in the lower half of Table 2.1, and the non-responsibility view in the upper half.

[52] Again, assuming he is now worse off than someone else in the relevant group, say Roberts.

[53] Marc Fleurbaey says that my position, according to which equality is never unjust, is 'not convincing, because this implies that luck egalitarianism would have no objection against a full equalization policy' ('Review of Shlomi Segall, "Health, Luck, and Justice"', p. 504). Indeed I don't. I find nothing implausible (or unconvincing) in the view that luck egalitarians will have no objection of *egalitarian distributive justice* to a policy of full equalization. Confiscating the hard-earned capital of the rich and industrious and distributing it equally among all members of society may be wrong for all sorts of reasons (e.g. it would violate legitimate expectations). But it does not necessarily offend egalitarian distributive justice.

IV. Equality and Redress

I hope to have shown so far that the non-responsibility view, an implication of which is that egalitarian distributive justice is bothered only by inequalities and never by equalities survives initial pangs of counterintuition. Moreover, if keeping a proper distance between egalitarianism and the ideal of desert is a virtue for an egalitarian formulation (something for which I have *not* argued here) then this should count in favour of the non-responsibility view, and against the responsibility view. Yet, even if the reader is persuaded by my discussion in the previous section, she might still feel uneasy about the conclusion that equalities are never unjust. Isn't it unjust, for example, for someone rich who lost much of his assets through reckless gambling to be as well-off as a very prudent (yet unlucky) poor person? Surely this is wrong, the critic might say. Notice, though, that the non-responsibility view would stipulate leaving the prudent poor as she is only so long as there is no one else *in the entire society* (or whatever the relevant reference group is) who is better-off than she is (and through no merit of their own). It seems to me that once attention is called to that fact, the sense of counterintuition triggered by the comparison of the prudent poor with the imprudent (formerly) rich subsides. In a two-person society it is plausible, I submit, to think of the equality that obtains between the reckless but lucky person and the diligent but unlucky one as a state of affairs that is not unjust.

Here is a different objection to the suggestion that egalitarian distributive justice concerns only inequalities. Suppose Jim and Jill occupy identical positions in a firm, but where Jill puts in twice as many hours (and, accordingly, let us also assume for simplification's sake, produces twice as much output). Yet, at the end of the month Jim and Jill receive identical pay checks. Many would protest that an injustice has taken place here, and one that the non-responsibility view does not condemn. This looks like an unassailable case of unjust equality. But notice, for one thing, that it could have been the case that the firm has actually stated in advance that no matter how much work one put in, everyone would be rewarded equally. (Think of the firm in question as a kibbutz or, indeed, as a department in a university.) If that were the case, then perhaps there would be no reason to suppose that Jill has been wronged after all. One would perhaps expect leading luck egalitarians, and especially ones with Socialist sympathies such as Cohen,[54] to endorse the

---

[54] See, for example, his 'Why Not Socialism?' in Edward Broadbent (ed.), *Democratic Equality: What Went Wrong?* (Toronto: University of Toronto Press, 2001), pp. 58–78, esp. p. 63.

practice of undifferentiated pay in kibbutzim or among faculty, which is why it might come as a surprise that he should condemn as unjust an equality that is coupled with unequal effort. Even under circumstances where the policy of equal pay was not made public in advance, it is still not obvious that the equality between Jim and Jill would then be an unjust one. It is plausible to think that if the state of affairs (her getting as much as Jim despite working harder) is unjust, it is so because her legitimate expectations have been frustrated. On that account, Jill has less than she could have had because of a discriminating interference by the managers of the firm. The comparison with Jim only serves to *indicate* that. The equality between Jill and Jim is therefore not *constitutive* of the injustice that has been done to her; it is only potentially indicative of it. (In contrast, *in*equalities, on the non-responsibility view, *are* constitutive of injustice [unless of course excused by differential responsibility].) Thus, from the perspective of egalitarian distributive justice, there is nothing wrong with the equality that prevails between the two.

A further potential objection is a variant on Kymlicka's famous gardener and tennis player example.[55] The gardener's hard work, and the player's laziness have led, after a while, to an inequality (with respect to wealth, and consequently also with respect to their welfare, let us assume) in favour of the gardener. Luck egalitarians are unanimous in finding this consequence to be not unjust. In a subsequent twist of the story, though, the gardener's crop, despite being carefully selected to avoid known diseases, falls prey to an unknown pestilence. The tennis court next door, in contrast, is mysteriously improved by the demise of some weeds that have plagued it in the past. Through sheer brute luck the two individuals' levels of welfare have been equalized. Carl Knight writes:

> I submit that egalitarian justice requires that we redistribute from the tennis player to the gardener, and that it is a powerful objection to the idea that inequality is a necessary condition for egalitarian redistribution that such a condition precludes a transfer to the spectacularly unfortunate gardener from the lucky tennis fanatic. In refusing such distribution, Segall allows distributions to be much more dependent on brute luck than the core intuitions of luck egalitarianism permit. Indeed, I would argue, as Kymlicka and Cohen do, that giving to people like the gardener only as much as people like the tennis player amounts to treating them unequally, given the morally significant difference in their actions.[56]

---

[55]   Knight, 'Inequality, Avoidability, and Healthcare', p. 75–6.
[56]   Knight, 'Inequality, Avoidability, and Healthcare', p. 75–6.

There are three different objections here. The first one says that allowing the brute luck equality to stand is to treat the two unequally, 'given the morally significant difference in their actions'. But I deny both that my account implies an unequal treatment of the two, as well as the claim that their actions are different in a morally significant way. Both assertions are precisely that which is at stake here. The second objection concerns the fact that my account 'allows distributions to be much more dependent on brute luck than the core intuitions of luck egalitarianism permit'. I deny, as I did already, that that in itself captures something essential about luck egalitarianism. An equal distribution of manna-from-heaven is very much dependent on brute luck, but no luck egalitarian I know, including Cohen, would object to it. The third objection, which is perhaps the strongest, appeals to a conventional intuition. The equality between the hard-working gardener and the lazy tennis player simply seems infuriating. But this might be because our intuitions in such cases are muddled. To stress again: there may be all sorts of regrettable aspects to the revised tale of the gardener and the tennis player (we might feel pity for the gardener for his failed effort), but a concern for *egalitarian distributive justice* is not necessarily one of them. We must not confuse equality with some ideal of redress.[57]

V. Talents and Effort

Let us turn, finally, to a different type of objection to the view that equalities cannot be unjust. Think of a hypothetical society that is composed of two individuals (or two classes of individuals), one diligent but untalented,

---

[57] For a similar view see Lake, *Equality and Responsibilty*, p. 103. Another worry that Knight raises is that my account is indeterminate. Since it objects neither to equalities nor to inequalities that are owed to option luck it remains indeterminate between them. (I concede that this is so.) This is problematic, says Knight, because: 'In one gardener/tennis player case equality might be chosen, and in another identical gardener/tennis player case option luck inequality might be chosen. This subjects the gardener in the first case to bad brute luck relative to the gardener in the second case...' ('Inequality, Avoidability, and Healthcare', p. 76). But the objection assumes that justice is concerned with comparing the relative holdings of the gardener in the first story with the gardener in the second story. Yet this is implausible. Egalitarian distributive justice is concerned with the relative holdings of different individuals occupying the same world (although not necessarily simultaneously). Justice does not concern (at least not without some further argument) the relative holdings of the same person (or even different persons) occupying two alternative states of the world. We may assess, of course, which world is fairer, but it is unintelligible to say that a person in one possible world has been disadvantaged compared to her existence in an alternate world.

and the other talented but lazy. Table 2.2 represents the different scenarios (regarding pay) available in that society. Notice that the tax scheme here kicks-in only once inequality obtains.

Table 2.2 Talent and effort

	A 4-hour workday		An 8-hour workday	
	Before tax	After tax	Before tax	After tax
Talented	40K	25K	80k	60K
Untalented	10K	25K	40K	60K

The first thing we may notice about Table 2.2 is that there is (income) equality between the two classes when T (Talented) works 4 hours while U (Untalented) works 8 hours a day. (As I said, no tax is levied when earning is equal, so pre-tax and after-tax earnings are identical in this particular scenario.) This may seem unjust and yet the non-responsibility view, counterintuitively perhaps, does not condemn it. Now of course, one thing to observe here is that this state of affairs might nevertheless be characterized as one of inequality, for while income might be equal, leisure is obviously not. But suppose we bracket this issue. Suppose all we are interested in assessing is individuals' income and how much effort they exert. (We may do so, for example, by switching from speaking of the length of the work day to speaking about the intensity of equally long work days.) In that case, isn't the resulting equality unjust? Notice, in reply, that the 8-hour working day of U is entirely a matter of her choice. Were she to reduce her working day to seven hours, say, something that, by hypothesis, she is perfectly entitled to do, her bundle would accordingly drop to below that of T. When that happens, taxation would kick in, and there would be a transfer from T to U (since the latter is now worse-off, and through no fault of her own).

The critic might not be content with that reply, though, and argue that this state of affairs between T and U is nevertheless unjust, even in the absence of inequality in their respective bundles. For it seems that U does not have here the same earning options as does T. To illustrate, looking at Table 2.2, we can see that U lacks the option of earning an 80k salary, for example. But, of course, a moment's reflection reveals that this option is not enjoyed by T either. If T chooses to work 8 hours a day then her 80k would be taxed, leaving her with just 60k, which is precisely what U would

get. Thus, if the situation is unfair this must be due not to T having different earning options, but to the fact that, arguably, it is she who, effectively, is
calling all the shots here. U's level of welfare seems to depend on the choices
made by T (and not vice versa). Suppose that T decides to work four hours a
day and surf the rest of the time. In that case, the extent of U's bundle is limited to the small amount of resources that T can generate in those four hours.
Only should T decide to increase her own bundle by working longer hours
would U become entitled to a transfer of resources. If T decides to work a full
working day (i.e. 8 hours), then U's salary would be 60k, and if T decides to
work a 4-hour working day, U's salary would be (at most) 40k. U simply does
not have the same sort of power. If she unilaterally decides to work longer
hours, and produce whatever little she can with her less-marketable talents,
she would gain no right to a transfer of resources from T. U, it turns out,
does not have an equal power over determining hers and T's bundles. This
seems unfair. But what exactly, we might ask, is the source of unfairness here?
Notice that for U to complain about being at 40k rather than at 60k is to complain against T for not exercising his talent to the maximum. But how should
we assess this? One interpretation is that U has a legitimate complaint about
T's laziness. If T had worked as hard as U then they both would be better-off.
But then T can justly retort that no one has ever forced U to work 8 hours. U
is entitled to work as many hours as T, and her overall income is guaranteed
(by the non-responsibility view) not to fall below that of T. Moreover, why
should T accept an 8-hour working day as some sort of a benchmark that
he ought to reach? Why not 12 hours (in which case, U herself would also
be at fault), or indeed 4? The accusation of laziness seems unwarranted. The
complaint against T, therefore, cannot simply be about his choice regarding
the length of his workday. Alternatively, then, the complaint might be that T
is not employing his talent to the benefit of society. If he did, everyone would
be better-off. But this again does not seem like a valid complaint. Suppose
that Wilt Chamberlain, to use Robert Nozick's famous example, prefers not
to play basketball and rather opts to be a Phys-Ed instructor. Does the rest of
society have a just claim for the tax-transfer that they *would have gotten* had
he decided to play basketball?[58] I don't see a reason to think so.[59] It is true that

---

[58] Thomas Pogge, in his critique of Cohen, entertains a similar possibility. 'On the Site
of Distributive Justice: Reflections on Cohen and Murphy', *Philosophy and Public Affairs* 29
(2000), p. 153.

[59] And neither does Cohen, for that matter. See his *Rescuing Justice and Equality*, ch. 5. On
p. 398, Cohen also remarks (in reply to Pogge's criticism): 'This conjures up a nightmare

Wilt holds the key here to how high the income of members of his society is. But that does not mean that he is committing an injustice by choosing not to practise his talent (or even for not practising it more often), nor that the society is thereby rendered unjust by that inequality in talent.

We have yet to see a reason, then, why the equality between the lazy talented and the hardworking untalented is, in some way, unjust. Now, it is important to notice that my rebuttal of the above objection does not depend on denying that inequalities in native talent can themselves be unjust. What I *am* denying is that the claim that the inequality in talent between T and U is in itself unjust (even if true) shows that the income *equality* between them (which the inequality in talent somehow facilitates) is also unjust. But suppose for a moment that we concede to the critic that it is indeed unjust that greater talent allows T more power in deciding the size of the social pie (even while it is divided equally). Supposing this is indeed an injustice, what can be done to correct it? The obvious solution would be to grant U some compensation for her lesser talent. Compensating the less talented is, in general, something that luck egalitarians are often happy to endorse.[60] But would it make sense in our story? Notice that giving U any additional compensation would, in our story, bring her bundle to *above* that of T. Now, I admit that it is not altogether implausible to suggest that individuals should get some compensation for having less of a say in collective decisions. But I do find it counterintuitive that if Wilt decides to become a teacher (rather than a basketball player) he should thereby be penalized by earning a salary that is lower than that earned by all other teachers (just because he happened to be born with a gift for basketball). To do so would amount to something akin to 'the slavery of the talented'.[61] It seems, then, that even when we do recognize that there is

---

scenario in which the duty that I advocate is interpreted as making the productive work as much as they can to make the wages of the less well paid as high as possible' (p. 402). Later on that page Cohen refers to this view as 'crazy'. Note that even Joseph Carens whose *Equality, Moral Incentives, and the Market* (Chicago: University of Chicago Press, 1981) is often cited as the closest that contemporary egalitarians come to holding such a position (namely, that individuals have a duty to work in the line of work to which their talents and skills make them most suitable) has subsequently modified his position. Carens's revised position is that individuals should make 'good use of their skills', which is different from a duty to work in what one is best at. See his 'Rights and Duties in an Egalitarian Society', *Political Theory* 14 (1986), 31–49.

[60]   See Ronald Dworkin, *Sovereign Virtue: The Theory and Practice of Equality* (Cambridge, MA: Harvard University Press, 2000), p. 85ff.

[61]   See Dworkin, *Sovereign Virtue*, p. 90; Cohen, *Rescuing Justice and Equality*, ch. 5.

some injustice involved in the unequal distribution of talents (for reasons of greater influence that it grants the talented), it would still be wrong to compensate individuals merely for having inferior talent. (Over and above, that is, the distributive scheme that would tax any benefit the talented earn with their superior talents.) Notice, finally, that if there was some other way of rectifying the inequality in talent between T and U, the non-responsibility view may very well require that we pursue it. If it were possible, for example, to, literally, redistribute the talent between T and U (perhaps by some genetic procedure) the non-responsibility view gives us a pro tanto reason to do so (or at the very least, it does not militate against it).

Conclusion

Dworkin's egalitarianism, Cohen famously wrote, incorporates into egalitarian thought one of the powerful weapons of the anti-egalitarian right, namely the ideal of responsibility.[62] It is important, however, to be clear about why egalitarians might be concerned with responsibility. Suppose there is a certain ultimate high level of welfare possible for humans, and suppose, happily, that members of society all possess that equal maximum level. Yet suppose also that members of this society differ in their degree of prudence. Would the egalitarian (qua egalitarian) see this hypothetical world as in some way defective? I cannot see a reason why. Or suppose, alternatively, a state of utter abundance. Would egalitarians condemn an equal distribution under these idyllic circumstances if it reflected unequal levels of effort? In other words, would it be better, from an egalitarian perspective that Lazy gets less than Prudence *even if* taking from Lazy does not in any way improve Prudence's position? It is hard to think of a reason why this would be so.[63] Egalitarians, including luck egalitarians, should not care about responsibility in that way at all. Rather, (luck) egalitarians' interest in responsibility only kicks in on the

---

[62] 'On the Currency of Egalitarian Justice', p. 933.

[63] The critic might say that invoking a state of abundance does not prove anything in the present context for the simple reason that it conflicts with Humean circumstances of justice. Justice simply does not obtain in these circumstances and thus the question 'should egalitarians condemn an equal distribution that reflects unequal prudence?' becomes unintelligible then, thereby saving the skin of the equality-condemning egalitarian. Now, even if this objection is correct (which I doubt), it need not detain us here. The reason is that the type of egalitarians with whom I am concerned here, namely luck egalitarians, in fact reject the premiss of the 'circumstances of justice', and moreover reject the claim that these circumstances inform what justice consists of. See Cohen, *Rescuing Justice and Equality*, pp. 331–6.

event of inequality. To be disadvantaged (that is, to be worse-off than others), say luck egalitarians, is unjust only when that disadvantage comes about in the absence of personal responsibility. Responsibility (and conversely, luck), thus, only begins to play a role in egalitarianism in the absence of the one and only thing that egalitarians (qua egalitarians) care about, namely, equality. This, in turn, reflects on our defence of radical equality of opportunity. Striving for equality of opportunity is a requirement of justice *only* in so much as it contributes to curbing inequality of outcome. The latter, I have sought to establish here, should always be the ultimate concern for egalitarians.

Appendix: How the Non-responsibility View Meets Susan Hurley's Critique

Let me point out a potential advantage of the non-responsibility view, which may hopefully serve to show that it provides a perhaps more attractive view of egalitarianism than does the responsibility view. This concerns Susan Hurley's unique critique of luck egalitarianism.

I mentioned in Section II Hurley's simple but effective observation, namely that neutralizing luck cannot serve as a basis for egalitarianism. When luck is neutralized, she argues, the default we fall back on is not necessarily an equal distribution. This is so for the reason that equality may also be the result of luck, whereas inequality may be the result of choice.[64] This startlingly simple observation shows that neutralizing luck does not necessarily lead to equality. Hurley employs this insight to cast doubt on the egalitarian credentials of the luck-neutralizing approach adopted by leading luck egalitarians such as Cohen, Arneson, and Roemer. I cannot, of course, delve into how each of these philosophers may respond to Hurley's critic.[65] Rather, what I want to show in this appendix is how adopting the non-responsibility view may help luck egalitarians avoid Hurley's objection. The point is this: the understanding of egalitarianism that I have attempted to defend here does not take the neutralization of luck to be its starting point. Rather, the starting position of the non-responsibility view, recall,

---

[64] Hurley, *Justice, Luck, and Knowledge*, esp. ch. 6. In fact a similar point was made already in Lake, *Equality and Responsibility*, p. 12. See also Arneson, 'Justice is Not Equality', p. 386.

[65] See Cohen's and Arneson's reply to Hurley to that effect. Cohen, 'Luck and Equality'; Arneson, 'Luck and Equality'. See also Lippert-Rasmussen, 'Hurley on Egalitarianism and the Luck-Neutralizing Aim'.

was the (potential) injustice of inequalities. Inequalities are unjust, that formulation holds, unless they are the outcome of choice. This understanding of egalitarianism does not, therefore, take luck-neutralization to be its starting point (or reason of being, or what have you). With the hindsight of Hurley's critique we may summarize the difference between the two views of egalitarianism (presented in this chapter) in the following way: on the responsibility view, it is luck-neutralizing first, equality second (at best); on the non-responsibility view, in contrast, it is equality first, luck-neutralizing second (at best).[66] It is easy to see, then, that a conception of egalitarian justice that kicks-off from the injustice of inequality rather than from the arbitrariness of luck would not be vulnerable to the (Hurley-type) objection that luck-neutralizing is not necessarily egalitarian.[67] (But it does so, it might be objected, at a price of using equality as a mere default position, thus ending up *not justifying* equality, a problem I shall address in a moment.)

Understanding egalitarianism as condemning inequalities that are owed to brute luck (and thus permitting all equalities, as well as all inequalities that are generated by choice) has further advantages in facing up to Hurley's critique. Consider her claim that luck-neutralizing, or responsibility, cannot perform a patterning role in egalitarianism, let alone that of *justifying* an egalitarian pattern. Using the badness of inequalities as a starting point, I maintain, avoids that problem. For, on the non-responsibility view, responsibility (or choice, and conversely, luck)

---

[66] Kok-Chor Tan gets it right when he writes: '...it is the commitment to equality that moves luck egalitarians in the first place. As I see it, luck egalitarians need not start off with some independent obsession with luck and the importance of neutralizing differential luck per se.' *Justice, Institutions, and Luck: The Site, Ground, and Scope of Equality* (Oxford: Oxford University Press, 2012), p. 90.

[67] See also Arneson, 'Luck and Equality', p. 79; 'Justice is Not Equality', p. 388. I think that Hurley herself admits as much: 'It is critical for my purposes to distinguish the aim to neutralize only differences that are a matter of luck from the more general aim to neutralize luck. Only by distinguishing them can we register that the general aim to neutralize luck neither specifies nor justifies aiming to neutralize only differences that are a matter of luck', *Justice, Luck, and Knowledge*, p. 154. Her criticism, thus, does not seem to affect a conception of egalitarianism that is concerned solely with inequalities. I mentioned Arneson, but it is useful to observe that his own position is also vulnerable as a consequence of my defence of the non-responsibility view. Put very briefly, Arneson argues for prioritarianism partly by way of denying that justice, understood as luck-neutralizing, results in equality. And he rests much of his case for that rebuttal on stressing that a luck egalitarian is committed to depicting both undeserved inequalities *and* undeserved equalities as unjust. (See 'Justice is Not Equality', p. 381, 386.) If the non-responsibility view is persuasive then it pulls the rug from under Arneson's contention that 'justice is not equality'.

may play both a currency and a patterning role. It tells us that inequalities are bad, *unless* they are the result of choice. Thus, luck (or responsibility) tells us *which* distributions require rectification, namely inequalities that are not owed to choice (hence performing a currency role). And, luck (or choice) also plays here a patterning role: it tells us *what* to do about those brute luck inequalities, namely, to level them. Hurley herself admits as much:[68] 'An exception to the claim that responsibility cannot play any patterning role at all is the case in which responsibility is used merely to permit departures from an independently specified default pattern'.[69] If we specify equality as that default which fairness requires, and allow only departures from it that could be attributed to choice, we seem to be within Hurley's exception, and thus escape her criticism.

To illustrate that last point, consider Hurley's claim concerning manna-from-heaven.[70] On the responsibility view (or what she calls, the luck-neutralizing view), we should neutralize the luck aspect of this good. But that does not tell us, she says, whether we should redistribute the manna equally or otherwise (Maximinally, say.) On the non-responsibility view that problem is avoided. Since that position is not bothered by equalities, if equal amounts of manna fall on equally endowed individuals the non-responsibility view would not condemn this as unjust, let alone attempt to neutralize (whatever that may mean) it. If *un*equal manna falls on equally endowed individuals, thereby upsetting equality, the non-responsibility view *would* move to restore equality, thereby neutralizing the effects of differential brute luck. I therefore concede to Hurley that luck-neutralizing cannot perform the patterning role of telling us *how* to redistribute things, let alone equally.[71] Something else, namely fairness, must do so. On the non-responsibility account, the starting point is equality *as* the demands of fairness. Fairness, on this account, says, quite simply, that inequality is unfair, unless it is the result of choice. Responsibility and luck therefore play only a limited patterning role in the non-responsibility version of luck egalitarianism. They do, very much so, play a defining role in the ideal of desert, say. An

---

[68] As already pointed out by Nir Eyal, 'A Review of S. L. Hurley's *Justice, Luck, and Knowledge*', *Economics and Philosophy* 21 (2005), p. 167.

[69] Hurley, *Justice, Luck, and Knowledge*, p. 159, n. 7.

[70] *Justice, Luck, and Knowledge*, p. 151.

[71] See for example, *Justice, Luck, and Knowledge*, p. 155.

ideal of desert which is prudential, mandatory, and comparative,[72] tells us to allocate to individuals no less and no more than what they are prudentially responsible for. An egalitarian account that approximates this ideal of desert would therefore be vulnerable to Hurley's critique. The non-responsibility view, in contrast, denies luck or responsibility this extensive patterning role.

Hurley's critique, as I mentioned, goes both ways, as it were: not only is it, she says, that luck-neutralizing does not specify, nor justify, an equal distribution. But also, an egalitarian pattern of distribution may not necessarily end up neutralizing luck.[73] Whether or not this is true of Cohenite luck egalitarianism, it is not true of the view defended here, we can now see. In aspiring only to curb inequalities, inequalities for which individuals are not responsible, the non-responsibility view concedes, and thereby avoids, both problems pointed out by Hurley: the non-responsibility view does not aspire to neutralize luck as a means of achieving equality; nor does it aspire to achieve equality *as a means* of neutralizing luck.

Still, one might say that it is no great achievement that the non-responsibility view ends up recommending equality (whereas the responsibility view cannot). Its starting point, recall, is one that concerns only inequalities, and therefore it is true *by definition* that it will end up justifying equality.[74] Here is how Hurley puts this objection: 'On the interpersonal understanding of neutralizing bad luck, the aim is to eliminate just *in*equalities for which people are not responsible. *Equalities* for which people are not responsible are ignored. So of course the result of the exercise will be to equalize people in respects for which they are not responsible! But there is no inherently luck-related basis for favouring or defaulting to equality.'[75] Hurley is no doubt correct here. Perhaps, by taking it to be its starting point, the view adopted in this chapter (and indeed, the book) does make the justification of equality appear too easy (or circular). And perhaps, further, by doing so it denies itself the

[72] See my *Health, Luck, and Justice*, pp. 16–18. A non-comparative ideal of desert may recommend making a person worse-off (than *she* currently is) as such (e.g. making sure that a sinner suffers), something which can never be true of comparative desert *nor* of egalitarianism. See Christiano, 'A Foundation for Egalitarianism', p. 74, for a similar point.

[73] *Justice, Luck, and Knowledge*, p. 167.

[74] See also Lake, *Equality and Responsibility*, p. 15.

[75] *Justice, Luck, and Knowledge*, p. 157 (emphasis added).

title of being a luck-neutralizing account, properly speaking. So the non-responsibility view might be facing two (final) objections here, in fact. One is that by not taking luck-neutralization to be its starting point it cannot be labelled 'luck egalitarian'. And, second, that by taking equality (rather than the neutralization of luck) to be its starting point it does not end up justifying equality, and is therefore perhaps circular in that respect. I admit to not being too bothered by the first problem.[76] My aim in this chapter has been to provide an egalitarian account that is plausible and coherent. If that account cannot be said to be luck egalitarian then so much the worse for luck egalitarianism. As for the second, more principled point: I concede that by taking equality, rather than the neutralization of luck (or the rewarding of responsibility), to be its starting point the non-responsibility view does not end up *justifying* equality. But neither is this true, notice, of the responsibility view. Even those who take luck-neutralization to be their starting point do not seem to intend it as a means of justifying equality (which, in any case, it cannot do, as Hurley has convincingly shown), rather than as one *specifying* what it requires. Cohen, for example, says that the luck egalitarian does not oppose luck as such. He opposes luck *in the name of fairness*. 'Since we are against luck in the name of fairness, we have to rejig what luck produces in a specific way, by, that is, removing or counterbalancing the inequalities that are caused by luck in particular.'[77] Luck-neutralization as such does not therefore tell us all that we need to know about egalitarianism. We only oppose differential brute luck in the name of fairness, which means that we still need to stipulate what it is that fairness requires. It turns out, then, that, at the very least my account in this chapter does no worse in this respect, compared to the rivalling account: it specifies equality as its starting point. It

---

[76] Carl Knight has characterized my position as 'a halfway house between luck egalitarianism and outcome egalitarianism' ('Inequality, Avoidability, and Healthcare', p. 77). I have no problem with that characterization. In a sense, my argument in this chapter could be characterized as an attempt to rescue luck egalitarianism from its false association with desert, and rather bring it closer (although, not all the way) to outcome egalitarianism.

[77] 'Luck and Equality', p. 444.

cannot justify equality, nor did it ever presume to do so.[78] (That, indeed, was the task of the previous chapter.) The non-responsibility view of egalitarianism only tells us that if we care about fairness then we should go about achieving it by making sure that people are not worse-off (than others) through no fault of their own.

---

[78] I have already mentioned in the previous chapter that the question 'equality of what' is distinct from the question 'why equality'. The claim that recent arguments about what it is that fairness requires distributing equally do not end up providing a foundation for egalitarian justice therefore misses the point. For one such claim see Christiano, 'A Foundation for Egalitarianism', pp. 45–6. Cohen, as Lippert-Rasmussen points out ('Hurley on Egalitarianism and the Luck-Neutralizing Aim', p. 254), begins his seminal article on the currency of egalitarian justice by stating that he takes it *for granted* that there is something which justice requires people to have equal amounts of' ('On the Currency of Egalitarian Justice', p. 906, emphasis added), thus, not presuming to justify equality, but only intending to specify what it requires.

3

Inequality of Risks

Consider two smokers, Steve and Eve, identical in all relevant aspects (the same starting age for smoking, same number of packets of cigarettes smoked per day, same number of years spent smoking, same socio-economic and ethnic background).[1] The two smokers differ in one crucial respect, though, namely their genetic propensity to contract lung cancer as a consequence of smoking, of which they are unaware. Steve, let us suppose, has twice as much the risk of contracting the disease compared to Eve. The two smoke away, and, sure enough, by the time they both reach the age of 50 Steve, alone, contracts cancer. He subsequently endures ten years of ill health, and eventually dies at 60. Eve, on the other hand continues to puff away until the age of 85. Is there anything unfair about this state of affairs?

It may seem that for egalitarians the answer should clearly be affirmative, and for the following reason. It is bad, with respect to equality, for one to suffer graver risk than another, and crucially, for no fault of one's own. This chapter seeks to rebut that view. It argues that, ex post, having unequal ex ante risks pursuant to an imprudent conduct is *not* unfair. If I am correct then this further limits the scope of our concern with equality of opportunity. Namely, the story of Eve and Steve will establish that we need not be concerned with inequality of opportunity pursuant to imprudent conduct, by which I shall mean actions that it would not have been unreasonable to expect the agent to avoid. If the previous chapter established that egalitarian justice is concerned only with unequal outcomes (and never with equal ones), this chapter seeks to establish that of those unequal outcomes, justice is concerned only with those that the agent could not have reasonably avoided.

---

[1] The latter premiss was, of course, the main concern of John Roemer's discussion of justice between smokers. See his *Equality of Opportunity* (Cambridge, MA: Harvard University Press, 1998), ch. 8.

The question before us (which is curiously underexplored)[2] poses a dilemma, in particular, for luck egalitarians. Take the standard understanding of luck egalitarianism as holding that it is unfair for an individual to be worse-off than another for reasons that are outside her control. Critics have noted an interesting, perhaps unintended, implication of this standard formulation of luck egalitarianism.[3] If it is indeed unfair for a person to be worse-off than another for reasons that were outside her control then it follows that it is unfair for two individuals who take the same calculated risk to end up with unequal outcomes. What differentiates these risk-takers' unequal outcomes is something that lies outside their control, namely luck. Some luck egalitarians, sometimes known as 'all-luck egalitarians' (or 'choice egalitarians'), have come to see this implication as a rather attractive feature of luck egalitarianism. They have, in effect, employed this observation to extend the concern of standard luck egalitarianism from brute luck inequalities into option luck inequalities as well (hence 'all-luck egalitarianism').[4] All-luck egalitarianism thus argues, for example, that it is unfair for two individuals who smoke the exact same number of cigarettes to end up with (radically) unequal fates (one gets sick and the other does not). If this outcome-inequality between lucky and unlucky smokers is indeed unfair, then some rectification would be called for. One way in which the injustice could be neutralized is through

---

[2] Richard Arneson in his seminal paper does not explicitly discuss the potential injustice of unequal risks pursuant to an imprudent action. See his 'Equality of Opportunity for Welfare', *Philosophical Studies* 56 (1989), 77–93. Peter Vallentyne, likewise, never discusses unequal risks in the face of option luck. The closest he comes to the issue is in saying that there is no requirement of justice to leave the unlucky smoker to suffer. 'Brute Luck, Option Luck, and Equality of Initial Opportunities', *Ethics* 112 (2002), p. 553.

[3] Thomas Christiano, 'Comment on Elizabeth Anderson's "What Is the Point of Equality?"' http://www.brown.edu/Departments/Philosophy/bears/9904chri.html.

[4] See Kasper Lippert-Rasmussen, 'Egalitarianism, Option Luck, and Responsibility', *Ethics* 111 (2001), pp. 548–79, and 'Hurley on Egalitarianism and the Luck-Neutralizing Aim', *Politics, Philosophy, and Economics* 4 (2005), p. 259; Marc Fleurbaey, 'Egalitarian Opportunities', *Law and Philosophy* 20 (2001), 499–530, esp. pp. 513–22, 'Equal Opportunity or Equal Social Outcome?' *Economics and Philosophy* 11 (1995), pp. 25–55, and *Fairness, Responsibility, and Welfare* (Oxford: Oxford University Press, 2008), esp. ch. 6; Alexander W. Cappelen and Bertil Tungodden, 'A Liberal Egalitarian Paradox', *Economics and Philosophy* 22 (2006), p. 394, 'Relocating the Responsibility Cut: Should More Responsibility Imply Less Redistribution?' *Politics, Philosophy, and Economics* 5 (2006), pp. 353–362; Alexander W. Cappelen, 'Responsibility and International Distributive Justice', in A. Follesdal and T. Pogge (eds), *Real World Justice: Grounds, Principles, Human Rights, and Social Institutions* (Dordrecht: Springer, 2005), pp. 215–28; Nicholas Barry, 'Reassessing Luck Egalitarianism', *Journal of Politics* 70 (2008), pp. 136–50.

taxes on cigarettes, where the collected revenue could be used to care for unlucky smokers. Taxes on cigarettes can thus be used to help level (at least some of) the inequality between lucky and unlucky smokers.

This chapter aims to refute this all-luck egalitarian (henceforth ALE) argument. But before doing so I want to first acknowledge two attractive features of it. First, ALE appears to deliver luck egalitarianism from an objection that has been dogging it from its inception. If luck egalitarianism is concerned with rectifying disadvantages for which the agent is not responsible, it follows, or so critics claim, that luck egalitarians are oblivious to disadvantages for which the agent *is* responsible. Luck egalitarians are consequently often accused of 'abandoning the imprudent' (such as smokers); those whose predicament could be traced to their own choice.[5] (I shall say more in the next section on what I mean by 'imprudence' in this context.) In contrast, if the inequality between lucky and unlucky smokers justifies taxes on cigarettes, as ALE holds, and if the revenue from that tax can be used to care for sick smokers, then this helps luck egalitarianism escape that objection.[6] Still, one problem with this response is that meeting the needs of unlucky smokers would depend on a more or less 50–50 distribution of luck between smokers. If most (not to mention all) smokers turn out to be unlucky then the revenue from cigarette tax may not be sufficient to care for all affected smokers, and thus the abandonment objection is not completely averted.[7] (This is not to deny, of course, that even averting part of it is also a commendable achievement.)

The other attractive feature of the ALE argument is that it provides a unique justification for taxation on cigarettes, one that is distinctly egalitarian. This is no mean feat because taxes on cigarettes are normally thought to be justified *only* by the paternalist and efficiency considerations of discouraging smoking.[8] Justifying taxes on cigarettes on the basis of pursuing egalitarian justice (that is, *between* lucky and unlucky smokers) thus avoids

---

[5] Elizabeth Anderson, 'What is the Point of Equality?' *Ethics* 109 (1999), esp. pp. 295–302; Fleurbaey, 'Equal Opportunity or Equal Social Outcome?' p. 40.

[6] Alexander W. Cappelen and Ole F. Norheim, 'Responsibility in Health Care: A Liberal Egalitarian Approach', *Journal of Medical Ethics* 31 (2005), 476–80; Julian LeGrande, 'Responsibility, Health, and Health Care', in Nir Eyal, Samia A. Hurst, Ole F. Norheim and Daniel Wikler (eds), *Inequalities in Health Concepts, Measures, and Ethics* (Oxford: Oxford University Press, 2013).

[7] I have discussed this in *Health, Luck, and Justice* (Princeton, NJ: Princeton University Press, 2010), pp. 48–9.

[8] In fact, cigarette taxation is often seen as the quintessential example of taxes that are motivated by concerns *other than* egalitarian justice. See, on this, Liam Murphy and Thomas Nagel, *The Myth of Ownership: Taxes and Justice* (Oxford: Oxford University Press, 2002), p. 165.

the charge of paternalism that is often levelled against cigarette taxation. But this second attractive feature of ALE also has a downside. Namely, the same egalitarian argument that justifies cigarette taxation also justifies some rather less intuitive schemes of compensation. An unsuccessful casino gambler, for example, is worse-off compared to a successful such gambler for reasons that were beyond the control of both of them, namely whether or not they had Lady Luck on their side. Thus, all-luck egalitarians are forced to judge the inequality between gamblers to be unjust, which seems counterintuitive. [Of course, one need not deny that there are important differences between gamblers and smokers. Gamblers often pursue their gambles *for the sake* of the risk, whereas smokers pursue smoking, mostly, *despite* the risk.[9] But the division is not clear cut: some casino gamblers pursue gambling for the sake of the (presumed) easy cash; and some smokers, we may plausibly assume, smoke partly because it is bad for them.][10] I do not deny, notice, that it may be desirable (for all sorts of reasons) to pool gains and losses between gamblers, but that is different from a requirement of egalitarian justice to do so, which seems rather counterintuitive.[11]

---

[9] See Lippert-Rasmussen, 'Egalitarianism, Option Luck, and Responsibility', p. 555.

[10] I have elaborated on this in *Health, Luck, and Justice*, p. 50.

[11] 'It is *insane* to compensate victims of deliberate gambles. It is not insane (whatever else it may be) to compensate the imprudent contractor of cancer'. G. A. Cohen, personal communication (original emphasis). Nir Eyal similarly writes that compensating gamblers for their losses is 'an absurd view of luck egalitarianism'. See his 'Egalitarian Justice and Innocent Choice', *Journal of Ethics and Social Philosophy* 2 (2007), p. 10. Some luck egalitarians, however, are willing to bite this bullet. This is the position taken in Fleurbaey, *Fairness, Responsibilty, and Welfare*, e.g. p. 154. Most others, including Arneson and Dworkin, shy away from endorsing such a conclusion. [See Richard J. Arneson, 'Equality and Equal Opportunity for Welfare: A Postscript', in Louis P. Pojman and Robert Westmoreland (eds), *Equality: Selected Reading* (New York and Oxford: Oxford University Press, 1997), pp. 239–40.] Dworkin's argument to the same effect is that taxing the winners in order to give to the losers amounts, in effect, to a prohibition on gambling, and thus deprives individuals of the ability to pursue a particular life plan that they find appealing, namely gambling. [Ronald Dworkin, *Sovereign Virtue: The Theory and Practice of Equality* (Cambridge, MA, and London: Harvard University Press, 2000), pp. 74–6. See also Michael Otsuka, 'Luck, Insurance, and Equality', *Ethics* 113 (2002), p. 41, fn. 5; Eyal, 'Egalitarian Justice and Innocent Choice', p. 14.] But notice that Dworkin's rationale only gives us a reason to refrain from levelling inequalities between gamblers when: (a) gambles are pursued for their own sake; (b) when they are a matter of a zero-sum game. Dworkin's argument does not give us a reason to refrain from taxing winners and redistributing to losers when they are both gambling against the house, say. It certainly does not give us a reason to refrain from compensating for bad option luck more generally. (This last point has been observed already by Thomas

The story of Steve and Eve represents a slight but potentially important variation on the dilemma. It is different in the crucial respect that Steve and Eve did not, to begin with, face an equal risk. The eventual inequality between Steve and Eve is thus potentially unfair in a way that the outcome-inequality between the casino gamblers was not. If the (ex post) state of affairs between Steve and Eve is indeed unfair then this would seem to rescue luck egalitarianism from incoherence (i.e. from the counterintuitive conclusion of neutralizing inequalities between gamblers). My claim in this chapter is that, ultimately, this is not so. In other words, I want to claim that the story of Eve and Steve, when viewed ex post, represents no unfairness. This conclusion, however, brings back the question we started off with: does luck egalitarianism consider differential option luck, like that which leads to eventual inequalities between risk-takers, to be unjust or not. If it does not, as my conclusions suggest, we would need a formulation of luck egalitarianism that would reflect that. I shall try to do precisely that in the concluding section. I shall try to offer there a luck egalitarian formulation which, unlike ALE, is not forced to depict the inequality between Steve and Eve (not to mention ordinary lucky and unlucky gamblers) as an unjust one.

I start my inquiry into the potential unfairness between Steve and Eve, in the next section, by unpacking the potential unfairness of inequalities in initial chances. In Section II I ask whether lucky and advantaged (in terms of initial risk) risk-takers, such as Eve, have duties of justice towards risk-takers that are unlucky and disadvantaged (such as Steve). Concluding that they do not, I go on to rebut the view that Steve's (ex post) predicament is, on the whole, unfair. I then elaborate (in the concluding section) a luck egalitarian formulation that captures that judgement, concluding that this formulation is more coherent than the one suggested by all-luck egalitarianism.

Christiano in his 'Comment on Elizabeth Anderson's "What Is the Point of Eqaulity?"'.)
Notice that my claim is not merely that it is unjustified, all things considered, to equalize gains and losses between gamblers (a claim which all-luck egalitarians might agree with). The claim is rather the stronger one, according to which this is not even a requirement of justice. I concede, though, that this may be a contentious matter. (In any case, this last point is intended only to motivate our inquiry, but plays no role in my argument below.)

I.   What's Wrong with Unequal Risks?

We are asking, then, whether, viewed ex post, an initial inequality of risk, one which is pursuant to an imprudent action, is unjust. Perhaps the first step in addressing that question is to say what we mean by 'imprudent action'. There is a rich literature, of course, on how precisely imprudence, and conversely option luck, ought to be understood,[12] and it is not part of my argument to engage with it here.[13] I inquire here into the potential injustice of unequal risks pursuant to imprudent action, *however* the latter might be understood. Furthermore, I use smoking as an illustration of that question,[14] but I am agnostic with regard to whether smoking is indeed imprudent. (I am, for example, open to the possibility that smoking might not be reasonably avoidable for the poor.)[15] I simply assume that it is for the sake of illustration (and if the reader resists that depiction she is free to replace smoking with any other activity she does consider to be imprudent, e.g. rock-climbing). Still, it would be useful to have a working understanding of what I take prudence, and conversely option luck, to consist of. An action should be understood as prudent, on my understanding, when it would be *unreasonable to expect the agent to avoid it* (or undertake it, in the case of omission).[16] Notice that this understanding of option luck substitutes the more common 'responsibility' with the more nuanced (albeit, more ambiguous) concept of 'reasonable unavoidability'. Let me give three examples by way of illustrating the significance of this difference. A person may avoid traffic accidents by staying indoors at all times. If she steps outdoors (say, in order to go to work or take her children to school), and is then hit by a car while walking on a crosswalk, she could be said to be

---

[12] Martin E. Sandbu, 'On Dworkin's Brute-Luck-Option-Luck Distinction and the Consistency of Brute-Luck Egalitarianism', *Politics, Philosophy, & Economics* 3 (2004), 283–312; Zofia Stemplowska, 'Making Justice Sensitive to Responsibility', *Political Studies* 57 (2009), 237–59; Vallentyne, 'Brute Luck, Option Luck, and Equality of Initial Opportunities'; Lippert-Rasmussen, 'Egalitarianism, Option Luck, and Responsibility'.

[13] I have done so extensively elsewhere. See for example, 'Health, Luck, and Justice Revisited', *Ethical Perspectives* 19 (2012), 328–30.

[14] Smoking is often used as a paradigmatic example of imprudence, by both critics and adherents of luck egalitarianism. On the adherents' side, see Roemer, *Equality of Opportunity*, ch. 8; on the critics' side, see Anderson, 'What is the Point of Equality?' p. 327.

[15] See also Zofia Stemplowska, 'Responsibility and Respect: Reconciling Two Egalitarian Visions', in Carl Knight and Zofia Stemplowska (eds), *Responsibility and Distributive Justice* (Oxford: Oxford University Press, 2011), p. 129.

[16] For a similar account see Vallentyne, 'Brute Luck, Option Luck, and Equality of Initial Opportunities', p. 532.

responsible for the resulting injury.[17] But it would obviously be unreasonable to expect individuals, as a rule, to stay indoors at all times. Thus, stepping outdoors cannot be considered imprudent. Second, getting pregnant is most often something for which the expecting mother is responsible, yet we baulk at portraying pregnancy and the normal risks it carries as a case of option luck. Understanding imprudence in terms of reasonable unavoidability captures this: it would be unreasonable to expect women (as a rule) to avoid getting pregnant. Third, an on-duty fire-fighter who enters a burning building to save a child is, strictly speaking, responsible for the slight burns that she herself may suffer. But again this does not strike us as a case of option luck or imprudence. Instead, we may say that it is unreasonable to expect a fire-fighter to abstain from risking her health in the line of duty. It would *not* be unreasonable to expect a bystander to avoid doing so (when there is a sufficient force of fire-fighters on the scene). And therefore, as far as strict egalitarian justice is concerned, such a bystander may be charged the expenses of her heroic rescue attempt.[18] There is no doubt a lot more that could be said about this understanding of imprudence, but for the purpose of our discussion this working definition should suffice.[19] In any case, this characterization is only meant to facilitate the discussion and is not part of the argument itself. My claim, then, says that *in so far as* an activity counts as imprudent, the inequality of ex ante risks pursuant to it is not itself unjust, when evaluated ex post.

So, is the eventual state of affairs between Steve and Eve unfair? Let me begin by sketching two reasons to think that it is, but ones that, in my view, we should dismiss rather quickly. One such reason to think that, ex post, the outcome is unjust, it might be suggested, is that there is something unfair about the fact that Eve made imprudent choices and yet got out scot free. In other words, she did not end up paying the true price of her choices.[20] If this suggestion is true, then it would mean that the eventual

---

[17]   I follow here Arthur Ripstein, *Equality, Responsibility, and the Law* (Cambridge: Cambridge University Press, 1999), p. 36 ff.

[18]   Cf. Eyal, 'Egalitarian Justice and Innocent Choice'.

[19]   I elaborate this understanding of option luck in *Health, Luck, and Justice*, pp. 19–24, and 'Health, Luck, and Justice Revisted'. For a similar account see Stemplowska, 'Responsibility and Respect', pp. 129–30.

[20]   Dworkin, I think, is sometimes misinterpreted to imply this position: '... equality of resources requires that people pay the true cost of the lives they lead...'. *Sovereign Virtue*, p. 76. I think that this would be a misinterpretation, thought, because in 'true cost' Dworkin means the cost *to others*, rather than some 'cosmic' or 'natural' cost of actions.

inequality between them is unfair. One difficulty with this suggestion, and this is not a mere epistemic matter, is that it is not obvious what the price of smoking is or should be. There is certainly no reason to think that a serious illness, of all things, is the true price of smoking.[21] Even if the illness was in some way the natural outcome (whatever that may mean) of smoking, this still would not yet mean that it is the appropriate 'price' for smoking. A slightly more plausible complaint, then, is that Eve was not held responsible for her imprudent conduct. She would thus seem to fall short of the requirements of luck egalitarianism which is reputedly a responsibility-sensitive conception of egalitarian justice. This claim, however, assumes that there is value (independent of fairness) in holding people responsible for their actions. But as we saw in the previous chapter, this is far from obvious. Even if it is true that fairness ought to be informed by considerations of responsibility it does not follow that responsibility, as a pre-institutional notion, holds some independent value within egalitarian justice.[22] Once again, we must be careful not to confuse here (luck) egalitarianism with the ideal of desert. According to (a certain) ideal of desert, it is a requirement of justice that individuals be made to bear some punishments (and rewards) for their actions. I shall not delve here again into the discussion of what distinguishes LE from desert (see the previous chapter),[23] but what we can say here is that it is rather easy to see that desert is concerned with rewarding and punishing actions (and omissions) for which the agent is responsible *independently* of equality (i.e. independently of comparative assessments). With the risk of stating the obvious, then: if there is something unfair about the story of Steve and Eve this must be for reasons of fairness, not responsibility.

We are searching, then, for intrinsically egalitarian reasons for thinking that distributive justice judges the ex post state of affairs between Steve and Eve to be unfair. Now, the most obvious such reason is that Steve and Eve

---

[21] A similar worry is raised in Avner de Shalit and Jonathan Wolff, 'The Apparent Asymmetry of Responsibility', in Carl Knight and Zofia Stemplowska (eds), *Responsibility and Distributive Justice* (Oxford: Oxford University Press, 2011), p. 217; Zofia Stemplowska, 'Luck Egalitarianism', in G. Gaus and F. D'Agostino (eds), *The Routledge Companion to Social and Political Philosophy* (Abingdon: Routledge, 2012), p. 18; Serena Olsaretti, 'Responsibility and the Consequences of Choice', *Proceedings of the Aristotelian Society* 109 (2009), 165–88.

[22] See also Marc Fleurbaey on this, *Fairness, Responsibility, and Welfare*, p. 260.

[23] I have done so also in *Health, Luck, and Justice*, pp. 16–18. Cf. Daniel M. Hausman, 'Review of Shlomi Segall, "Health, Luck, and Justice"', *Economics and Philosophy* 27 (2011), 190–7.

did not, to begin with, face equal decision trees. From the standpoint of equality this should be of obvious concern. As Richard Arneson wrote in his seminal formulation of the luck egalitarian ideal of 'equality of opportunity for welfare': 'Equal opportunity for welfare obtains among persons when all of them face equivalent decision trees—the expected value of each person's best (=most prudent) choice of option, second-best,... nth best, is the same.'[24] Moreover, in the case of Eve and Steve we have inequality of opportunity with regard to one of the most important goods imaginable (life itself). Our first thought, then, might be that justice, and certainly, luck egalitarian justice, requires equality in initial chances.[25] Inequality of opportunity obtains whenever individuals face non-equivalent decision trees, that is, the state of affairs whereby identical decisions would yield unequally good outcomes. That is not the case between Steve and Eve, hence, arguably, the unfairness.

But is this true? Is the inequality of opportunity between Steve and Eve an unfair one when (importantly) viewed ex post? Suppose Steve and Eve, despite having unequal propensity to contract lung cancer, nevertheless *both end up contracting it* (and at the same time). (Or, suppose they both stay healthy.) Is there anything unfair about this state of affairs? One reason to think that this is still unfair is the fact that compared to Eve, Steve has endured much more stress and anxiety over his smoking (agonizing over his weaker genetic disposition and increased risk of contracting the disease). But this is something we have already set aside at the outset, having assumed that Steve and Eve are both ignorant of their unequal genetic disposition. Holding on to this simplifying assumption of ignorance, then, is there anything unfair about the state of affairs just described (them starting off with unequal risks, but ending with the same outcome)? Upon

---

[24] Arneson, 'Equality and Equal Opportunity for Welfare', pp. 85–6. Arneson, following criticism, seems to have later modified this position. 'People have equal opportunity for welfare, roughly, if each faces an initial array of life options such that each would get the same welfare over the course of his life if each behaved *as prudently* as it would be reasonable to expect.' Richard J. Arneson, 'Equality of Opportunity for Welfare Defended and Recanted', *Journal of Political Philosophy* 7 (1999), p. 493 (my emphasis).

[25] As for what counts as 'initial': typically egalitarians will speak of individuals reaching maturity (say, the age of eighteen), but this is also a contentious matter. See Clare Chambers, 'Each Outcome is Another Opportunity: Problems with the Moment of Equal Opportunity', *Politics, Philosophy, & Economics* 8 (2009), 374–400. I postpone addressing that issue until Chapter 6.

reflection, it is hard to think of a reason to hold such a view.[26] This seems pretty clear to me, but to see this even more clearly suppose Eve and Steve do both contract the illness and now seek medical care, and suppose it can only be given to one of them. Recall that all else is equal between them, including how prudent they have been in looking after themselves. Should the discovery, now, that, ex ante, Steve was twice as much at risk compared to Eve give him (or her, for that matter) any stronger claim on the medical treatment? This seems implausible. This shows (what to me seems to begin with rather obvious) that, ex post, having unequal risk to contract cancer (or, in other words, having unequal *opportunity* to stay healthy) is not in itself unfair.[27]

Now suppose, alternatively, that Steve and Eve, having started with unequal initial chances to contract cancer, do end up unequally well-off, only now it is Eve, the one with the better genetic disposition, who actually got sick, and Steve, having the weaker disposition to begin with, somehow, against the odds, did not. Is there anything unfair about this state of affairs? Perhaps there is, but if so, it is obviously not on account of the unequal initial chances. The presumed unfairness in this case follows solely from the fact that two individuals made exactly the same choices yet ended up with radically unequal outcomes. If there is anything unfair about this state of affairs, it is an unfairness which has nothing to do with the unequal initial chances. Here is a third and final variant: suppose Steve, who was, to begin with, at a greater risk of contracting cancer, not only smoked (which Eve did as well), but also imprudently exposed himself to some unnecessary radiation. And suppose it is established that it is in fact the radiation, and not the smoking, that was the cause of his cancer. Is that state of affairs unfair? Perhaps. But here it would seem wrong to accord Steve compensation *on account* of his initial aggravated risk compared to Eve. That inequality in initial risks had nothing to do with his eventual disadvantage.

---

[26] This point was made already in Kasper Lippert-Rasmussen, 'Arneson on Equality of Opportunity for Welfare', *Journal of Political Philosophy* 7 (1999), p. 484; 'Egalitarianism, Option Luck, and Responsibility', *Ethics* 111 (2001), p. 563.

[27] This may raise an objection: we often think it is wrong to expose people to risks. Indeed, doing so is often liable to legal sanctions, even if, ex post, the risk never materialized. But of course the reason grounding this legal practice might be the social value in setting incentives for prudent conduct. Put simply, exposing others to risk can be wrong for reasons other than fairness.

We may summarize our by-conclusions regarding an ex post evaluation of ex ante risks (option luck) in Table 3.1. (Recall that we are holding constant the level of prudence of the two agents.)

Table 3.1 An ex post evaluation of ex ante risks (option luck)

Chances	Outcomes	Unfair?
Equal	Equal	Not unfair
Equal	Unequal	Not unfair (at least according to standard luck egalitarianism)
Unequal	Equal	Not unfair
Unequal	Unequal, but *not* due to the unequal chances (e.g. Eve, rather than Steve, ending up ill)	Not unfair (at least not due to the unequal chances)
Unequal	Unequal (due to the unequal chances)	?

Following Table 3.1,[28] we shall restrict our investigation from now on to the last row. We need to investigate whether or not an unequal outcome with regard to smoking that was *caused by* an inequality in initial risk to contract a smoking-related disease is objectionable. Or to put this differently: is it unjust for some smokers to end up worse-off than other smokers *because* of having an initially worse propensity to get sick? And once again, more generally: is it unjust for an imprudent risk-taker to end up worse-off than someone taking the exact same action *because* of facing an initially worse risk?

---

[28] Notice that the table replicates the lesson from the previous chapter, namely that unequal outcome is a necessary condition for unfairness. As Arneson writes: 'I think that what matters fundamentally from the moral standpoint is not the opportunities one gets but the outcomes one's opportunities generate.' 'Equality of Opportunity for Welfare Defended and Recanted', p. 497. See also Lippert-Rasmussen, 'Arneson on Equality of Opportunity for Welfare'; Fleurbaey, 'Equal Opportunity or Equal Social Outcome?' esp. §7; and Arneson's amendment to his ideal of equality of opportunity for welfare: 'Equality and Equal Opportunity for Welfare: A Postscript', p. 239.

II. Is Outcome Inequality Between Unequally-situated Risk-takers Unfair?

There is a certain built-in difficulty in answering the question before us, I speculate, because much of the answer may depend on intuition. This may explain why the literature is divided on this issue, with all-luck egalitarians and standard luck egalitarians holding opposite views. But there is perhaps a way of unpacking this particular question, so that it yields a more principled and definite answer. To do so we need the following assumption, which might, at first blush, appear controversial. It says that unfairness cannot obtain if there is no agent (actual or potential) whose pro tanto duty (importantly, of fairness) it is to rectify it.[29] The premiss may seem controversial because it might be thought to give luck egalitarian justice a social-relative dimension, a somewhat Rawlsian feature from which luck egalitarians have long laboured to distance themselves. But this impression would be mistaken. To begin with, the premiss is consistent with our lesson from the first two chapters: there is no unfairness if there is no one who is under duty to justify her advantage. To see this more fully, consider some paradigmatic examples: in contrast to Rawlsians, luck egalitarians often claim that it is unfair for one to enter this world with less marketable talents, or similarly, that it is unfair (and not merely bad) to be struck by lightning (when some others are not). Identifying these states of affairs as unfair implies, I submit, that there is some agent(s), whose duty it is to rectify this unjust disadvantage, whether or not she is currently capable of doing so. The last qualifier is worth stressing. The test does not depend on some hypothetical requirement, according to which for injustice to obtain, its rectification must be (physically) feasible. The impossibility of matching my basketball skills to those of Michael Jordan, or the medical impossibility of making the lightning-stricken individual walk again, does not detract, in the eyes of luck egalitarians, from the unfairness of the said disadvantage. What the premiss in question does require is that there is somebody (society as a whole or some particular individuals) for whom it is a duty of egalitarian justice to rectify the unfairness. There is probably much more that could be said about correlating unfairness with

---

[29] Here I find myself in a surprising agreement with Elizabeth Anderson. See her, 'The Fundamental Disagreement between Luck Egalitarians and Relational Egalitarians', *Canadian Journal of Philosophy* 36 (2010), p. 5, 9.

an agent whose duty of justice it is to alleviate it, but I hope what I have said suffices for our purposes here.

If Steve suffers some unfairness, there must be someone whom luck egalitarian justice identifies as having the duty to rectify that disadvantage. Who might that be? All-luck egalitarians, I noted in the introduction, target Eve (that is, smokers who are both lucky and genetically better endowed) as the one exclusively under that duty. Incidentally, locating the duty of fairness exclusively with Eve, notice, is crucial for the ALE justification of cigarette taxation as a means of pursuing justice *between* smokers (because if not, the scheme would encompass society as a whole, as opposed merely to smokers).[30]

But it is questionable whether Eve, as distinct from society as a whole, owes Steve some compensation. Eve, for example, might very plausibly claim that it is not her fault that Steve got sick. They both undertook an activity knowing full well that it risks grave consequences. (What they did not know was only the exact unequal degree of the risk.) Moreover, it would not have been unreasonable to expect Steve to refrain from the activity in question. The fact that Eve also smoked does not reduce Steve's imprudence and consequently, his liability. Still, might not Steve and Eve's liability be a shared one? After all, there is nothing to distinguish between their stories save from their differential luck. Now, there may have been, perhaps, a case to target Eve (as distinct from society as a whole) if smoking was somehow seen to generate duties of fair play among all smokers. To fully see this, compare the case under investigation with the following one. Suppose an organizer of an extreme sport event proposes to hire two skiers for a double act. And suppose the two skiers agree to do it, only they know in advance that one of them faces a greater risk of a compound fracture should he do so. In this case, there may well be a good reason to impose some mutual insurance (to be derived from the prize money) on the two skiers. This seems to me quite plausible. But it is hard to see anything of that sort pertaining to the smoking case. Smoking is not a joint venture. To pursue and enjoy smoking it is not necessary for it to be undertaken together, nor does it yield some mutual benefit. People can, and usually do pursue it alone and for their own gratification. There is

---

[30] See again Cappelen and Norheim, 'Responsibility in Health Care: A Liberal Egalitarian Approach'.

therefore nothing mutual or joint about that undertaking, 'social smoking' notwithstanding.[31] There seems, therefore, to be no justification for duties of fair play that are exclusive to smokers. It is the case then, that it would not be right to target lucky risk-takers as those whose exclusive duty it is to compensate the unlucky ones.

There is nothing that Eve, as distinct from society as a whole, owes Steve as a matter of egalitarian justice. That fact does *not* yet show that the inequality between Steve and Eve is just, for it might be the case that society as a whole is under a duty of justice to alleviate Steve's disadvantage. We need to inquire, then, whether society (as opposed to Eve alone) owes Steve compensation. More to the point, we ask whether Steve is owed societal compensation on account of the fact that his disadvantaged outcome (his illness) was the result of a disadvantaged starting point, and crucially, one for which, we all agree, he was not responsible.

What claim of justice, then, might Steve have against society as a whole? I can think of three (and only three) such claims. The first, and most obvious one is that he is worse-off than Eve (namely, he is ill), and through no fault of his own (his illness, recall the last row of the table above, did stem from his weak genetic disposition). Now, society is (obviously) composed of both smokers and non-smokers. Do non-smokers have a duty of justice to compensate Steve? For luck egalitarians the answer should be straightforwardly negative. Steve's plight is ultimately a matter of option luck (on my account, or indeed any other luck egalitarian account). By hypothesis, his illness would not have occurred if it wasn't for his voluntary (so we assume) choice to smoke. His voluntary act of smoking is the sine qua non, as it were, for his current disadvantaged state. When the demand for compensation is directed not exclusively at other smokers but rather at society as a whole, Steve's claim loses whatever plausibility it might have had. On a luck-egalitarian reading (at least), his disadvantaged end-state (his illness) does not appear to be something that it is the duty of non-smokers to rectify. If Steve has a valid complaint against society as a whole, then, it must be grounded not in his end-state but rather in his disadvantaged starting-point vis-à-vis Eve.

---

[31] The 'social' in social smoking denotes that the benefit gained from smoking sometimes increases when it is done in company. But this does not yet imply that smoking is an undertaking of mutual benefit. It is hard to see, for example, what would constitute free-riding in 'social smoking'.

That, indeed, could be the basis of Steve's second potential claim. His disadvantaged starting point compared to Eve *did* lie outside his control. But we can quickly see that this alleged disadvantage also cannot ground a society-wide duty of compensation. This is something we have already established in Section I (recall Table 3.1). Viewed ex post, unequal ex ante chances cannot, in and of themselves, constitute an injustice. (It is the disadvantaged *outcome* which follows a disadvantaged starting point which is, if anything, unjust.) Steve, thus, cannot claim compensation for his disadvantaged starting point *independently* of some disadvantaged outcome. Just to illustrate once again, if his initial disadvantaged starting point *was*, on its own, a source of a valid claim, Steve should then have received compensation even if he never got sick, or indeed, even if he never smoked! But that is counterintuitive.[32]

This latest point may hint at a third (and final) source of disadvantage suffered by Steve. This potential source of disadvantage entails, however, revising our initial example, something I am happy to do for the sake of argument. Suppose that upon turning eighteen, Steve was informed of his greater risk of contracting smoking-related illnesses (compared to Eve), and so decides not to become a smoker. He would have, he informs us in good faith, taken up smoking had he had normal chances of contracting the disease. But finding out that he has an even greater risk (compared to the average smoker) of getting sick he decides that he is better-off, in that case, not tempting luck. Should Steve now at least get some compensation for *that* disadvantage, that is, for the fact that, compared to Eve, he cannot, for all intents and purposes, take up an activity he craves? At first blush, it might seem absurd of Steve to claim compensation for something that may have well spared him the horrors of smoking-related diseases. If anything, he ought to be grateful for being informed of that so-called disadvantage, since it is the implications of this aggravated risk that deterred him from smoking. Still, there might be something to his complaint. At least so far as first-order preferences are concerned, Steve does appear to be at a disadvantage compared to Eve.[33]

---

[32] Vallentyne's 'equality of initial chances' suffers from precisely this weakness, I think. He admits that his principle may well require that those with good prospects but (eventual) miserable lives would have to compensate those with poor prospects but adequate lives. See his 'Brute Luck, Option Luck, and Equality of Initial Opportunities', pp. 547–8.

[33] Notice, incidentally, that this would constitute a more modest claim for compensation compared to compensation for the illness itself.

To see whether Steve has a (residual) justice-based claim here, it would be instructive to compare his case with an example of a rare allergy. Consider aspartame, a common ingredient in dietetic soft drinks. One of the residues of aspartame upon ingestion is a high dosage of an amino acid called phenylalanine. For most people phenylalanine is completely safe. However, some, who are born with a rare genetic disorder (called Phenylketonuria), do not have the ability to break it down. For those people, especially at a younger age, the consumption of more than a very small dose of phenylalanine or of products causing its production in the body (such as aspartame) will cause brain damage, mental retardation, seizures, and even death.[34] It is plausible to suppose that for this minority it would be imprudent to go on drinking dietetic soft drinks. This follows directly from our working definition of imprudence: it would *not* be unreasonable to expect someone with Phenylketonuria to avoid drinking dietetic drinks. Crucially, the inequality in initial risk represented in this case, it seems to me, *is* unfair. There is a clear disadvantage here for which neither group is responsible: those sensitive to aspartame effectively cannot do something which the rest of us, for all intents and purposes, can. Drinking Diet Coke (say) is safe for most people but unsafe for the diagnosed group. To be prudent, the latter must refrain from it. These individuals are thus at a disadvantage compared to the rest of society, for whom Diet Coke is very much on the menu. It is therefore the case that those vulnerable to aspartame have a claim for compensation. It is compensation, note, for the disadvantage entailed by the fact that drinking Diet Coke is off the menu for them; it is *not* compensation for the outcome that would ensue if they drank it nevertheless. This, in turn, helps us reflect back on Steve's third claim. Assuming that *smoking is prudent for no one*, there is no action X which is on the menu for Eve (or anyone else for that matter) but off the menu for Steve. Steve therefore has no claim for compensation even for the residual disadvantage of not being able to smoke (safely).[35]

[34] R. Surtees and N. Blau, 'The Neurochemistry of Phenylketonuria', *European Journal of Pediatrics* 169 (2000), S109–S113.

[35] This, however, seems to open the door to an obvious objection. Suppose we discover that there is this one individual for whom smoking proves completely safe. This person has, miraculously, a genetic makeup which immunizes her body to the dangerous effects of smoking. The existence of that one individual would then seem to hijack my entire case. But I don't think this is a weakness for my account. If there is someone for whom smoking is prudent then it *would be* right for Steve to claim compensation at least for the disadvantage entailed in not being able to smoke safely. With respect to *egalitarian justice*, it is indeed bad that there is something which is prudent for some (even if one person) yet is imprudent for others.

III. Revising the Luck Egalitarian Formula?

Let us take stock of what has been established so far. First, I noted that, judged ex post, a disadvantaged initial risk is potentially unfair only if it causes a disadvantaged outcome. Then I noted that being disadvantaged in terms of initial risks does not give rise to a claim against lucky and better endowed risk-takers. And then (Section II) I showed that being disadvantaged in terms of ex ante risks pursuant to an imprudent conduct also does not give rise to a claim of justice against society as a whole. We must conclude, then, that (ex post) the inequality in initial risks between such imprudent agents as Steve and Eve is not unjust, even when it does lead to Steve being disadvantaged later on in life.

Is this conclusion embarrassing for luck egalitarians? Recall that we began this inquiry noting the luck egalitarian commitment to eradicate disadvantages for which individuals are not responsible. If it is unjust for individuals to be worse-off through factors that are outside their control then how can it be not unfair for Steve to be worse-off than Eve? After all, as we noted at the outset, the inequality between them is something that lay outside their control. I want, then, to propose a way out of this dilemma. The key is a somewhat overlooked comment made by Thomas Nagel quite a while before the onset of all-luck egalitarianism. Egalitarians, Nagel wrote, object not to '*inequalities* for which the parties are not responsible, but only to the parties' being unequal in goods or evils for *the possession of which* they are not responsible'.[36] In other words, egalitarians (qua egalitarians) object to a person suffering some evil for no fault of her own when that misfortune results in her being worse-off compared to others. Egalitarians, then, indeed object to people being worse-off than others for reasons that are beyond their control. But the clause 'reasons beyond their control' refers not to being worse-off than others, but to suffering some absolute bad (which, in turn, leads them to be worse-off than others). Brute luck is therefore the property of the absolute bad that has befallen a person; not of her disadvantaged position vis-à-vis others.[37] To sum up the point, being unfairly disadvantaged

[36] Thomas Nagel, *Equality and Partiality* (Oxford: Oxford University Press, 1991), p. 72. Cf. Lippert-Rasmussen, 'Egalitarianism, Option Luck, and Responsibility', p. 573, n. 47.

[37] This understanding of fairness may, unsurprisingly, help solve the puzzle of moral luck. Advocates of the moral luck thesis such as the early Nagel [see his 'Moral Luck', in his *Mortal Questions* (Cambridge: Cambridge University Press, 1979)] hold that it is unjust for

has two necessary conditions according to this interpretation of luck egalitarianism: an interpersonal aspect and an intrapersonal one. First, the person must be worse-off than others (the interpersonal aspect). (This was the conclusion of the previous chapter.) Second, the person must be worse-off than she would otherwise have been (the intrapersonal aspect), and, crucially, for reasons that were beyond her control. This understanding of luck egalitarianism rids it of the alleged incoherence: it advocates a duty to compensate those who suffer a disadvantage, the absolute badness of which they could not have avoided. Luck egalitarians are not, in contrast, forced to compensate for disadvantages the relative badness of which the sufferer could not have controlled. Thus, they are not forced to compensate unlucky gamblers, including unlucky smokers.

Conclusion

I have not argued here that the Nagel formula is the correct interpretation of luck egalitarianism. I do, however, claim that it is a plausible interpretation of luck egalitarianism, and moreover, one that escapes its alleged incoherence. The story of Eve and Steve, I hope to have shown, helps illustrate that lesson. I should, perhaps, end by saying that the plight of Steve may arouse all sorts of ethical concerns, ones having to do with compassion,[38] autonomy,[39] solidarity,[40] the concern for his basic needs,[41]

---

two individuals who undertake an identical action, to end up with unequal outcomes, and merely on account of how their luck turned out. To use a standard example, consider two reckless drivers, only one of which ends up in an accident (and injuring a passenger, say). The only difference between the two is owed to luck. Thus, there should not be any difference in our moral evaluation of the two drivers. The approach taken here handles the example differently. It is not unjust for the two risk-takers to end up with unequal outcomes (e.g. one has to pay damages and the other does not). And the reason is that it is only bad for two agents to be unequal with regards to goods or evils the occurrence of which they could not have reasonably avoided. Since we assume that both drivers could have reasonably avoided driving recklessly, it is the case that the eventual inequality between them is not unjust.

[38] Roger Crisp, 'Equality, Priority, and Compassion', *Ethics* 113 (2003), 745–63.

[39] For an autonomy-based account of aiding Steves and other smokers see Seana Valentine Shiffrin, 'Paternalism, the Unconscionability Doctrine, and Accommodation', *Philosophy and Public Affairs* 29 (2000), p. 239ff.

[40] See my 'In Solidarity with the Imprudent: A Defence of Luck Egalitarianism', *Social Theory and Practice* 33 (2007), 177–98.

[41] See my *Health, Luck, and Justice*, pp. 75–8.

civic capabilities,[42] and so forth. In this chapter I have only tried to argue that, upon reflection, egalitarian distributive justice is not one of those concerns.

The lesson from this chapter and the previous one taken together can be summarized in a sentence. Unequal opportunities are unfair only when pursuant to prudent conduct and when resulting in unequal outcomes. This is the scope of equality of opportunity with which justice ought to be concerned, and it is that scope of equality of opportunity that I shall be addressing in the rest of the book. I next turn to see how the radical understanding of equality of opportunity bears on something which has been the traditional subject of EOp, namely the allocation of office.

---

[42] Anderson, 'What is the Point of Equality?'

PART II
Hiring

4

Luck Egalitarian Justice in Hiring

What does luck egalitarianism say about justice in hiring? You might think that it says that hiring is discriminatory when based on traits for which the candidate is not responsible (or that it must be *only* according to traits for which one *is* responsible). But that would be mistaken. Instead, I want to suggest in the course of the next two chapters that the luck egalitarian, radical account of equality of opportunity says, very simply, that jobs ought to be allocated in such a way so as to equalize (opportunity for) welfare across society.[1]

This radical principle of justice in hiring is motivated by (at least) three premisses. The first, basic, premiss is the requirement of non-discrimination. For now we shall understand non-discrimination as the negative requirement of not allocating jobs on the basis of arbitrary considerations. (Section III is devoted to providing more content to this account of non-discrimination.) Second, radical, luck egalitarian (I shall use these interchangeably) equality of opportunity (EOp) does not see qualifications as entitling an individual to any particular job. And third, radical EOp does not accord jobs any privileged position within the account of justice it adheres to, and therefore does not see them as distinct from all other goods.[2] We may term these premisses of the radical position as, respectively, *non-discrimination*, *non-meritocracy*, and *monism*. The combined effect of

---

[1] In this I follow the position first introduced by luck egalitarian Richard Arneson. See Richard J. Arneson, 'Against Rawlsian Equality of Opportunity', *Philosophical Studies* 93 (1999), pp. 77–112. But I shall later note an important difference between my account and his.

[2] See also Arneson, 'Against Rawlsian Equality of Opportunity'. I should say that two other leading luck egalitarians, Cohen and Roemer, explicitly reject this requirement and hold that jobs are special in a way that other advantages are not. See G. A. Cohen, *On the Currency of Egalitarian Justice, and Other Essays in Political Philosophy* (Princeton and Oxford: Princeton University Press, 2011), p. 63; John E. Roemer, *Equality of Opportunity* (Cambridge, MA; London: Harvard University Press, 1998), pp. 86–7.

these three premisses is that luck egalitarian justice may use the allocation of jobs to offset inequalities in overall opportunity for welfare. Consequently, and very simply, luck egalitarian justice allocates jobs not according to qualifications but according to need. (By 'need' I do not mean 'need for the particular job' but rather 'being worse-off' more generally.) On the luck egalitarian view, then, individuals may have a claim for a certain job not on the grounds of their qualifications for it, but on the grounds of their position in the distribution of well-being in society. We may formulate that luck egalitarian account of justice in hiring thus. *Negatively, hiring must not be based on morally arbitrary considerations, and positively, the allocation of jobs must be used to equalize welfare across society.*

The two chapters in this part of the book are devoted to grounding that account. I begin, in this chapter, by arguing against the meritocratic view (Section I). Having defended the non-meritocratic element of luck egalitarian justice in hiring, I then introduce the other two elements of that account (Section II). In Section III I address the objection that luck egalitarian justice in hiring may license discrimination *against the rich* (or more accurately, the better-off). I meet that objection by introducing and elaborating (Section IV) on the abovementioned non-discrimination component. Section V then shows that the luck egalitarian account provides an attractive response with regard to the tricky issue of statistical discrimination. The whole of the next chapter is then devoted to addressing the objection that luck egalitarian justice in hiring licenses discrimination *against the poor* (or more accurately, the worse-off).

I should say that for the sake of simplicity my discussion in this chapter and the next is restricted to justice in hiring, namely the allocation of existing jobs, rather than to the broader issue of justice in employment, which would also encompass justice in the creation and restructuring of jobs.[3]

I. Against Meritocracy

The meritocratic ideal says that individuals have a claim of justice to the positions for which they are the best qualified.[4] In incorporating a

---

[3] That is largely the preoccupation in Paul Gomberg, *How to Make Opportunity Equal? Race and Contributive Justice* (Malden, MA: Blackwell, 2007).

[4] See David Miller, *Principles of Social Justice* (Cambridge, MA: Harvard University Press, 1999), ch. 8; George Sher, 'Qualification, Fairness, and Desert', in N. Bowie (ed.), *Equal*

non-meritocratic premiss, luck egalitarian justice in hiring goes against much of the accepted view, and finds itself in (uneasy) company with libertarians, mainly.[5] In this section I will try to show that the meritocratic ideal is indefensible, and devote the next one to showing why rejecting that ideal is nevertheless compatible with an attractive account of justice in hiring.

By 'meritocracy', I mean the view that individuals are entitled to certain positions because they possess some qualifications that make them suitable for carrying out the tasks associated with these jobs. It is easy to see that meritocratic considerations are of the forward-looking kind. This distinguishes merit from the related ideal of desert, which is generally understood as a backward-looking consideration.[6] When applied to jobs, the ideal of desert would state that individuals are entitled to certain positions because of something they have *done or achieved*. Obviously, a lot more can be said about deserving jobs as opposed to meriting them, and this will surface in the discussion below, but this brief characterization should suffice for the moment.

So, do individuals have a special claim on the jobs for which they are the best qualified, and if so, why? One suggestion along these lines is that the best qualified have worked hard to acquire the skills that make them suitable for a job, and it is this that entitles them to the job in question. But this argument, we can immediately see, would justify allocating jobs based on effort rather than merit. It does not tell us to appoint the person who has the most qualifications but the one who has worked the hardest to try and gain them. A related explanation concerns legitimate expectations: individuals have laboured hard to acquire the skills required under the expectation that the job in question would be given to the person who turns out to be the most qualified. This is plausible enough. Moreover, this reasoning *would* justify appointing the most qualified person rather than the one who has worked the hardest to earn qualifications. After all, that was the

---

Opportunity (Boulder, CO: Westview, 1988); Andrew Mason, 'Equality of Opportunity, Old and New', *Ethics* 111 (2001), 760–81.

[5] E.g. Matt Cavanagh, *Against Equality of Opportunity* (Oxford: Oxford University Press, 2002).

[6] See Miller, *Principles of Social Justice*, p. 137. [See also Norman Daniels, 'Merit and Meritocracy', *Philosophy and Public Affairs* 7 (1978), 206–23 for an earlier invocation of a similar thesis.] Miller's position, it should be noted, represents a mix between the forward-looking concerns of merit and the backward-looking concerns of desert.

expectation everyone were labouring under. However, like any argument about legitimate expectations, this one only provides a contingent defence of the ideal. It only tells us to meet a certain set of expectations once they have been formed.

A third reason can be found in Rawls's theory of justice. In defence of his Fair Equality of Opportunity Principle (FEOp), Rawls says that unless we fill positions on the basis of open competition we would be depriving people of the good of self-realization that comes from a fulfilling job. He says:

> if some places were not open on a basis fair to all, those kept out would be right in feeling unjustly treated even though they benefited from the greater efforts of those who were allowed to hold them. They would be justified in their complaint not only because they were excluded from certain external rewards of office but because they were debarred from the realization of self which comes from a skilful and devoted exercise of social duties. They would be deprived of one of the main forms of human good.[7]

This says nothing yet about appointing the best qualified, but Rawls couples this requirement of open competition with the requirement of 'careers open to talent'.[8] His FEOp thus stipulates that competition for jobs should be based on qualifications.[9] For Rawls, then, to appoint individuals on grounds other than their qualifications would be to deprive them of the important good of self-realization. This is also Rawls's main justification for placing the allocation of jobs under the auspices of the strictly egalitarian FEOp rather than under the maximinizing difference principle (DP). But it is doubtful that the concern for self-realization can provide a justification for meritocracy.[10] For why should the self-realization of the best qualified be of greater value compared to that of the person who is only slightly less qualified? [The same point applies even in the absence of meritocratic considerations: why should the self-realization of those who were selected through *lottery* (assuming it represents an open and fair competition) be of greater concern than the self-realization of those who have

---

[7] John Rawls, *A Theory of Justice* (Oxford: Clarendon Press, 1972), p. 84.

[8] *A Theory of Justice*, pp. 72–3.

[9] See also Seana Valentine Shiffrin, 'Race, Labor, and the Fair Equality of Opportunity Principle', *Fordham Law Review* 72 (2004), p. 1649.

[10] This has been noted already in Arneson, 'Against Rawlsian Equality of Opportunity', p. 97; Andrew Mason, *Levelling the Playing Field: The Idea of Equal Opportunity and its Place in Egalitarian Thought* (Oxford: Oxford University Press, 2006), p. 85.

lost out?] There seems no reason to think that it should. Moreover, based on the reasoning provided by Rawls here, we would have to allocate jobs not according to qualifications but according to their ability to improve the self-fulfilment of the worse-off. One thought that might be motivating Rawls here is that the likelihood of deriving a sense of self-fulfilment from one's job is strongly correlated with one's qualifications for it. People do often enjoy doing things that they are good at, and conversely, are frustrated by jobs, even prestigious ones, for which they are either over- or under-qualified. But we must not of course suppose that this will *always* be true.[11] In any case, this is an empirical matter. To establish a principle of justice according to which an individual *always* has a claim to the job for which she is the best qualified, the link between qualifications and self-fulfilment would have to be more than merely a contingent one.

Given all these difficulties, the meritocratic case seems to have settled, in recent years, on the view that to refrain from appointing the most qualified person would be disrespectful to her.[12] When individuals who possess the relevant skills for a given job are passed over in favour of a lesser applicant they rightly feel slighted, or so the claim goes. Notice that this is not necessarily a claim about legitimate expectations. The claim is that even absent such institutionalized expectations individuals have good grounds for feeling that their moral agency has been disrespected when a lesser candidate is preferred over them. This is an attractive and increasingly popular line of reasoning in support of appointing the best qualified. It is also one that luck egalitarians should have no qualms endorsing (at least in so far as the qualifications refer to cultivated skills rather than innate talents).[13] Notice that this argument may be appealing on both deontological and consequential concerns. Consider, first, the consequential version of the argument, according to which when the best qualified is passed over she is likely to suffer dignitary harm. For this argument to be true, notice, it has to be the case that the best qualified actually knows that from all those who have applied, she herself was the best qualified for the particular position. But this condition of course may not always hold. It is not always so easy

---

[11] See also Daniels, 'Merit and Meritocracy', p. 213.

[12] Mason, *Levelling the Playing Field*, pp. 56–64; George Sher, *Approximate Justice: Studies in Non-Ideal Theory* (Lanham, MD: Rowman and Littlefield, 1997), p. 128.

[13] This is in fact Mason's position, and his main argument for his hybrid position of 'meritocratic responsibility-sensitive egalitarianism'. See his 'Equality of Opportunity, Old and New'.

for someone to ascertain that she is the very best candidate. This means that, if anything, the concern for self respect would only rule out appointing a blatantly less-qualified person, rather than justifying a commitment to appoint *the very best* candidate. Consider, then, the deontological version of the argument, according to which to refrain from appointing the best qualified is to show disrespect towards her, which is wrong, whether or not she is aware of being disrespected. The problem with this version of the argument is that it is not clear that passing over the best qualified is always a manifestation of disrespect. As Arneson has pointed out, it is not obvious that appointing a person who is almost as qualified as the top candidate, but who is worse-off (and thus arguably more deserving) in other respects, would be disrespectful of that top candidate.[14] It is certainly difficult to see why that would be disrespectful given due publicity constraints and given how legitimate expectations would be duly formulated to take candidates' needs into account.[15] Finally, even if it were disrespectful to pass over the top candidate (whether for deontological or consequential grounds), it is still not obvious that the concern for self-respect (a good which, one need not dispute, is of concern for justice) should trump all other considerations of distributive justice.

The self-respect argument proves even weaker when we enter the thorny field of affirmative action (at which we shall look more carefully in the next chapter). If it is always disrespectful to appoint anyone but the most qualified person then how could it ever be just to prefer a member of a disadvantaged group who is nearly but not as qualified as the top candidate? Proponents of the self-respect view say, in response, that affirmative action need not, in fact, be disrespectful. For, the person appointed *would have been*

---

[14]   Arneson, 'Against Rawlsian Equality of Opportunity', p. 97.

[15]   To be fair, Mason, one of the advocates of the self-respect argument, acknowledges that 'there is a range of cases where taking into account considerations other than the candidates' abilities to perform the job does not appear to be disrespectful to their agency' (*Levelling the Playing Field*, p. 61). He, therefore, reverts to arguing that the self-respect argument does not give us a reason to always appoint the best qualified, but only a presumption in favour of doing so. There ought to be a presumption in favour of appointing the best qualified, says Mason, because doing so is a good rule of thumb for ruling out disrespect-based discrimination. But of course, the fact that the practice of appointing the best qualified is a good way of preventing discrimination does not yet imply that the best qualified have a justice-based reason to be appointed, which is what we are investigating here. And, moreover, the fact that appointing the best qualified is a good way of avoiding discrimination does not mean that it is the *only* way of doing so. Indeed, I shall offer a non-meritocratic alternative for non-discrimination in the next chapter.

the most qualified candidate if it weren't for the systematic disadvantage of the group to which she belongs.[16] This is a nice argument, but I speculate that even its proponents would admit that it is pulling at the seams of the notion of respect, and for the following reasons. First, the argument is contingent on the fact that those currently most qualified (that is, those who would have been selected if it wasn't for the policy of affirmative action) would readily recognize that the other candidate would have been better qualified than them if it wasn't for the historical discrimination. This is highly speculative.[17] But the proponent of the self-respect view could bypass that problem by simply speaking of people having 'good grounds' for feeling slighted, rather than of whether or not they are in fact slighted. So, second, even setting the speculative nature of the claim aside, do we really know whether absent the systematic disadvantage the person in question would have been the best candidate? We may have grounds for thinking that she would have been *good enough*, but knowing that she would have been the very best seems a bit of a stretch. It follows, then, that, at best, the self-respect argument could still justify affirmative action but only at the cost of sacrificing the requirement of appointing the best qualified person.

The self-respect argument seems to be the most sophisticated justification for meritocracy, but even it proves inadequate in justifying appointing the *best* qualified. But what if the meritocrat gave up on the ideal of appointing the best qualified, and settled instead for the closest second best, namely *appointing according to qualifications and qualifications alone*? This could perhaps prove a fruitful way of resurrecting a measure of the meritocratic ideal. One problem with this suggestion, however, is that again it would seem to rule out affirmative action (unless, implausibly in my view, disadvantaged-group-membership is considered a qualification for a job).[18] Another problem is that it is not entirely clear what 'appointing according to qualifications' exactly means. If it simply means—'giving

---

[16] Sher, *Approximate Justice*, ch. 3.

[17] Admittedly, though, this is no more a speculative claim than others according to which non-meritocratic practices would be disrespectful. On this general abuse of respect-based arguments see Nir Eyal, *Distributing Respect* (Oxford: Oxford University DPhil Thesis, 2003).

[18] This is the strategy adopted by Ronald Dworkin: 'If a black skin will, as a matter of regrettable fact, enable another doctor to do a different medical job better, then that black skin is by the same token "merit" as well.' [Ronald Dworkin, *A Matter of Principle* (Cambridge, MA, and London: Harvard University Press, 1985), p. 299.] In a later piece, Dworkin somewhat modifies this argument, stating that he never meant to depict skin colour as source of merit. [*Sovereign Virtue: The Theory and Practice of Equality* (Cambridge,

some consideration to the person's qualifications'—then that does not tell us much. Almost everyone has *some* qualifications for performing brain-surgery, by virtue of having opposable thumbs, or by virtue of the ability to tell a skull from a ribcage. 'Giving consideration to qualifications' is therefore critically uninformative. The most plausible interpretation of 'appointing according to qualifications' is therefore, probably, the idea of 'selecting individuals for jobs *in correlation* to their degree of qualification'. As a policy this sounds plausible enough, and is certainly much more informative compared to the alternative just mentioned. But in trying to spell out what that requirement precisely means, it quickly turns out that the commitment to appoint in correlation to qualifications inevitably ends up as the commitment to appoint the *best* qualified. For when we rank correlations between the requirements of a job and the qualifications a person has for it, the best qualified simply comes up at the highest rung of the correlation. Appointing in correlation to skills turns out to be simply another way of describing the commitment to appoint the best qualified (and as such, subject to all the problems we already witnessed with regard to that requirement).

Alternatively, if one is determined to avoid being committed to appointing according to qualifications then the only possible recourse is to select a candidate by lottery from a pool of *sufficiently* qualified candidates.[19] But, of course, then the dilemma shifts to how to determine that threshold. What distinguishes a person who is sufficiently qualified and thus meriting inclusion in the draw, from one who is insufficiently qualified, and thus being denied *any* chance of landing the job? There seems to be no credible

MA, and London: Harvard University Press, 2000), p. 404. But he then goes on to say that skin colour can act as 'a qualification' for a place in a university, akin to height for a basketball player. So his position seems effectively to remain the same.] To see why this argument is implausible we need to distinguish two ways in which skin colour (say) could be meritorious in the case discussed. One way concerns clients' (in this case, patients') reactions. Some patients, especially elderly ones, prefer being treated by doctors of their own race, and since there is a shortage of black doctors this may give us a reason to prefer black candidates. But as Miller correctly points out, on that rationale it would be equally right to prefer white doctors in hospitals serving predominantly white populations, and that seems wrong. (Miller, *Principles of Social Justice*, p. 174.) The other way in which Dworkin might mean skin colour to potentially count as merit is if it serves as an encouragement for black youth to strive and become doctors (the 'role model effect'). But notice that in that case skin colour cannot be said to allow the black candidate to *perform the job* better. Rather, she is a better candidate for reasons other than job-performance.

[19] See for example Roemer, *Equality of Opportunity*, p. 1.

way of drawing that line that escapes arbitrariness. The meritocrat would be hard pressed to show (with regard to each and every job) that applicants divide into neat categories of the qualified and unqualified. Instead, we normally think of qualifications for jobs as spanning some continuum. Notice that my claim is not that it is impossible, practically speaking, to draw such a guideline. Neither is my claim that it is impermissible (because it is arbitrary) to use such a cut-off as a rule of thumb. We employ such arbitrary cut-offs all the time (e.g. 17 years of age and no day less in qualifying for a driver's licence). My objection is not directed against the employment of arbitrary cut-offs as a practical policy;[20] it is rather that we may not use arbitrary cut-offs when formulating fundamental principles of justice. We may fuse arbitrary cut-offs with fundamental principles of justice to form rules of regulations, but before we do *that* we need to know what justice, pure and simple, requires.[21] 'Lottery between the sufficiently qualified' may serve as a good rule of regulation but it lacks specification and justification to serve as a principle of justice.

It seems, therefore, that the attempt to switch from 'appointing the best qualified' to 'appointing according to qualifications' quickly ends up back at the commitment to appoint the best qualified, and as such, subject to the same problems of justification already witnessed earlier.

II. Radical Equality of Opportunity in Hiring

Can egalitarians give up on the meritocratic requirement to appoint the best qualified (or even simply, the qualified) and still offer a plausible and attractive account of justice in hiring? I suggested that they can, and that *luck* egalitarians are particularly, if not exclusively, well positioned to do

[20] Frederick Schauer offers a very good discussion of the permissibility of using arbitrary cut-offs. See his *Profiles, Probabilities, and Stereotypes* (Cambridge, MA, and London: The Belknap Press of Harvard University Press, 2003).

[21] See G. A. Cohen, *Rescuing Justice and Equality* (Cambridge, MA, and London: Harvard University Press, 2008), ch. 6. There is an important qualification I must make here. I am not denying that arbitrary cut-offs can never be used at the fundamental level of theorizing. We may, perhaps, take recourse to such a rule of thumb while fusing justice with some other conflicting value (as part of some value-pluralist approach). (I am grateful to Zofia Stemplowska for this observation.) But even then, notice, we would still need to get an independent grip on what justice, pure and simple, requires, before we take recourse in the rule of thumb.

so. This is not trivial, for luck egalitarianism has been criticized precisely for its position on justice in hiring. Andrew Mason for example writes: 'If responsibility-sensitive egalitarianism [essentially, luck egalitarianism, SS] were unable to accommodate the meritocratic view, then this would count against it. This is not because the meritocratic view is beyond question. It is because it occupies a place in our thought and practice which militates against abandoning it lightly.'[22] Against this claim, I will attempt to argue in what follows that luck egalitarian justice can indeed abandon the meritocratic view and still offer a plausible and attractive conception of justice in hiring. Let me stress once again that in speaking of radical EOp, or of 'the luck egalitarian view' here I do not presume to trace the views of this or that philosopher, nor claim that the account of justice in hiring below is the only one that follows from luck egalitarianism.

Luck egalitarian justice in hiring, then, abandons meritocracy and instead requires that the allocation of jobs offset inequalities in overall (opportunity for) welfare. This suggestion should rightly raise a whole host of puzzles and difficulties. Here is a preliminary one. Suppose that all jobs pay an equal salary, and thus vary only in non-pecuniary terms. To pursue the suggested luck egalitarian policy it would be necessary to rank jobs according to their non-pecuniary qualities before we can go on to use them to offset inequalities in welfare. This, it might be suggested, forces the state to pass judgement on the relative quality of jobs, something which may turn out to be demeaning for their current as well as future occupants. A person may find herself occupying a job she happens to like but one which the Ministry of Equality has now decreed to be a pretty lousy job.[23] Of course, one way to avoid such a problem is to ensure that all jobs are equally good *also* in their non-pecuniary aspects. This is in any case something that an egalitarian conception of justice in jobs (to be distinguished from the narrower business of justice in *hiring*)

[22] Mason, 'Equality of Opportunity, Old and New', pp. 780–1. This dilemma was recognized already in James S. Fishkin, *Justice, Equal Opportunity, and the Family* (New Haven and London: Yale University Press, 1983), esp. ch. 3.

[23] I am grateful to Alon Harel for raising this worry. This has echoes, of course, of Elizabeth Anderson's critique of luck egalitarianism. See her 'What is the Point of Equality?' *Ethics* 109 (1999), 287–337; 'How Should Egalitarians Cope with Market Risks?' *Theoretical Inquiries in Law* 9 (2008), pp. 249–50. For an effective reply to this general complaint against luck egalitarianism see Zofia Stemplowska, 'Luck Egalitarianism', in Gerald Gaus and Fred D'Agostino (eds), *The Routledge Companion to Social and Political Philosophy* (Abingdon: Routledge, 2012).

would be happy with. But suppose, as I have said at the outset, that we limit our discussion to allocating existing jobs only. Even then, note, it is not necessary for the luck egalitarian state to pass an insulting judgement on the relative quality of jobs. While we may still need an ordering of jobs according to their quality, nothing mandates that it is the state who should determine this ordering. For example, the task may be carried out through some hypothetical auction (Dworkin-style). The auctioneer (namely, the state), would not then be involved in passing any judgement, demeaning or otherwise, over the quality of the jobs to be distributed.

Here is another, perhaps more obvious, worry. Does the fact that the account of justice proposed here recommends filling jobs according to needs rather than qualifications mean that it is of no significance whether or not people occupying certain positions have the proper qualifications for these positions? Do we not want brain-surgeons to be qualified for their job? Of course we do. There are weighty moral reasons to do so, some of which are even reasons of justice (such as meeting the medical needs of patients). But one need not resort to an alleged justice-based entitlement of the best qualified in order to reach the conclusion that it would be desirable to appoint brain surgeons that have good dexterity and some knowledge of how the brain works.[24] On the luck egalitarian reading, then, qualifications do not give a person a *claim* for a certain job but if anything give society a *reason*, one among many, to appoint her.[25]

Does the rule of regulation (to be distinguished from a requirement of justice) according to which we ought to appoint brain surgeons who are qualified imply a *compromise* between justice and maximizing utility (or some other value)? Not necessarily. According to the non-meritocratic component of the luck egalitarian reading, we said, *no one* has a justice-based claim to becoming a brain surgeon. The best qualified person does not have a valid complaint if she does not get that job. She never had a claim over it to begin with. But notice, further, that this is true also of the *neediest* (that is, the worst-off) person in society. On my account,

[24] See Roemer, *Equality of Opportunity*, p. 85, Amartya Sen, *Inequality Reexamined* (Cambridge, MA: Harvard University Press, 1992), pp. 145–6. Notice that the duty to appoint qualified doctors is one owed to patients and not to the (aspiring) surgeons, and second, that it is doubtful that this implies a duty to appoint the *best* qualified. See also Cavanagh's discussion of this point. *Against Equality of Opportunity*, p. 65.

[25] See Broome's distinction, with regard to fairness, between claims and reasons. John Broome, 'Fairness', *Proceedings of the Aristotelian Society* 91 (1990), 87–101.

there is nothing unjust in *not* appointing the worst-off person to a certain job, provided her welfare could be boosted by other means (by being given a higher salary, say, or indeed, by having qualified doctors treat her if and when she is in need of medical care). The monist component of luck egalitarianism (namely, the view that jobs are not special) requires boosting the worse-off person's level of welfare; it does not require giving her this or that job.[26] Appointing qualified brain surgeons is therefore neither a (direct) requirement of justice,[27] nor, importantly, an infringement of (or compromise with) justice. What I have just said allows us to see that the proposed account shifts the focus from the job bearer to those who are dependent on the way in which the job is carried out. Justice requires levelling the social gradient in welfare. It tells us to fill positions in such a way as would boost the welfare of the worse-off to the greatest extent. This might be achieved, on the one hand, by appointing unqualified members of that class to the remunerating and respected position of brain surgeons, but it may be equally—and probably better—achieved by appointing qualified brain surgeons (who can then treat those worse-off individuals).

The combination of non-meritocracy and monism survives initial pangs of counterintuition. We have yet to see a reason (contra Mason) why such a principle cannot yield an attractive account of justice in hiring. Let us now turn to examine the compatibility of these two components with the third one, namely that of non-discrimination.

III. Does Luck Egalitarian Justice in Hiring Discriminate Against the Rich?

The luck egalitarian account of justice in hiring rejects meritocracy. It is concerned, instead, with whether or not hiring flattens inequalities in welfare across society. Here are two important objections to that account. The first

---

[26] Monism has other advantages. It explains why we do not find disproportionate representation of a certain group in a given field of work as necessarily troublesome. White people's under-representation in American basketball and football are not unjust, the radical egalitarian says, because it is overall welfare which counts (in which case whites are not the worse off group). Cf. Robert S. Taylor, 'Rawlsian Affirmative Action', *Ethics* 119 (2009), p. 498.

[27] Notice, I do not deny that appointing the best qualified brain surgeons *could* potentially be a requirement of justice. It is a requirement of justice if doing so *always* serves to narrow inequalities in welfare in society. I am grateful to Zofia Stemplowska for pressing me on this point.

says that luck egalitarian justice allows wrongful discrimination *against the rich* (or more accurately, the better-off). At the same time, the other objection says, the account may allow for wrongful discrimination *against the poor* (or more accurately, the worse-off). I will reply to the first objection in this section, and devote the next chapter to replying to the second one.

The thought that an egalitarian (or more accurately in his case, prioritarian), non-meritocratic account may license wrongful discrimination against the rich has occurred already to Richard Arneson. Suppose, for example, that Harvard University decides to revive its system of quota for Jews.[28] From now on, Jews may make-up no more than 15 per cent of all new admissions, say. Arneson's account (on his own admission) does not rule against this obviously repugnant policy.[29] Jews represent one of the better-off segments of American society and limiting their numbers is likely to allow (let us suppose for the sake of argument) more blacks and Hispanics to enrol. The policy can therefore be said to level welfare inequality across American society. My account escapes that problem. Recall that the luck egalitarian account of justice in hiring has a negative clause according to which hiring must be based on non-arbitrary considerations. Consider, then, the example in light of that requirement. Levelling welfare inequalities is, of course, not an arbitrary reason. But limiting the number of Jews for that purpose is. Why target Jews of all people? If Harvard's policy had been to limit the enrolment of members of *all* better-off segments of society, in order to allow higher enrolment by the worse-off, then the policy would of course cease to be arbitrary. In fact, it would amount, it is easy to see, to affirmative action. (I do not claim here that affirmative action is necessarily just; only that it is not arbitrary.) Notice that nothing in my account relies on the prevalence of some racist intentions on the part of selectors (more on which in the next chapter). Suppose Harvard's policy had the intention to allow more disadvantaged individuals to enrol by limiting the number of better-off individuals. And suppose to avoid bias the University decided to undertake a lottery, whereby pieces of paper inscribed with 'Jews', 'WASPs', and 'Asian-Americans' (all of whom, let us

---

[28] Harvard University has unofficially pursued such a policy up until the end of WWII, leading to the reduction in numbers of Jewish students, as of 1930, from 27 per cent to around 12.5 per cent. See Marcia Synnott, 'The Half Opened Door: Researching Administration Discrimination at Harvard, Yale, and Princeton', *The American Archivist* 45 (2) (1982), p. 186.

[29] Arneson, 'Against Rawlsian Equality of Opportunity', p. 93.

assume, represent better-off groups) were thrown in a hat and one name drawn out. This would still strike us as wrong. My account explains why: it is arbitrary to select one well-off group, *any* group, when it is possible (at a reasonable social cost) to make members of *all* well-off groups share the burden of affirmative action.[30]

The addition of the non-arbitrariness clause seems to save the luck egalitarian account of justice in hiring from the objection that it discriminates against the better-off. But there may still be some uneasiness about the inclusion of that clause. Here is an initial worry. Doesn't the need to resort to an add-on of a non-discrimination proviso reflect badly on the luck egalitarian account of justice in hiring? After all, meritocratic accounts of justice in hiring already have their non-discrimination proviso built into their account and may thus be considered superior in that respect. Let me make two quick points in reply. First, the fact that meritocratic accounts of justice in hiring do already entail non-discrimination would certainly work in their favour, but only, of course, if they are actually able to justify a justice-based entitlement of the best qualified to be appointed (something for which, as we saw in Section I, there is still no evidence). Second, it is worthwhile noting that the 'ad-hoc' challenge is not peculiar to luck egalitarianism. Indeed, any non-meritocratic account of justice that is focused on ensuring some patterned end-state (whether equal or not) would require the add-on of a non-discrimination clause. For example, sufficientarians, such as Harry Frankfurt, also recognize the need to supplement their distributive account with the requirement of non-discrimination.[31] There is nothing peculiar, then, in the need for the account offered here to be supplemented with the requirement of non-discrimination. (We shall see, in the next chapter, that the account contains, perhaps, an even better reply to this ad-hoc challenge.)

---

[30] But let us try and pose an even harder case. Suppose that Jews are by far the most well-off group in society. Suppose that the entire top percentile of American society is made up exclusively of Jews. The radical account may then seem to allow limiting their numbers in order to allow in members of worse-off groups. For here subjecting Jews to *numerous clausus* can no longer be considered arbitrary. But notice that even this outlandish empirical supposition would not allow discrimination against Jews *as such*. For it is not obvious why the university should be relying on ethnicity rather than directly on socio-economic status (in curbing inequality of opportunity). Put simply, it would be wrong, in general, and on my account in particular, to target all Jews rather than just the very wealthy ones.

[31] Which Frankfurt derives from the independent requirement of treating people with respect. Harry Frankfurt, 'Equality and Respect', *Social Research* 64 (1997), p. 8.

IV. Discrimination without Meritocracy

The challenge of course, is to fill in the details of what the non-discrimination component, understood here as non-arbitrariness, means. Now, I should start by noting that a non-discrimination requirement is not peculiar, of course, to luck egalitarianism, but is rather a basic requirement that is shared by any plausible view of justice in hiring. (Recall what we said in the introductory chapter about formal EOp.) It is also worth stressing that this is quite a minimal requirement.[32] Using a lottery, say, in appointing brain surgeons would be enough to satisfy that requirement. It would be foolish perhaps to do so but it would not be discriminatory (and therefore not, as such, unjust).[33] A luck egalitarian (or any other) account of justice in hiring thus builds on a prior premiss of non-discrimination. (The premiss of non-discrimination is 'prior' to the account of justice in hiring only in the sense that it tells us what selectors may *not* do while filling jobs, which, it is plausible to think, is prior to the question, *who* should eventually get the job, which it is the task of a principle of justice to answer.) This entails the not-so-easy task of defining what should count as arbitrary for the purposes of non-discrimination, which is what I will attempt to do in this section. I should stress that there is nothing particularly radical or luck egalitarian about what I have to say of arbitrary discrimination in this section. However, as I have pointed out above, there is something that is particular to all non-meritocrats (including luck egalitarians) in the need to provide such an independent account. Furthermore, it may be suggested that it is impossible to defend a principle of non-discrimination in a way that does not, eventually, boil down to the ideal of appointing the best qualified.[34] I hope to show in this section that this is not true. If I succeed in accomplishing that then I will have

---

[32] See also Richard Arneson, 'Equality of Opportunity', *The Stanford Encyclopaedia of Philosophy* (2002) §6.

[33] Foolish (non-arbitrary) procedures of appointment may be unjust only when there is a fiduciary duty involved, such as the one toward patients. [See also Richard J. Arneson, 'What is Wrongful Discrimination?' *San Diego Law Review* 43 (2006), p. 784.] But crucially, the putative injustice is suffered by the patients, not by the applicants. There is, I should say, a line of thinking that links foolishness (or irrationality) with unfairness. It argues that for the state to act irrationally is for it to act unfairly. I do not find this even remotely persuasive, but for an effective rebuttal of this line of reasoning see Cavanagh, *Against Equality of Opportunity*, pp. 45–8.

[34] Mason, *Levelling the Playing Field*, pp. 29–30.

provided a non-discrimination requirement that is compatible with the two other premises of the luck egalitarian account of justice in hiring (non-meritocracy and monism).

Now, a lot of ink has been shed in attempts to define arbitrary discrimination in hiring. People most often associate discrimination with allowing hiring to be affected by the candidate's *race* or *sex*. But there are by-now-familiar counter-examples of preference for female gynaecologists in certain religious districts or for black police officers in predominantly black neighbourhoods which suggests that allowing race or sex to affect hiring is not always wrong.[35] Moreover, such understanding of discrimination would once again condemn any practice of affirmative action.[36] (Affirmative action is of course not beyond controversy.[37] My point is simply that whether or not one thinks affirmative action is *justified*, one will be hard pressed to show that affirmative action is by definition discriminatory.) Another suggestion is that to employ *considerations other than the candidates' qualifications* is discriminatory. But, in fact, we already saw that this would imply that giving some consideration to how badly an individual needs a job would be discriminatory, which seems false. (Notice, again, that I do not claim that failure to entertain considerations of need in the allocation of jobs is *unjust*. I only deny that entertaining such considerations is discriminatory.) A better criterion, it might be suggested, would speak of hiring *for relevant reasons alone*. This quite minimal criterion may comprise qualifications but also efficiency, need, and social benefit. This would also allow for affirmative action to be considered non-discriminatory. The relevance criterion thus seems promising. Still, that criterion runs into the familiar problem of 'reaction qualifications', and of identifying what counts as relevant reasons for hiring.[38] An example cited in this context is the practice of appointing white quarterbacks. Most football fans, it turns out, prefer their teams to

---

[35] Alan Wertheimer, 'Jobs, Qualifications, and Preferences', *Ethics* 94 (1983), p. 99; Mason, 'Equality of Opportunity: Old and New', p. 777.

[36] Lesley A. Jacobs, *Pursuing Equal Opportunities: The Theory and Practice of Egalitarian Theory* (Cambridge: Cambridge University Press, 2004), p. 111.

[37] See for example, George Sher, 'Diversity', *Philosophy and Public Affairs* 28 (1999), 85–104. We shall revisit some of these objections in the next chapter.

[38] Patrick Shin rejects the relevance criterion test. Hiring based on irrelevant criteria can sometimes be un-objectionable, he says. Suppose I search for someone to work as a toll-booth operator and I select Jones over Smith because while the latter graduated second of his class at the Harvard Law School, Jones has graduated first. The reasoning seems

be lead by a white quarterback, thus the practice of rejecting non-white candidates could be described as beneficial both in terms of enjoyment and revenue.[39] Crucially, the practice can be described as based on relevant reasons alone (teams' owners need not be racist in order to endorse it).[40] (A slightly different type of case would be hiring a white-only workforce out of the desire to avoid friction between whites and blacks in the workplace, and thus achieve greater harmony and productivity.)[41] Yet, this strikes us as discriminatory.[42] And, on the other hand, we do not consider it discriminatory for NFL teams to refrain from hiring disabled or untalented athletes.[43] How can we, then, pry these cases apart? One thing we could do is to altogether discount reactive attitudes as grounds for hiring. On that view, individuals' prospective performance ought to be 'considered in isolation from the abilities and dispositions of the workforce, customers, and clients'.[44] Such a criterion would explain why it is wrong to intentionally refrain from hiring black quarterbacks simply because the crowd tends to prefer white ones. The preference against those who cannot throw accurately, in contrast, is *not* discriminatory (according to the principle). Still, the principle captures too much.[45] It would condemn hiring individuals who possess a cheerful disposition (as opposed to morose types) to serve as sales-personnel (on the basis of the reaction they tend to elicit from customers), even though that practice appears benign.[46] The principle would also not allow the abovementioned preference for female

---

irrelevant for the position, and yet the action does not seem wrong, or so says Shin. [Patrick Shin, 'The Substantive Principle of Equal Treatment', *Legal Theory* 15 (2009), p. 153.] But if the criterion is genuinely irrelevant then, on my intuition at least, the decision would be wrong. The employer would have done better to choose by flipping a coin.

[39] Arneson, 'Against Rawlsian Equality of Opportunity', p. 79; Cavanagh, *Against Equality of Opportunity*, p. 194.

[40] Wertheimer, 'Jobs, Qualifications, and Preferences', p. 102.

[41] See Mason, 'Equality of Opportunity, Old and New', p. 776; Miller, *Principles of Social Justice*, p. 169.

[42] Kasper Lippert-Rasmussen provides a nice summary of the literature on reaction qualifications in his 'Reaction Qualifications Revisited', *Social Theory and Practice* 35 (2009), 413–39.

[43] Larry Alexander, 'What Makes Wrongful Discrimination Wrong? Biases, Preferences, Stereotypes, and Proxies', *University of Pennsylvania Law Review* 141 (1992), p. 151.

[44] A possibility entertained, but ultimately rejected by Mason. See his 'Equality of Opportunity, Old and New', p. 776.

[45] See also Lippert-Rasmussen, 'Reaction Qualifications Revisited', pp. 415–16.

[46] Wertheimer, 'Jobs, Qualifications, and Preferences', p. 103.

gynaecologists (for, a male gynaecologist may be no less competent in performing the job considered in isolation from the clients' reactions).

We need not, however, give up on an attempt to identify discrimination.[47] It seems, rather, that a complete account of discrimination should take account of customers' (as well as co-workers') preferences, but subject them to scrutiny.[48] So, in differentiating the preference against black quarterbacks compared to the preference against untalented quarterbacks, we may say that the preference for watching people who can throw far and accurate is not a *bigoted* one whereas the preference for not watching non-white athletes do so, is.[49] (In the same way, the preference for watching a black actor play Othello is not bigoted.[50]) So we may say that discrimination occurs when *a selector (an agent who is in a position of power over others with regard to the distribution of the position in question)*[51] *fills that position according to non-relevant considerations*, where *catering for bigoted reactions*[52] (of customers or co-workers) *cannot count as a relevant consideration*.

Notice two features of the above bigotry clause. First, notice that it applies to reactive attitudes, that is, to the attitudes of customers and co-workers. It does *not* apply to the selector herself. This is important because it means that this account of discrimination does not rely on this or that intention on the part of the selector. (I shall expand on that issue in the next chapter.) Second, ruling out reactive attitudes that are bigoted

---

[47] Contrary to what Wertheimer seems to suggest ('Jobs, Qualifications, and Preferences').

[48] This is also Mason's position. See 'Equality of Opportunity: Old and New', p. 778.

[49] I draw here on Miller's understanding of non-discrimination: 'only job qualifications based on legitimate reactions (on the part of customers, colleagues, and so on) are relevant when we are assessing applicants' desert.' *Principles of Social Justice*, p. 169. Although I am generally sympathetic to the account Kasper Lippert-Rasmussen provides (in 'Reaction Qualifications Revisited'), I think that 'bigoted preference' is better here than 'preferences that are antimeritocratic in a nonindividualized way' (see pp. 424–5). The latter may, for example, rule out preferring a member of a disadvantaged group as such (affirmative action), a preference that the anti-bigotry requirement would allow.

[50] Dworkin, *A Matter of Principle*, p. 318.

[51] See Deborah Hellman on this pre-condition of asymmetry of power. *When is Discrimination Wrong?* (Cambridge, MA: Harvard University Press, 2008), p. 37.

[52] Notice that it does not matter, on this account, whether the selector is aware of the fact that the preferences she is catering to are bigoted or not. Suppose a Norwegian pub owner in Prague follows his clientele's preferences, ending up dismissing all Roma waiters and retaining only ethnically Czech ones. His action is not racist (he is unaware of the significance of what he is doing), but the dismissed Roma waiters still have a valid complaint of having been discriminated against.

implies that we must not take into account reductions of welfare that are allegedly owed to it. This is important for the following reason. Suppose that the worst-off member of society is a white racist. Her welfare might further drop as a consequence of appointing a black person to serve as her doctor (something that my egalitarian account of hiring might seem to be compelled to act against). The bigotry restriction rules out such a consequence.

V. Statistical Discrimination and Other Tough Cases

I want, finally, to examine how the proposed account of radical justice in hiring copes with three difficult cases of discrimination. These concern statistical discrimination, preference against women for reasons of maternity, and hiring in small family businesses.

Statistical discrimination occurs when a selector rejects an applicant based on adverse statistical data on her group (however it is defined), for example that they tend to indulge more in absenteeism or are more involved in crime. If the statistics are valid, then the considerations that statistical discriminators appeal to are relevant. This is a potential problem for my account in those cases where statistical discrimination is deemed wrongful. (Statistical discrimination may very well be justified in many instances of crime fighting, car insurance, and also hiring.[53]) What, then, does the account offered here say about statistical discrimination?

Luck egalitarian justice in hiring, we said, holds that hiring practices are justified if they help level inequality of welfare. In light of that, statistical discrimination would be justified, on this account, in so far as it helps curb inequality. Think of the following case. In hunting for serial killers, the police in the USA often look for white males, based on the overwhelming evidence regarding the profile of such killers. We do not (at least I don't) find this case of racial profiling troublesome. My account explains why: white men (as such) are not a worse-off group. The same reasoning obtains in hiring. Suppose a government agency is recruiting individuals

[53] See Mathias Risse and Richard Zeckhauser, 'Racial Profiling', *Philosophy and Public Affairs* 32 (2) (2004), 131–70; Kasper Lippert-Rasmussen, 'Nothing Personal: On Statistic Discrimination', *The Journal of Political Philosophy* 15 (2007), 385–403; Schauer, *Profiles, Probabilities, and Stereotypes*, esp. ch. 7.

for an alpinist rescuing unit.[54] We know that some countries produce, on average, much better skiers than other countries. It will thus be efficient to keep all the Scandinavian- and Austrian-sounding names but throw out all the Dutch- and Chinese-sounding names, say. (The funds saved by having this more efficient hiring process, we may suppose for the sake of argument, can be then invested in some social policies that will benefit the worse-off members of society.) Given that those discriminated against are not particularly worse-off, and given the expected gain to the worse-off (due to the saving of communal resources), the practice proves benign. Compare that case with another case of statistical discrimination, that of a preference against African-Americans based on solid statistics that they require more sick days compared to whites. In difference to the Alpinist example, here, it seems plausible, the gain in terms of efficient hiring process (as well as the gain in terms of less absenteeism) is outweighed by the harm (entailed in not being hired) to an already disadvantaged group. The luck egalitarian account would thus rule against such practice.[55] Luck egalitarian justice in hiring thus offers a simple but compelling test as to which cases of statistical discrimination are acceptable and which are not. (I elaborate on this in the next chapter.)

The second difficult case concerns discrimination against women for reasons of maternity. Explaining why such discrimination is wrong is more difficult than it may initially seem, even for meritocrats.[56] The problem stems from the fact that this particular preference against women can be seen as relevant and non-arbitrary, for the simple reason that maternity contributes to absenteeism. So although this practice appears manifestly unjust, it is not so easy to say exactly why that is so.[57] One reason to think

---

[54] Arneson, 'Against Rawlsian Equality of Opportunity', pp. 105–6.

[55] For a similar intuition see Paul Bou-Habib, 'Racial Profiling and Background Injustice', *The Journal of Ethics* 15 (2011), 33–46. My account has similar aims and ambitions as Mason's. But they differ, among other things, in the way they treat a case such as the one just discussed. Mason's approach would be to treat skin colour (say, being black) as a qualification for a job if that trait is associated with being worse-off (thus contributing to overall EOp). But this seems an unnecessary and convoluted approach to justice in hiring. Qualifications are one consideration in hiring rules of regulation; equality (of opportunity) another. There is no point (con)fusing the two. (See for example, 'Equality of Opportunity: Old and New', p. 779.)

[56] See for example, Cavanagh, *Against Equality of Opportunity*, pp. 195–6; Miller, *Principles of Social Justice*, pp. 168–9.

[57] For one thing, it is out of step with legal practice (such as The Pregnancy Discrimination Act, which is an amendment to Title VII of the American Civil Rights Act of 1964). See <http://www.eeoc.gov/types/pregnancy.html>.

that rejecting female applicants (on the basis of maternity) is wrong is that it is based on prejudice. Not all women can or want to have children. Thus, to deny a woman a job based on such a prediction is like denying a black applicant a job based on the (let us assume for the sake of argument, equally valid) statistics that blacks are more likely to indulge in absenteeism than do whites. Not hiring a female applicant because some women tend to become pregnant can therefore be characterized as based on a bigoted view. It fails to judge the applicant's future performance based on who she is. But this explanation won't do. For one thing, it still leaves open cases of women who are already (visibly) pregnant or who out of their own initiative state that they are, or intend to be, pregnant. Here, the employer is using a substantiated, not a bigoted, judgement in his rejection of the female applicant. And yet the preference still seems problematic, to say the least.[58] The radical account, in contrast, accounts for the wrongfulness of the preference against women for reasons of maternity rather easily. Since women are worse-off compared to men, the preference against them exacerbates rather than reduces inequality of welfare across society. Luck egalitarian justice in hiring thus rules out the practice of discrimination against women for reasons of maternity.[59]

The third and final challenge concerns the hiring practices of small family businesses. We commonly think of nepotism (preference for one's family members in allocating public office) as paradigmatically wrong. Yet, at the same time we think it is permissible for a corner-store owner to simply hire his niece to help him out rather than go to the trouble of advertising the position and interviewing candidates for it. We do not

---

[58] In any case, it is not obvious that not to treat someone as an individual is sufficient to make an act discriminatory. To give an example from Lippert-Rasmussen: If I stop and search everyone wearing a Rolex, then I fail to treat them as individuals, but I do not necessarily discriminate against them. ' "We are All Different": Statistical Discrimination and the Right to be Treated as an Individual', *The Journal of Ethics* 15 (2011), p. 56.

[59] Paula Casal offers a similar rationale in 'Why Sufficiency Is Not Enough', *Ethics* 117 (2007), pp. 302–33. Now, what if women were to become better-off than men? The radical account would then cease to condemn discrimination on the basis of maternity, which seems perhaps embarrassing. But I submit that if, under those (utopian?) circumstances, we still think a preference against child-bearers is wrong, then this is so not for reasons of discrimination but for reasons of lack of gratitude (for a worthy social service), or something of that nature. In any case, the counter-example in that case would be too outlandish for us to trust our current intuition about it. Notice, finally, that if in some distant future men could become pregnant (and still remain better-off overall than women) then my account would allow a preference against pregnant individuals as such.

think that he is under an obligation to advertise the position, nor do we think that it is wrong for him to give preference to his niece for nothing other than their family relation. How can we account for this? One possible explanation is that positions requiring no specialized skills, as is the case in small family businesses, are outside the purview of discrimination. But this cannot be true: if a supermarket chose not to hire cashiers that are black we would still think it wrongful discrimination. Another possible explanation is that the preference against 'anyone who is not a family member of mine' is not repugnant or bigoted in the same way as a preference against individuals based on their salient group membership (i.e. ethnic, racial, religious, sexual, and sexual orientation).[60] Arguably, then, it is the benign intention that explains why the practice is acceptable. But of course, in many other cases a hiring preference against non-family members is wrong (say, if one happens to be the mayor). Intentions, therefore, cannot be the key here. The radical account does a better job in prying these cases apart. The preference of these small businesses for their family members is not wrongful because it is not likely to undermine equality of opportunity for welfare across society.[61] The practice, generalized across society, is not likely to exacerbate welfare inequalities. Notice that the principle holds even in extreme examples: suppose that all jewellery shops in Antwerp are owned by ultra-orthodox Jews (not an outlandish supposition). And suppose further that all of these shop owners hire only family members, so that jewellery retail is exclusively the domain of ultra-orthodox Jews. Even in that case, on my intuition at least, no discrimination or injustice obtains. In contrast, nepotism outside the petit-bourgeoisie is a very different matter. Given the tendency of offices in the public sector and civil society to in fact correlate with other advantages, preference for family members *would* exacerbate welfare inequalities, and thus would be unjust.

---

[60] The US Supreme Court identifies something pretty close to what political philosophers refer to when they speak of salient groups. The Court calls this a 'suspect class', and defines it as a group 'saddled with such disabilities, or subjected to such a history of purposeful unequal treatment, or relegated to such a position of political powerlessness as to command extraordinary protection from the majoritarian political process'. [Cited in Dworkin, *Sovereign Virtue*, p. 412.] For the significance of social-salience for discrimination see also Kasper Lippert-Rasmussen, 'The Badness of Discrimination', *Ethical Theory and Moral Practice* 9 (2006), 167–85.

[61] See also Arneson, 'Against Rawlsian Equality of Opportunity'.

Conclusion

It is commonly held that people's access to jobs should not be affected by other people's prejudices. That is why, for example, it is generally wrong to discriminate in hiring on the basis of sex or race. But from the judgement that individuals' access to jobs should not depend on considerations that are morally arbitrary, it does not follow that individuals should be judged *only* according to their qualifications. Non-meritocrats, such as libertarians, are therefore correct in pointing out the falseness of this move.[62] The luck egalitarian finds herself in a surprising agreement with the libertarian here. She agrees that justice in the allocation of jobs requires neither a competition, nor appointment according to qualifications. Where the luck egalitarian does part from libertarians (no doubt), as well as from meritocratic egalitarians, is in holding that justice in hiring must be informed by, and only by, offsetting overall inequalities of welfare.

Dismissing meritocracy, I have addressed the worry that this egalitarian, non-meritocratic account of justice in hiring may in fact license discrimination. In particular, we saw, it is thought to license discrimination against the rich. The negative requirement not to hire based on arbitrary considerations, I said, takes care of that objection. Endorsing the understanding of non-discrimination as a prohibition on resorting to non-relevant (or arbitrary criteria) in filling jobs, I showed that luck egalitarian justice in hiring need not, in fact, discriminate against the rich. Does it succeed, however, in preventing discrimination against the poor? The next chapter addresses that worry.

---

[62] See Cavanagh, *Against Equality of Opportunity*, p. 134.

5

Discrimination without Inequality?

Luck egalitarian justice in hiring says that there is nothing unjust in a hiring practice that fails to appoint the worst-off person (let alone any other person) for a given position, provided that person becomes as better-off as possible as a consequence. It might follow that it is permissible not to appoint, or indeed discriminate against, worse-off individuals provided they are otherwise compensated. This is a point picked up, for example, by Andrew Mason in his critique of luck egalitarianism. He accuses luck egalitarians (at least of the welfarist strand) of licensing the denial of jobs from some applicants simply on the basis of their skin colour or sex. Luck egalitarianism entails that embarrassing conclusion, Mason says, because such minority applicants could be 'compensated by adjusting the overall distribution of benefits and burdens, through some system of redistributive taxation'.[1] In other words, the luck egalitarian account allows for discrimination in hiring so long as the 'global' end result (in terms of levels of welfare, say) is not made more unequal, or so is the claim. This chapter is devoted to trying to defend luck egalitarian justice in hiring from this charge. I shall do so by showing that striving for radical equality of opportunity (EOp) in fact eliminates discrimination. This is so because undermining EOp (for welfare) is in fact a necessary condition of discrimination. An EOp-based account of justice in hiring, therefore, cannot, by definition, be discriminatory (and least of all, towards the worse-off). Inequality of opportunity is not only a necessary condition of

    [1] Andrew Mason, *Levelling the Playing Field: The Idea of Equal Opportunity and its Place in Egalitarian Thought* (Oxford: Oxford University Press, 2006), p. 154. See also Jonathan Wolff, 'Fairness, Respect, and the Egalitarian Ethos', *Philosophy and Public Affairs* 27 (1998), p. 117; Jonathan Wolff and Avner de Shalit, *Disadvantage* (Oxford: Oxford University Press, 2007), pp. 28–9.

discrimination, I want to argue, it is also what makes discrimination bad in the first place.

Let me make some qualifications. First, by searching for the root cause of the badness of discrimination, I do not presume to be saying something about what makes discrimination unique. In other words, I am not searching for what distinguishes discrimination from other injustices, but rather for what makes it bad. Second, I refer to the badness of discrimination 'as such'. Particular incidents of discrimination might be bad for a variety of reasons. In speaking of the badness of discrimination as such I search for what source of badness, if anything, is common to *all* incidents of discrimination. Third, by 'equality of opportunity', recall, we refer to radical EOp. In other words, I mean not EOp for a certain job or position, but I refer rather to overall EOp (e.g. EOp for welfare). Finally, in speaking of 'equality of opportunity' I do not presume to say anything about what the relevant group for assessing it is: one's city, country, or the globe as a whole. For the purposes of this chapter, I claim that discrimination is bad when it undermines EOp, in whatever the relevant reference group is taken to be.

Discrimination, I argue then, is bad when and only when it upsets EOp. The view may not seem all that controversial, perhaps. But in fact, it is almost universally rejected.[2] Indeed, some have gone so far as to say that if there is a 'connection between anti-discrimination laws and equality it is at best negligible, and in any event is insufficient to count as a justification.'[3] The EOp account seems in fact to be very much the minority view.[4] I shall begin my defence of that view by looking into alternative accounts of what might be bad about discrimination, and showing why

[2] Harry Frankfurt, 'Equality and Respect', *Social Research* 64 (1997), p. 8; Sophia Moreau, 'What is Discrimination?' *Philosophy and Public Affairs* 38 (2010), 143–79; 'Discrimination as Negligence', *Canadian Journal of Philosophy* 36 (2010), 123–49, esp. p. 145; Deborah Hellman, *When is Discrimination Wrong?* (Cambridge, MA: Harvard University Press, 2008); Matt Cavanagh, *Against Equality of Opportunity* (Oxford: Oxford University Press, 2002); Elisa Holmes, 'Anti-Discrimination Rights without Equality', *The Modern Law Review* 68 (2005), 175–94; Larry Alexander, 'What Makes Wrongful Discrimination Wrong?' *University of Pennsylvania Law Review* 141 (1992), 149–219; Richard J. Arneson, 'What is Wrongful Discrimination?' *San Diego Law Review* 43 (2006): 775–807; Peter Westen, 'The Empty Idea of Equality', *Harvard Law Review* 95 (1982), 537–96; Christopher Peters, 'Equality Revisited', *Harvard Law Review* 110 (1997), 1201–64; Patrick Shin, 'The Substantive Principle of Equal Treatment', *Legal Theory* 15 (2009), 149–72.

[3] Holmes, 'Anti-Discrimination Rights without Equality', p. 194.

[4] Owen Fiss has put forward an account basing discrimination on equality between *groups*. [Owen Fiss, 'Groups and the Equal Protection Clause', *Philosophy and Public Affairs* 5 (1976), 107–77.] My account, in contrast, is not restricted to groups. Similarly, Cass Sunstein

none of them is successful in accounting for the badness of discrimination as such. This is the concern of Section I. Section II takes on the challenge (to the EOp thesis, let us call it) presented in cases which appear discriminatory despite not involving inequality of opportunity. The notable case here is that of segregation. Section III looks at advantages of the radical EOp account, and most notably at the way it accommodates affirmative action. Finally, in Section IV, I address some potentially tough cases for the EOp account; these concern the confinement of discrimination to salient groups, 'buying off' discriminatees by means of financial compensation, 'discrimination' in the selection of life partners, and the duties that non-discrimination might place on employers.

I. Why is Discrimination Bad?

Discrimination could be bad for a variety of reasons. We may initially divide relevant accounts between those that locate the badness of discrimination in the harm to the person being discriminated against (the discriminatee), as opposed to accounts that locate it outside her.[5] The latter group of reasons, which I first want to address, may be further divided into two: badness which resides with the person committing

---

has argued that anti-discrimination laws are better understood as an anti-caste requirement, where the concern is for the impact of policies on the overall status of members of vulnerable groups. ['The Anticaste Principle', *Michigan Law Review* 92 (1994), 2410–55.] His account is, nevertheless, different from mine. Sunstein's principle is concerned with turning 'highly visible differences' into social disadvantage. My account is not limited to discrimination on the basis of those highly visible differences. In a more recent paper, Kasper Lippert-Rasmussen ['The Badness of Discrimination', *Ethical Theory and Moral Practice* 9 (2006), 167–85] has claimed that discrimination is bad when and because it disadvantages the discriminatee. Although he invokes 'disadvantage', Lippert-Rasmussen, in fact, focuses on what counts as *harm* for the purposes of discrimination. The account I attempt to provide here, in contrast, is more specifically focused on delimiting discrimination to undermining EOp. To put this differently, while Lippert-Rasmussen focuses on 'harm', I focus on the narrower concept of 'disadvantage'. This is important because, obviously, some harms do not constitute disadvantages: a progressive tax policy may harm the interests of the very rich without disadvantaging them. Matthew Clayton ['Equality, Justice, and Legitimacy in Selection', *Journal of Moral Philosophy* 9 (2012), pp. 8–30] also seeks to defend the connection between egalitarianism and discrimination, although his argument shows only why equality is not alien or redundant to discrimination, whereas mine has the more ambitious task of showing that inequality (of opportunity) is indispensible to discrimination.

[5] Some accounts of discrimination offer a 'bifurcated' account, namely addressing these two quite distinct sources of badness. See John Gardner, 'Liberals and Unlawful Discrimination', *Oxford Journal of Legal Studies* 9 (1989), 1–22.

the discrimination (the discriminator, or selector), and badness residing in society as a whole. Looking at the first sub-group, we may say that discrimination is bad because it corrupts the discriminator. When discrimination is wrong (and in this chapter I shall always refer to 'discrimination' in the pejorative, rather than the literal and neutral sense, namely to imply wrongful discrimination) then we might think that to commit it is to undermine one's own moral virtue or perfection. This is familiar enough to us from characterizations of discrimination that focus on the morally repugnant intentions of selectors.[6] Bad intentions are therefore a necessary condition of discrimination under this badness account. But is this defensible? Consider the following example (borrowing from Kasper Lippert-Rasmussen).[7] Think of an employer who, while not a Scandinavian herself, has a favourable and somewhat inflated view of Scandinavians. (It is not, notice, that she thinks Scandinavians constitute some super-race. She just happens to have a very favourable view of them.) Consequently, whenever a Scandinavian applicant comes along, she gives careful consideration to all other candidates but then, perhaps somewhat unconsciously, judges the Nordic applicant to be superior, even when that is not the case. This seems like a case of discrimination, even though there is nothing obviously repugnant about the employer's intentions. Corrupting the moral character of the selector is therefore a type of bad which while plausibly associated with discrimination, does not seem to be true for discrimination as such. The fact that bad intentions are not a necessary condition for discrimination may be further witnessed with regard to cases of what is known as 'disparate impact'. This occurs when a procedure which is seemingly neutral ends up disadvantaging a vulnerable group. A typical example is incorporating tests for upper-body strength as part of the hiring process for fire-fighting or bus-driving, thereby ending with selecting far fewer women. We tend to think of such cases as constituting discrimination, even though the intention is not necessarily repugnant.[8]

Another reason why discrimination might be bad, switching now to badness which resides in society as a whole, concerns efficiency reasons. Namely, discrimination is bad because it deprives society of the benefit of

---

[6] For one such account see Arneson, 'What is Wrongful Discrimination?'
[7] Lippert-Rasmussen, 'The Badness of Discrimination', p. 181.
[8] See Arneson's struggle with responding to this challenge. 'What is Wrongful Discrimination?' pp. 793–4.

having a workforce made up of the best qualified.[9] We are, indeed, often repelled by discrimination for the waste in talent which it typically harbours. But, again, it is possible to think of counter-examples, where discrimination is not necessarily inefficient. Think of some of the examples discussed in the previous chapter, such as discrimination against women for reasons of maternity, statistical discrimination against minority groups who are likelier to engage in absenteeism or crime, and discrimination on the basis of reactive attitudes (not hiring someone based on the fact that one's clients prefer not to be served by members of that minority). We normally think of these as discriminatory and yet it would be difficult to show that they are necessarily inefficient.

A third source of badness is one which it is not so easy to categorize (at least not initially) in terms of whether the badness resides within or outside the discriminatee. This particular account of badness says that discrimination is bad because it manifests a lie. Discrimination represents the discriminatee as lacking in qualifications which in fact she does have. Wrongly depicting someone as lacking some qualifications which she does in fact have may lead to the even worse lie regarding her very moral worth.[10] Notice that this claim is different from a related, and more common, account of discrimination (which we shall discuss shortly), according to which discrimination is bad because it is disrespectful. According to the claim under investigation here, the badness lies with the false representation, independently of any disrespect it may convey. Now, this badness claim could be interpreted in (at least) two ways. First, the view might be that it is harmful for individuals to be falsely represented. And second, it could be claimed that it is bad when actions (hiring) convey untruths, independently of any harm they may cause. That is, a world which contains actions that manifest some untruth is worse

---

[9] An argument famously made in John Stuart Mill, *On the Subjection of Women*: 'The second benefit to be expected from giving to women the free use of their faculties, by leaving them the free choice of their employments, and opening to them the same field of occupation and the same prizes and encouragements as to other human beings, would be that of doubling the mass of mental faculties available for the higher service of humanity. Where there is now one person qualified to benefit mankind and promote the general improvement, as a public teacher, or an administrator of some branch of public or social affairs, there would then be a chance of two.' John Stuart Mill, *Three Essays* (Oxford and New York: Oxford University Press, 1975), pp. 525–6.

[10] This is Larry Alexander's account. Discriminatory practices are wrong, he says, 'because they reflect incorrect moral judgments'. 'What Makes Wrongful Discrimination Wrong?' p. 161. See also Harry Frankfurt, 'Equality and Respect', p. 12.

than one which does not. Looking at the first variant of the claim we may notice the following implication. Since the putative badness resides in the lie (rather than, we have distinguished, in the message of disrespect) this badness account is forced to condemn, in equal measures, falsely representing someone as having *better* qualifications than they actually have.[11] (It might be said in reply that representing Jones as better than she is invariably entails representing Smith as worse than he in fact is. But as Lippert-Rasmussen has pointed out, this does not follow: I may discriminate against Smith, having a correct view of her, by virtue of having an inflated view of Jones.[12]) Yet, it does not seem harmful to the person selected to be represented as better qualified than she really is. (Being under-qualified for one's job, a likely outcome of such practice might, admittedly, end up harming the person in question. But the inflated representation, in itself, does not appear harmful.) So falseness, on its own, cannot be the source of badness here. Notice that this is not a weakness for the second variant of the claim. That version of the claim says that it is simply bad for there to be acts which manifest lies (regardless of harms to the misrepresented individual). But this view is vulnerable to other problems. Namely, this claim, while manifesting a plausible enough bad, does not account for the badness of discrimination as such.[13] Not all practices that we commonly consider as discriminatory entail a putative lie. Think of a hiring process that picks the candidate that everyone concerned considers as the obvious choice for the job, but crucially, by not giving the other applications even cursory consideration. The practice seems wrong, but it is not one that necessarily manifests a lie.

A fourth potential source of badness is the already mentioned disrespect account. This account, again, might locate the badness of discrimination either in the discriminator or in the discriminatee. Discrimination might be bad because it is bad for selectors to manifest disrespect.[14] Alternatively, discrimination is bad when and because it causes the discriminatee loss of (self-) respect. We already saw that concern for the moral virtue of the

---

[11] This has been noted already in Kasper Lippert-Rasmussen, 'Private Discrimination: A Prioritarian, Desert-Based Account', *San Diego Law Review* 43 (2006), p. 845.

[12] Lippert-Rasmussen, 'The Badness of Discrimination', p. 181.

[13] But nor does, I should say, Alexander seem to intend it to be.

[14] Matt Cavanagh offers this account of the badness of discrimination, whereby he speaks of treating people 'with unwarranted contempt' as the source of discrimination's badness. See his *Against Equality of Opportunity*, p. 166.

selector cannot account for all cases (e.g. the admirer of Scandinavians, or cases of disparate impact), so let us focus on the badness residing in the discriminatee, and the loss of respect she[15] might suffer. This account of badness is vulnerable to the obvious counter-example of covert discrimination of which the discriminatee is unaware. Think of a policy whereby only male employees receive a bonus and the female employees never find out.[16] They are unlikely to experience a denial of self-respect and yet we think they were nevertheless discriminated against.[17] If the badness of discrimination lies with the loss of self-respect experienced by the discriminatee, then cases of covert discrimination would have to lie outside the sphere of discrimination, which seems implausible. It therefore cannot be the case that the underlying badness of discrimination lies in some demeaning effect.[18]

A fifth account locates the badness of discrimination squarely with the discriminatee. It says that discrimination is bad for reasons of desert, namely because it deprives the most qualified person of the job to which she is entitled. This account relies, obviously, on a series of contentious premises. First, it must assume that desert is, in fact, a principle of justice, which is controversial.[19] Second, it assumes (the no less controversial view) that individuals deserve rewards for their natural talents. And third, it assumes that these rewards must take the shape of jobs, of all things.[20]

---

[15] Or the group to which she belongs. Discrimination against a woman as such will likely cause a sense of disrespect to other women.

[16] Let us assume that the male employees also do not know that women did not get the bonus. This assumption might be necessary because if they did know that, this might prompt them to correspondingly disrespect their female colleagues.

[17] This point is also, I think, fatal for an account of discrimination as denial of some 'deliberative freedoms', such as Sophia Moreau's. She says that what underlies the badness of discrimination is the (absolute) harm to the discriminatee's ability to conduct herself without having to think of the obstacles that others might force on her due to her gender, race, disability, etc. While I think there is something important that Moreau captures here, her account is vulnerable to the present objection. Her response to it, namely that the lack of opportunity undermines one's deliberative freedom whether or not she is aware of it, does not strike me as very persuasive. See Moreau, 'What is Discrimination?' pp. 170–1.

[18] Lippert-Rasmussen offers a series of additional counter-examples to show why discrimination need not involve a demeaning message. See his 'Intentions and Discrimination in Hiring', Journal of Moral Philosophy 9 (2012), 55–74.

[19] See John Rawls, A Theory of Justice (Oxford: Clarendon Press, 1972), p. 313.

[20] For the most sophisticated such account see David Miller, Principles of Social Justice (Cambridge, MA: Harvard University Press, 1999), chs 7–8. For an early rejection of this view see Thomas Nagel, 'Equal Treatment and Compensatory Discrimination', Philosophy and Public Affairs 2 (1973), 348–63.

Notice that this account locates the source of badness not simply in the inefficiency that society must endure due to not recruiting the best qualified (which we have already examined and dismissed), but rather in the wrong committed *against the talented* who are arguably deserving of those jobs. Even setting aside the series of controversial premises that one would have to swallow in order to accept this account, it is still doubtful that desert successfully explains the badness of discrimination as such. We have already discussed and rejected this account when examining, in the previous chapter, different meritocratic justifications, but let me nevertheless say the following. One obvious problem with the desert account, and one which we have already mentioned in the previous chapter, is that it would have to condemn any act of affirmative action as discriminatory. I have said that desert theorists such as David Miller try to bypass this problem by arguing that affirmative action is not discriminatory because it selects the person who would have been the best qualified if it hadn't been for the social injustice that made the affirmative action necessary to begin with. But notice that this reply smuggles in considerations of egalitarian justice in its understanding of discrimination. I have no quarrel with the latter, of course, but it does mean that desert theorists do not provide us with a badness account of discrimination that is independent of equality.

The final competing badness account I can think of is the view that discrimination is bad for reasons of prejudice. Namely, it is bad for people's lives to be determined by other people's prejudice. Paradigmatic cases of discrimination, we may observe, typically do involve prejudice (e.g. on the basis of race or sex). Thus, some people hold that discrimination is bad because we do not 'want to see people succeeding or failing because of other people's prejudice'.[21] Now, it is hard to deny that for people to fail because of other people's prejudice is bad. But why exactly is it bad for people to *succeed* on the basis of someone else's prejudice? Some of the reasons we have already mentioned may serve as an answer: it is inefficient to hire on the basis of prejudice; hiring on prejudice does not reward talent; and it is potentially demeaning to be hired for the colour of your skin rather than for your ability to perform the job. So at best, this view relies on other badness accounts, and ones which we have already dismissed. Now, one reason, of course, why hiring Smith on prejudice might be bad

---

[21] Cavanagh, *Against Equality of Opportunity*, p. 137. This seems to be also Holmes' view ('Anti-Discrimination Rights without Equality').

is that it implies *the failure of Jones* to get the job because of prejudice, which is certainly bad. But if this is where the badness of discrimination resides then we are back at a concern for equality of opportunity. Hiring Smith on prejudice is bad, here, because Jones did not really get an equal opportunity to compete for the job. So the claim that discrimination is bad for reasons of prejudice inevitably boils down to one about equality of opportunity.[22] Prejudice, then, does not provide an independent badness account.[23]

None of the potential sources of badness reviewed so far captures what is bad about discrimination. It might be suggested, however, that discrimination is bad for a multitude of compatible, overlapping reasons, and that there is no point searching for one source of badness that captures all incidents of discrimination.[24] It would follow that it is wrong to dismiss this or that account of badness when it fails to account for the badness of a particular incidence of discrimination. Now, it is certainly true that particular incidents of discrimination could be bad for a variety of reasons. But if discrimination is to make sense as an independent concern, there must be at least one reason underlying why it is bad *as such*. Consider, in contrast, the implications that would follow were discrimination to have only overlapping, non-exhaustive sources of badness, some accounting for the badness of incidence X and some accounting for the badness of incidence Y. In many particular incidents of discrimination the different sources

---

[22] In that respect, Sophia Moreau's account improves on Cavanagh. For she locates the badness of discrimination not in people succeeding or failing due to others' prejudice but only in the un-freedom of being at the mercy of someone else's prejudice. This is what she calls the deliberative freedom 'to live insulated from the effects of normatively extraneous features of us, such as our skin colour or gender'. Moreau, 'What is Discrimination?' p. 147. As mentioned, however, this account is vulnerable to the counter-example of covert discrimination.

[23] There is, however, one other way for its proponents to resurrect the prejudice account. They could say that discrimination is bad not when and because it is based on prejudice but rather when there is some *appearance* of prejudice. [At one point, Cavanagh, one of the proponents of this view, says so explicitly. He talks about tinkering with the 'message' of discrimination (*Against Equality of Opportunity*, p. 137).] A public display of prejudice in hiring might be bad whether or not it involves unequal opportunities. This is no doubt true. But, of course, this revised account cannot, once again, explain the badness of covert discrimination.

[24] This, implicitly, is Gardner's view, for he sees a separate source of badness for direct discrimination (what he calls 'harm'), and another for indirect discrimination (distributive justice, or equality of opportunity). (Gardner, 'Liberals and Unlawful Discrimination'.) Another 'bifurcated' account is Larry Alexander's, for whom some discrimination is wrong because of the animus it manifests and others for the harm they cause.

of badness clash. Think of the following example. Suppose an employer adopts a consciously racial hiring policy, preferring members of his own race just for that reason. Virtue-wise the action seems bad. It could also be bad due to reasons of efficiency: preferring members of his own race, the selector overlooks other, perhaps better qualified candidates. (And the same could be said for the deceit and desert accounts: the action does not truthfully represent the fitness of the appointee for the job, and it does not reward the desert of those truly suitable for the job.) Suppose, however, that the action is desirable from the perspective of EOp. Suppose the employer in question is hiring disproportionately more (sufficiently qualified) blacks. To decide whether this case constitutes discrimination we would first need to know which source of badness here trumps, as it were, the others. Ought the bad intentions, inefficiency, deceit, and desert trump the concern for EOp? In a case similar to this (*United Steelworkers v Weber*), the US Supreme Court decreed that the action, which it characterized as 'private affirmative action', is not discriminatory.[25] We may deduce from this that, at least in the Court's view, equality of opportunity was the weightier concern, even when all other concerns were stacked up against it. What this case shows, quite apart from the primacy of EOp in discrimination (at which we shall arrive shortly), is that even if there are overlapping sources of badness in different instances of discrimination, there must be at least one that captures the badness of discrimination as such. My point, to stress, is not that the court's decision proves any philosophical point here. Rather it is to illustrate that different sources of badness may clash with regard to any given case of potential discrimination, and that if discrimination as such is bad, there must be at least one account that captures this. The bottom line, then, is that we are searching for a badness account that successfully explains all incidents of discrimination. We want to know, in other words, why discrimination is bad *as such*.

In the rest of this chapter, then, I shall defend the view that discrimination is bad because and only because it undermines EOp for welfare across society. To suffer unequal opportunity (that is, to be disadvantaged relative to others) is the one and only bad accounting for the badness of discrimination.

---

[25] Cited in Gardner, 'Liberals and Unlawful Discrimination', p. 14. Although, as Gardner comments, there is a proviso here that the corporation undertaking 'private affirmative action' must be atoning, as it were, for its own personal historical discrimination rather than for society's past wrongs. But that shouldn't affect the point I am making here.

II. Discrimination without Inequality?

Cases which appear discriminatory while not involving inequality of opportunity pose an obvious challenge to the view defended here. Think of the following example (discussed by Deborah Hellman):[26] A head-master addresses his students and orders the black students to sit on the right of the hall and the white students to the left. The headmaster's order appears offensive.[27] Importantly, there seems to be no disadvantage here. Seats on the left are no better than seats on the right. Still, given the his-torical and social context of race relations, the headmaster's order strikes us as offensive. This seems a difficult case for the EOp account, and is easily explained by its rival accounts. For example, what is bad here, it might be suggested, is the headmaster's racist motive, which would sug-gest corruption of moral virtue as the source of badness.[28] Alternatively, and more plausibly, the order is bad because it is disrespectful towards the black students.[29] Alternative accounts, then, seem to fare better than the EOp account on this particular case. Still, we might also be able to understand the badness of such acts of segregation in terms of EOp. The headmaster's order is wrong in that it separates two groups and, given the particular historical context, brands the historically disadvantaged one as inferior. (This explains why sitting black-eyed students on the left, and brown-eyed ones to the right, would not be offensive or discriminatory.

---

[26] Hellman, *When is Discrimination Wrong?* pp. 26–8.

[27] Of course, his order might be part of some educational experiment meant to convey the repugnance of segregation, in which case we would probably not think the overall action to be wrongful. (Notice that the specific action, taken out of context, would still be wrong, and it is the overall educational context which makes it permissible. If the specific, isolated action were not wrong, then the educational experiment would not be effective to begin with.) But suppose the order has no educational purpose and thus no redeeming justification. Also, it might be useful to notice that the extent of offensiveness may depend on, among others, the following two variables. First, the case would carry slightly less offence were it to be a request rather than an order. And second, it would be slightly less offensive if made by one of the teachers, rather than the headmaster. The latter corresponds with our intuition that discrimi-nation is made worse the higher the selector is located in the hierarchy. (A point I shall return to in the last section.) In the particular example before us, we could think of variations on it which would not be offensive. For example, if the separation was along eye colour rather than skin colour then this would strike us as idiosyncratic but not offensive. Or, the headmaster could have ordered the seating to be based on some alphabetic order of surnames, which is neither offensive nor idiosyncratic.

[28] Then again, he might do so because he likes the aesthetic effect of this form of seating, not an obviously wrong motive. Hellman, *When is Discrimination Wrong?* p. 26.

[29] This is Hellman's position. *When is Discrimination Wrong?* p. 27.

There is no historical context of injustice towards either group.) 'Separate but equal' treatment is thus bad, we may say, when and because given a certain context it affords one group a *lesser opportunity for respect*. Respect is (obviously) a social good, and what segregation (when it is bad) does is to lower the social standing and opportunity for respect of the vulnerable of the two (or more) groups. Notice that this is *not* a disrespect-based account. Respect features here as a good, as a component of individual well-being; not as a deontic requirement. This is captured in the following case. Suppose segregation somehow ended up affording lesser access to respect to an already overall advantaged group. On that occasion, the EOp account would *not* deem segregation as discriminatory.

Segregation poses no threat to the EOp account of discrimination. More challenging, perhaps, are special cases where segregation actually works to the benefit of the worse-off group. I can think of two (real) examples to that effect, both concerning education (to which we turn our full attention in the next part of the book). Empirical research shows that separate classrooms for boys and girls, and, in a different case, native-born and newly arrived immigrants, boost the educational achievements of the latter groups (that is, girls and immigrant children, both of which we may plausibly consider to be the worse-off group).[30] It is hypothesized that girls find it more congenial to actively participate (say, ask questions or offer correct answers) in the absence of the dominating and pestering presence of boys. A similar mechanism may explain the success of students in classrooms composed exclusively of newly arrived immigrants, where shyness about one's perceived inadequate language skills might be at play. Now, one need not deny that there is an obvious price here to be paid in terms of integration, and for that reason, the practice might not be desirable all things considered. But from a strict fairness assessment it would be hard to argue that there is something wrong—if anything quite the opposite— about such (voluntary, let us assume) segregation.[31] This judgement, once again, is neatly captured by the EOp account.

[30] For a good review of the evidence on girls see Janice L. Streitmatter, *For Girls Only: Making a Case for Single-Sex Schooling* (Albany, NY: State University of New York Press, 1999), pp. 38–43. The evidence on immigrants is reported in Harry Brighouse and Adam Swift, 'Educational Equality versus Educational Adequacy: A Critique of Anderson and Satz', *Journal of Applied Philosophy* 26 (2009), p. 123.

[31] Elizabeth Anderson's account of segregation does not engage with tough cases (for her thesis) of this kind. See her *The Imperative of Integration* (Princeton, NJ, and Oxford: Princeton University Press, 2010).

But there are other prominent challenges to the thesis that discrimination is bad always and only for reasons of inequality of opportunity. In the infamous *Palmer v. Thompson* case a mayor in the south of the USA, following Federal de-segregation legislation chose to close down a public swimming pool, declaring that he wanted to end the spectacle of whites and blacks splashing in the same waters. The case seems to present a challenge to my thesis since there is no obvious inequality of opportunity here and yet the action is manifestly condemnable. Notice, though, that for this case to present a challenge it has to be the case that prior to the closure the public pool was used in equal measures by whites and blacks [rather than it being the (more probable) case, say, that proportionally, white folks had better access to private swimming pools, or to recreation facilities more generally]. We must suppose, to make the challenge an effective one, that the closure did not, in fact, undermine EOp (suppose whites and blacks were equally harmed by it). In that case the radical view would say that the mayor's decision might be repugnant (for the racist views it manifests, or for obstructing integration), but it was not discriminatory. The fact that we find the Mayor's decision to be repugnant, while involving no inequality does not imply that equality is irrelevant for discrimination.[32] It rather implies that some actions can be repugnant without being discriminatory.[33] This may sound strange at first, and so it needs to be stressed: mere expression of racism, repugnant as it is, does not necessarily amount to discrimination.

Here is another challenge to the view that discrimination is bad for reasons of EOp. Suppose, says Matt Cavanagh, that two towns are hit by some natural disaster and that you are a captain of a rescue ship that can save people in either of the towns. To simplify matters, assume that all relevant features (number of inhabitants, distance from the rescue ship, etc.) are equal between the two towns. Suppose also that the captain knows nothing about the identity of the inhabitants in the two towns. Under those circumstances, it is safe to assume, the captain should quickly flip a coin to choose which town to head for. All the same, says Cavanagh, we do not think it impermissible

---

[32] Contra Westen, 'The Empty Idea of Equality', p. 590.

[33] This is, incidentally, precisely what the Supreme Court reasoned in allowing the mayor's racist decision to stand. Justice Black wrote: 'Nothing in the history or language of the Fourteenth Amendment nor in any of our prior cases persuades us that the closing of the Jackson swimming pools to all its citizens constitutes a denial of the "equal protection of the laws"'. Cited in Helen M. Cake, 'Palmer vs. Thompson: Everybody Out of the Pool!' *Hastings Law Journal* 23 (1971), p. 889.

for the captain to skip the coin toss and to rather decide on a whim to head right or left to one of the towns. If we accept the story so far (which I do),[34] Cavanagh claims, then it follows that the moral constraints on the captain's conduct are those of avoidance of prejudice, and not those of EOp. What we care about in this case, in other words, is that the fate of the two towns would not depend on the prejudice of the selector. We would object, for example, if the captain chose one town over another because it contained fewer Jews. Our underlying concern here, then, is the avoidance of prejudice and *not* ensuring that the towns' inhabitants have some equal opportunity to survive the disaster. This is evidenced by our willingness to forgo the coin toss, or so says Cavanagh.[35] But notice that although a coin toss is, to be sure, a good way of ensuring equal chances, it is obviously not the only way. Allowing a choosing agent to act on a whim, *when it is truly a whim*, also accords equal chances. If the captain has no access to information that might bias his decision (anything from the composition of races to the number of individuals in each town) then his choice could be said to be truly made on a whim. And choosing on a whim, crucially, is a procedure that distributes equal chances. It is, in this sense, precisely like flipping a coin.[36]

Consider, finally, the following counter-example. Think of a society made up of five ethnic groups, whereby group A selects against group B, group B selects against C, and so forth. There is no inequality of opportunity here but the state of affairs nevertheless seems repugnant.[37] This proves, some may say, that the badness of discrimination is owed to reasons other than some unequal distribution of opportunities.[38] One thing

---

[34] One reason to deny the permissibility of a decision on a whim here is that, in contrast to a coin toss, it does not show respect for the occasion. Dworkin, for example, writes of a very similar case that acting in this way 'insults the gravity of the occasion'. *Justice for Hedgehogs* (Cambridge, MA, and London: The Belknap Press of Harvard University Press, 2011), p. 283. But this seems more like an external constraint, so I shall set it aside.

[35] Cavanagh, *Against Equality of Opportunity*, pp. 135–6.

[36] See also John Broome, 'Selecting People Randomly', *Ethics* 95 (1984), p. 55.

[37] See Lippert-Rasmussen, 'Intentions and Discrimination in Hiring', p. 14. Or consider a slightly different example whereby a multi-racial committee selects applicants, where in each case an applicant from one racial group is being rejected because of a racist vote of one of the committee members, and yet overall, no one is being disadvantaged, due to her race, compared to others. (See Lippert-Rasmussen, 'The Badness of Discrimination', p. 173.)

[38] Moreau, 'What is Discrimination?' p. 172. She gives an example of a community that has an equal number of restaurants each adversely selecting against a different clientele (Jewish, Muslim, etc.). She says that even though there is no inequality, there is still discrimination here.

that might be going on here is that this state of affairs involves (avoidable) dignitary harm. While each is equal to others in terms of opportunities, each has also suffered dignitary harm. If this state of affairs is bad, then, one reason explaining it might be that the treatment is demeaning. Crucially, however, and in difference from the paradigmatic cases of segregation, here the loss of respect is suffered equally by all. The EOp account therefore fails to detect something bad about this state of affairs. I suggest, once again, that this represents a case which is bad (perhaps even wrongful), but not discriminatory. It is bad because it entails some universal reduction in respect, but it is not discriminatory. To help see this, consider the following variant of the above story. Suppose that group A is viewed as quirky and idiosyncratic by group B, but its judgement is highly esteemed by groups C through E. And suppose that group B is viewed as quirky and idiosyncratic by group C (the group it will end up selecting against), but highly valued by everyone else, and so forth. It might be that when A selects against B (and B against C, and so forth) it causes a slight reduction in B's self-respect but an increase in C's through E's self-respect (and one whose accumulated amount is larger than the decrease in B's). It is easy to see where this is going. We have here what seems like multiple acts of adverse selections (consistent, recall, with EOp) which results, on the whole, in an increase in the absolute level of self-respect in society (or, at the very least, no decrease in that absolute level). Is there something bad about this state of affairs? Perhaps there is, but if so, it does not seem to be owed to reasons of discrimination (but if anything, to something like social cohesion), and thus does not pose a problem for the EOp account.

III. Radical Affirmative Action

I now want to point out three, perhaps rather obvious, advantages of the thesis advanced here. These concern disparate impact, so-called age-discrimination, and affirmative action. Consider first disparate impact, which occurs, recall, when a procedure which is seemingly neutral (e.g. physical tests for upper-body strength as part of a fire-fighting hiring process) ends up adversely selecting against an already disadvantaged group (e.g. women). I said earlier that cases of disparate impact are normally seen as presenting a challenge for intent- or respect-based (or in general, deontological) accounts of discrimination,[39] and it is not difficult to see why. Such cases demonstrate that some action may constitute wrongful discrimination even if there was no discriminatory intent and even if there was no loss of respect, either manifested or incurred. My account, in contrast, easily accommodates such cases. Discrimination, I said, is wrong when and because it exacerbates inequality of opportunity. That is precisely what disparate impact does and, more pertinently, why we think it is bad. Think, next, of so-called ageism or age-discrimination. My account sides with the practice of many European countries that opted *not* to follow the USA in abolishing mandatory retirement. Mandatory retirement is not discriminatory precisely because, over their whole lives, the old are not disadvantaged (compared to the young) with respect to employment opportunities.[40]

Consider, finally, affirmative action. Affirmative action, we said, poses a challenge to merit-based accounts of discrimination.[41] In contrast, affirmative action is undertaken precisely *for* the sake of equality of opportunity, and is thus easily accommodated in my account.[42] Now, there is of course a lot of objection to affirmative action (AA). Some of these objections are more challenging than others. (George Sher has done probably more than anybody else to generate egalitarian doubts with respect to affirmative action.) I cannot and do not intend to offer here a comprehensive defence of AA. But I do want to illustrate how the radical account of justice in hiring can handle such objections. Here are what I consider the four most pertinent ones:

1. Past discrimination is not the fault of those harmed by AA (e.g. poor whites).[43]

---

[39] See Arneson's struggle with responding to this challenge. 'What is Wrongful Discrimination?' pp. 793–4.

[40] See also Lippert-Rasmussen on this ('The Badness of Discrimination', p. 177).

[41] See Miller, *Principles of Social Justice*, ch. 8.

[42] The radical egalitarian's endorsement of affirmative action is rooted simply in the imperative to level inequalities in welfare. As such it does away with what many see as a problematic aspect of many accounts of affirmative action, namely the requirement to predict a counterfactual that would have been reached in the absence of systematic discrimination. [See for an example of such criticism, Robert S. Taylor, 'Rawlsian Affirmative Action', *Ethics* 119 (2009), p. 494.] The radical egalitarian's outlook, in that sense is forward-looking and does not rely on a backward-looking assessment of counterfactuals.

[43] George Sher, *Approximate Justice: Studies in Non-Ideal Theory* (Lanham, MD: Rowman and Littlefield, 1997), ch. 3.

2. Justifying affirmative action on the basis of equality between groups (men versus women, whites versus blacks) is problematic because it is not obvious that groups have moral standing.[44]
3. Affirmative action cannot be justified on the basis of equality because it generates unequal access to the job in question.[45]
4. Affirmative action helps individuals who are already better-off (middle-class blacks and middle-class women) rather than those harmed by it (poor whites).[46]

The first claim targets backward-looking justifications for affirmative action, while the other three target forward-looking justifications. I cannot do justice to all these objections, and there is by now a rich literature for and against AA).[47] Instead, I want to give a taste of how radical EOp handles these objections. Recall that the radical account of justice in hiring has three premises: non-meritocracy, monism, and non-discrimination. Non-meritocracy takes care of the first objection. On the radical account we said, no one has any special claim to a job; neither the most qualified, nor the most needy. Radical AA is therefore exempt from the need to find fault in anyone's past conduct in order to redistribute jobs in society. If no one has a prior claim to positions then no assignment of blame, and no backward-looking justification more generally, is required.

Radical AA shares the methodological individualism that is at the basis of the second objection (and thus easily averts it). It sees individuals, not groups, as its object of concern. The question, of course, is whether it (radical AA) can avoid relying on the moral status of groups. This would not be the case, for example, if the third and fourth objections could not be met. The third objection is often overlooked, but in fact constitutes quite a persuasive objection to backward- as well as forward-looking justifications of AA. Notice for example how it would condemn using quotas. The use of quotas can result in giving a preference to Jane over equally-qualified (or even more qualified) John. This may be justified on all sorts of grounds (e.g. diversity), but not on the grounds of equality of opportunity *for jobs*.

---

[44] Sher, *Approximate Justice*, ch. 4.
[45] Sher, *Approximate Justice*, pp. 85–6; Carl Cohen and James P. Sterba, *Affirmative Action and Racial Preference: A Debate* (New York: Oxford University Press, 2003), p. 19.
[46] Sher, *Approximate Justice*, ch. 6.
[47] For a relatively recent contribution see Cohen and Sterba, *Affirmative Action and Racial Preference*.

Monism helps us avert this objection. Radical EOp never sought equality of opportunity for a certain job, or even for jobs more generally. Its objective, recall, is equality of opportunity for welfare. The fact that AA may breach EOp in the pursuit of a certain job is therefore no objection to the radical account.

What of the fourth and final objection? This is the familiar claim that AA ends up benefitting individuals who are already quite privileged (middle-class blacks and women, compared to economically disadvantaged whites). Monism alone cannot help radical EOp here. For the objection says that AA ends up advantaging those who are already better-off more generally, compared with those who are worse-off (in overall socio-economic terms). Now, one thing the radical egalitarian can say is that AA helps narrow inequalities between men and women, as groups. But this of course will run afoul of the second objection (regarding the dubious moral status of groups). So this is no help for the (methodologically individualist) radical egalitarian. Instead, I propose, there are two answers that the radical egalitarian can provide with regard to the fourth objection, concerning, respectively, the immediate and long-term effects of AA. The first is to point out that the objection overlooks the multifaceted way in which certain minorities are disadvantaged in our non-ideal societies. Some middle-class blacks may have better jobs and income than many other whites, but they still have lower access to respect, personal safety, and freedom from stereotype, compared to whites (of all economic strata). It is not obvious, then, that middle class blacks are better-off, overall, than working-class whites. The second point concerns the long-term effects of AA. We have good reason to think that boosting the status of women, even if middle-class, may help women of all socio-economic strata. A middle-class woman shattering a glass ceiling (of certain careers) is likely to benefit, in the long term, women from all socio-economic strata. Having said all that, *if* it were the case that a certain practice of AA truly ended up increasing inequalities of welfare, even in the long term, then radical EOp would rule against it. This is no embarrassment for radical EOp; it is precisely that which it mandates.

IV. Some Final Tough Cases

I want to end my inquiry by presenting four issues that pose a potential challenge for the EOp account. These are: the confinement of discrimination to salient groups, 'buying off' discriminatees through financial compensation, 'discrimination' in the selection of life partners, and the duties that non-discrimination places on employers. Here is the first challenge. Accounts of discrimination sometimes rely on what is called 'socially-salient groups'[48] or 'groups with HSD (history of social disadvantage) traits'.[49] The term helps explain why discriminating against a person based on a salient trait (race, say) is much more offensive than rejecting her on the basis of a non-salient trait (having freckles, say). Arguably, speaking of the badness of discrimination exclusively in terms of EOp fails to explain why discrimination on the basis of salient features is so much worse than discrimination based on non-salient features (even when both of them are arbitrary).[50] There are two points to be made in reply. First, perhaps the main reason why the concept of 'socially-salient groups' is central to discrimination is precisely that these groups are generally already disadvantaged in terms of opportunities.[51] That is why a race-based (say) discrimination against a majority group (whites in the USA) strikes us as no more repugnant than discriminating against the freckled. A concern for EOp thus easily explains the centrality of disadvantaged salient groups to discrimination. Second, recall the point made in Section II. One of the opportunities that individuals typically (and rightly) care about is the opportunity to gain the respect (or esteem) of others. Crucially, discrimination would typically cause a greater disadvantage (in terms of respect) when it is directed at members of salient groups compared to when it is directed at members of non-salient groups (such as 'people whose surname contains seven letters', 'the untalented', and 'people who are not family members of mine'). In other words, disadvantageous hiring on the basis of salient group membership presents much greater damage to one's equal opportunity to social-esteem, compared to discrimination on the basis of non-salient, idiosyncratic, traits.

Here is the second challenge. Suppose someone who is denied a job based on her skin colour is then offered some compensation (say, cash). And suppose that that package of compensation makes her as well-off

---

[48]   Lippert-Rasmussen, 'The Badness of Discrimination', p. 168.

[49]   Hellman, *When is Discrimination Wrong?* pp. 21–2. Cf. Arneson, 'What is Wrongful Discrimination?' p. 794. Arneson resists placing any moral importance on historically disadvantaged groups. Consequently, he is forced to say that if a procedure is neutral then the fact that it yields a disparate impact for black children is of as much consequence if 'the affected children were green in colour'.

[50]   Cavanagh raises an objection to that effect. *Against Equality of Opportunity*, p. 154.

[51]   See also Lippert-Rasmussen, 'Private Discrimination', e.g. p. 834.

as having the job would. Since the discriminatee is not made worse-off in this case, and given that my account makes exacerbating inequality of opportunity (for welfare, recall) a necessary condition, it would imply that there is no discrimination involved. Still, the practice seems quite repugnant. I bite the bullet on this: if, given the choice, Smith would not give up the package of compensation in favour of the denied job [thereby indicating, notice, that there is no inequality of welfare (recall the envy test from Chapter 1)] then I would indeed resist depicting this as a case of discrimination. We are assuming, of course, that Smith's preference for the compensation package is fully informed and not, in any way, coerced. It might also be useful to note that our sense of counterintuition in such cases might be motivated by some practical considerations for restricting anti-discrimination remedies to 'in-kind' measures. As Mark Kelman rightly observes, compensating a particular person for discrimination on the basis of her skin colour does little to prevent such future discrimination to other people of colour.[52] But this is of course a practical (instrumental) consideration and not a principled one.

The third challenge concerns discrimination in private spheres of life, where the paradigmatic case is that of selecting life partners. We normally think that, beyond certain obvious prohibitions (marrying the under-aged or one's sibling) the state should not regulate the way in which individuals select their partners. Still, that does not mean that the choices individuals make in that sphere are beyond moral assessment.[53] In particular, we may think that there is something wrong about individuals choosing a priori never to marry individuals of a certain ethnic group or skin colour. If this is a form of discrimination (allowing that it is one that the state would do well to steer clear of), then it is one that does not seem to concern EOp.[54] If we think there is something repugnant about individuals having such preferences then the problem does not seem to rest with some putative inequality of opportunity (for partnership) but is rather grounded in the morally reprehensible motive of the discriminator. I concede, in reply, that there is something morally wrong in the conduct of racist grooms

[52] Mark Kelman, 'Market Discrimination and Groups', *Stanford Law Review* 53 (2001), 833–96, p. 884.

[53] See Lippert-Rasmussen on a similar point. 'Private Discrimination', p. 851ff.

[54] Cavanagh, *Against Equality of Opportunity*, p. 201; Lippert-Rasmussen, 'Intentions and Discrimination in Hiring', p. 22.

and brides to-be. But I want, nevertheless, to make two points in reply. First, some cases of a priori rejection of certain life partners *does* potentially undermine equality of opportunity. Suppose, not implausibly, that most people prefer to marry what they consider as good-looking partners, and suppose further that some physical traits (certain eye colour, certain cheekbone structure, etc.) is universally considered unattractive in a given social context. Those bearing these traits might then be said to be disadvantaged in terms of marriage opportunities. Much of what is repugnant about the distribution of life partnerships *is*, therefore, captured as discriminatory on the EOp account. Second, admittedly some a priori marriage preferences need not result in inequality of opportunity and hence are not discriminatory. Think again of a thoroughly racist society composed of evenly numbered racial groups. Here no concern for EOp can arise, and in such cases I would insist that no discrimination takes place. Once again, the state of affairs might be regrettable for all sorts of reasons, such as the prevalent racism and the lack of integration, but it is nevertheless not discriminatory.

Here is the fourth and final challenge to the EOp account. My claim in this chapter has been that discrimination is bad because and only because it undermines EOp. This seems to suggest, the critic might say, that what is wrong about employers who discriminate is that they fail to promote EOp. To put this differently, discriminators are at fault for not using their power (the ability to allocate jobs) in a way that would curtail inequality of opportunity (and moreover, for welfare!). And this, the claim goes, is counterintuitive, and in at least two ways. On the one hand, this objection reveals the account to be potentially too wide. For it seems to suggest that employers are under a greater burden to advance distributive justice than are other citizens, which seems implausible.[55] On the other hand, the EOp account is revealed by this objection to be, in a different way, too narrow: it seems to miss the point of what is wrong about the employer's conduct. Our intuition is that she is at fault not for her failure to promote a worthy social goal (EOp) but for something else and something much more sinister (e.g. disrespecting the applicant, allowing prejudice to affect her judgement, etc.). One thing to note here, before replying, is that this latter objection may also apply to other accounts of discrimination. The view that discrimination as such is bad because of say, efficiency

---

55   Gardner also raises this doubt. See his 'Liberals and Unlawful Discrimination', p. 10.

reasons (it fails to appoint the person who would be the most useful one) would suggest, arguably, that the fault of discriminators is the failure to maximize the social good. This equally seems to miss the point of what is repugnant about the very act of discrimination. None of this, of course, gets the EOp account off the hook. Recall, then, that my claim was that discrimination *as such* is bad because and only because it undermines EOp. This is not to deny, I have said, that particular incidents of discrimination might be repugnant for additional reasons (such as disrespect or inefficiency). A discriminatory act might be offensive for a variety of reasons, but there is only one reason, I maintain, that explains why discrimination *as such* is bad. This is why, I think, the EOp account is innocent of the narrowness objection: it never purported to, and need not, capture everything that is condemnable about each and every instance of discrimination. Because it never purported to exhaust everything which is bad about particular acts of discrimination, it also never meant to exhaust discriminators' *culpability*. (And consequently, the EOp account does not purport to exhaust the range of morally permissible *punishments*, as well as potential remedies against a discriminating employer.) In short, the badness of discrimination as such is tied up with the person being discriminated against and is always one and the same. The extent of the culpability of the discriminator, on the other hand, will vary depending on her intent, knowledge, the grounds on which she chose to discriminate, etc. This may actually indicate the strength rather than weakness of the EOp account. For, it can potentially categorize as discriminatory even actions that appear to have a rather minimal level of culpability on the part of the selector (e.g. those concerning disparate impact). Turn now, finally, to the wideness version of the objection. The objection said that locating the badness of discrimination in EOp implies that employers are under a greater duty to promote distributive justice than non-employers. But we can now see that this does not follow. The objection would have been true had my claim been that undermining EOp is a sufficient condition for discrimination. This *would* have entailed that the sin of the selector was in not promoting social justice. But my claim, recall, was that it is only a necessary condition. Undermining equality of opportunity therefore does not purport to exhaust why discriminating selectors are culpable; what exactly they are culpable of; nor what their duty in terms of hiring was to begin with (recall the arbitrariness condition from the previous chapter).

Conclusion

I defended here the view that the badness of discrimination (as such) is rooted in one and only one evil, namely the undermining of equality of opportunity for welfare. I tried to argue that other accounts of the badness of discrimination, such as those concerning intent, efficiency, false representation, prejudice, respect, and desert are unsatisfactory. I then argued that inequality of opportunity captures everything that is bad about discrimination as such, and I tried to show that this account successfully handles the toughest cases associated with discrimination, such as those concerning segregation, salient group membership, and the duties of employers. If and when discrimination is bad (as such) it is so for the reason motivating radical equality of opportunity (namely, narrowing inequalities of welfare across society), and nothing else. Thus, an account of justice in hiring that is premissed on equality of opportunity, as the luck egalitarian account is, cannot possibly be discriminatory, neither towards the rich, nor towards the poor.

PART III

Upbringing

6

Against Equality of Opportunity in Education?

Few would object to equality of opportunity.[1] Fewer still, Christopher Jencks wrote some twenty years ago, would object to equality of opportunity in education.[2] Interestingly, this is no longer the case: equality of opportunity in education has become in recent years a contested issue, in practice and in theory.

Taking a step back from equality of opportunity, we may observe two different reasons why people who call themselves egalitarians may be suspicious of pursuing equality (and not just equality of opportunity) in education. The weaker (and more widely shared) reason is that doing so requires intruding into the family. Many egalitarians understandably baulk at telling parents how to spend their money and time on their children even if they acknowledge that doing so may exacerbate educational inequalities. The stronger (and more recent) objection to equality in education is that, independently of the conflict with the family and (legitimate) parental partiality, equality in education is not an ideal we should strive at. The present chapter will engage with (part of) the latter claim, and the next chapter will engage with the former one.

In thinking of objections to the very ideal of equality of opportunity in education (independently of the price it may exact from the family) it is possible to identify two sets of objections. One such set of objections claims that

---

[1] Matt Cavanagh, of course, wrote a book titled 'Against Equality of Opportunity'. But even he is not, in fact, against the ideal of equality of opportunity as such, but rather against its application to hiring. See Matt Cavanagh, *Against Equality of Opportunity* (Oxford: Oxford University Press, 2002).

[2] Christopher Jencks, 'Whom Must We Treat Equally for Educational Opportunity to Be Equal?' *Ethics* 98 (1988), p. 518.

the ideal misses the point of justice in education,[3] while the other claims that the ideal is incoherent.[4] I shall not engage with the first type of objection. I shall not do so not because it is a marginal one (it is not), but because I think that others have already done an excellent job in refuting it, and I have nothing interesting to add to their comprehensive critique.[5] This chapter thus aims to defend equality of opportunity (EOp) in education only from the latter accusation. More specifically, I argue that applying the *radical* ideal of EOp to education helps avert the claim that equality of opportunity in education is problematic and undesirable. According to that radical ideal, inequality in educational achievements is just when and only when it reflects unequal effort on the part of the child. The argument unfolds as follows. The first section delimits the scope of our discussion within the general concern for justice in education. Section II focuses the discussion on EOp in education by looking at the dominant account to date, namely meritocratic (or Rawlsian) EOp. Section III introduces radical EOp in education, and moves to defend it from some prominent objections. The final section then sketches some attractive features of the radical account.

I. Justice in Education

In thinking of EOp in education it would be helpful to disentangle that issue from other related questions of justice in education. Perhaps the most important one is the abovementioned question of legitimate parental partiality. Parents' interest in their children's education is, naturally, of supreme relevance to an ethical account of educational distribution. But there are some aspects of justice in education that can and ought to be discussed in isolation from how parents, legitimately or not, subvert EOp.

---

[3] Elizabeth Anderson, 'Rethinking Equality of Opportunity: Comment on Adam Swift's How Not to Be a Hypocrite', *Theory and Research in Education* 2 (2004), 99–110; 'Fair Opportunity in Education: A Democratic Equality Perspective', *Ethics* 117 (2007), 595–622; Debra Satz, 'Equality, Adequacy, and Education for Citizenship', *Ethics* 117 (2007), 623–48.

[4] Jencks, 'Whom Must We Treat Equally for Educational Opportunity to Be Equal?'; Janet Radcliffe Richards, 'Equality of Opportunity', *Ratio* 10 (1997), 253–79; Clare Chambers, 'Each Outcome is Another Opportunity: Problems with the Moment of Equal Opportunity', *Politics, Philosophy, and Economics* 8 (2009), 374–400; Kenneth R. Howe, 'Equality of Educational Opportunity and the Ideal of Equal Educational Worth', *Studies in Philosophy and Education* 11 (1993), 329–37; John Wilson, 'Does Equality (of Opportunity) Make Sense in Education?' *Journal of Philosophy of Education* 25 (1991), p. 28.

[5] See Harry Brighouse and Adam Swift, 'Educational Equality versus Educational Adequacy: A Critique of Anderson and Satz', *Journal of Applied Philosophy* 26 (2009), 117–28.

My first methodological suggestion, then, is to detach the issue of parental partiality from the question of justice in education. In a way, Jencks has already undertaken that by focusing on what his by-now famous Ms Higgins should aim at in her classroom. In focusing on what justice requires of the educational system narrowly understood, he thereby set aside the potential implications for legitimate parental partiality. (Admittedly, it does not set aside what Ms Higgins may do to offset the unequal effects of parental care, and it does not set aside whether parents are allowed to opt out of Ms Higgins' class altogether.) The question of legitimate parental partiality has, I concede, important implications for the pursuit of EOp and the next chapter is indeed devoted to it. In this chapter, we set parental partiality aside.

A further restriction on the discussion to follow is that I am concerned here only with children and therefore leave higher education aside. Obviously, individuals may obtain education at any given point of their life, and justice must be able to say something about the attainment of these educational opportunities throughout one's life. But there are nevertheless good reasons to confine the discussion to K–12 (kindergarten to Year 12) education. Part of the reason, it will shortly become apparent, is that some of the criticism of EOp in education centres, specifically, on some alleged counterintuitive implications of applying EOp to children.

Here is a third point of clarification. I said that I focus my discussion solely on primary and secondary education, and leave higher education aside. But in narrowing our discussion to basic education we must not, of course, ignore its effects later in life. Obviously, a large (if not the major) reason for our preoccupation with justice in basic education is precisely the way in which it shapes future adults' life chances. That goes without saying. Still, we must decide upfront, for the purpose of our discussion, whether we conceive of what follows high school, primarily higher education and the job market, in ideal or non-ideal terms. Importantly, if one assumes that higher education and the job market operate according to some ideal principle then that would obviously affect what, ideally, one would expect from a just basic education system. Think of a world in which education, both at K–12 and university level, does not affect job-placement (suppose jobs are allotted by lottery)[6].[7]

[6] See Barbara Goodwin, *Justice by Lottery* (Exeter: Imprints Academic, 2005).
[7] Or suppose we accept Debra Satz's surprisingly rosy portrayal of American society as one in which private education does not matter that much for one's higher-education and career opportunities. One proof for this that she cites is that: 'Even in the United States, many of the most visible chief executive officers have not graduated from selective

When education is, in this way, stripped of its positional value (let us assume) and is reduced to its intrinsic value it may well be the case that egalitarians would be less troubled by inequalities in educational outcomes at the primary level. In other words, a reform of higher education (and the job market) can help neutralize much of the positional value of primary education, and that, crucially, may have implications for what a just allocation of educational resources at the primary level is. This is important, because, in providing an account of justice in basic education one must choose between taking the distribution of subsequent related goods to be as they non-ideally are, or as they should be according to some ideal of justice. For what it is worth, it seems to me that it is a lot more informative to provide an ideal account of justice in basic education while taking the job market and higher education as they are.[8] (But that is not to claim that a comprehensive exercise in ideal theory is without merit.)

We are searching, then, for what justice in education requires, assuming the world as it is, but setting aside, for now, the issue of parental partiality. Notice that that latter qualification does not require the sort of idealizing that I have just warned against. We may, I said, look at a classroom in a public (state) school and ask how its resources ought to be distributed. What is it that Jencks's Ms Higgins ought to equalize, if at all? This calls

colleges and universities' (Satz, 'Equality, Adequacy, and Education for Citizenship', p. 644). Whether or not this is a good indicator of how private education affects career opportunity, it would be interesting to examine how many of these 'visible' CEO's have *attended* selective colleges, before the promise of huge sums of money distracted them from bothering to graduate.

[8] See also Harry Brighouse, *School Choice and Social Justice* (Oxford: Oxford University Press, 2000), p. 115. This is, in my view, one of the weaknesses in Elizabeth Anderson's argument for adequacy in education. Anderson combines an account of sufficiency in primary education with an ideal account of higher education and the job market. (Her latter account says that merit should be measured not solely in terms of academic qualifications but also in terms of one's familiarity with diverse socio-economic backgrounds.) I concede that both ideals are at least prima facie attractive. The point, however, is that Anderson often employs the latter ideal in defence of the former. In other words, to defend adequacy in primary school from egalitarian critics, Anderson claims that their worry about the unequal distribution of the positional value of primary education is premised on their non-ideal view of higher education. Under higher education as she conceives it (when college placement is meant to reflect diversity), the unequal achievement of primary education results will not matter as much. (See Anderson, 'Fair Opportunity in Education', e.g. p. 616.) Whatever else we might think of this argument, we must notice that it provides an account of justice in primary education that is premised on an ideal picture of higher education and the job market. That is precisely what I shall refrain from doing in this chapter. I shall attempt to spell out what justice in primary education requires, given the world as it is, and not as it should be.

for the fourth and final point of qualification. I have mentioned that in recent years EOp is no longer taken for granted in discussions of justice in education. But I have also said that I do not intend to engage in this chapter with what its critics alternatively propose. I refer to the view that what justice in education requires is some level of adequacy, rather than equality. Recently, this has become a rather prominent line of thinking (especially in the USA).[9] Nevertheless, I shall set this aside, and for two reasons. One reason is that I have already discussed (in Chapter 1) my reservations about whether sufficientarianism satisfies the requirements of egalitarian justice. And the other reason is that others have already thoroughly refuted, in my view, the sufficientarian case in education. More precisely, they have refuted the claim that sufficiency in education comes anywhere near exhausting the requirements of justice.[10] That is not to deny, of course, that reaching some level of sufficiency in education is an important policy goal. The point, rather, is that making sure that everyone reaches some level of sufficiency far from exhausts the requirements of *egalitarian* distributive justice in education (and in some cases may even conflict with those requirements).[11] To be clear, then, I ask in this chapter what egalitarian distributive justice requires with regard to education; not what the requirements of equal citizenship do. Equal citizenship may indeed spell some independent requirements for the allocation of educational

---

[9] Satz, 'Equality, Adequacy, and Education for Citizenship'; Anderson, 'Fair Opportunity in Education'; James Tooley, *Disestablishing the School* (Aldershot: Avebury Press, 1995), ch. 2.

[10] Brighouse and Swift, 'Educational Equality versus Educational Adequacy'; Brighouse, *School Choice*, pp. 133–4, 146–50; Colin Macleod, 'Justice, Educational Equality, and Sufficiency', *Canadian Journal of Philosophy* 36 (2010), 151–75. There is no need to rehearse here the series of decisive objections raised by Brighouse, Swift, and Macleod, but here is just one example. Like any sufficiency account, Anderson's and Satz's account suffers from 'threshold fetishism'. It favours aiding better-off Smith (because doing so would lift him above the sufficiency threshold) over aiding worse-off Jones, who, unfortunately for him, could only be lifted to just below the sufficiency threshold. This might be desirable for all sorts of reasons, but is nevertheless in conflict with our intuitions concerning distributive justice.

[11] Satz, for example, claims that egalitarian critics of sufficientarianism in education overlook the way in which the high level of adequacy in education that her model requires (the skills needed to serve on a jury, for example) would substantially curb contemporary inequalities in education. (See Satz, 'Equality, Adequacy, and Education for Citizenship', p. 636.) This argument is similar in form to the argument utilitarians sometimes make, according to which maximizing utility would lead, by virtue of diminishing marginal utility, to narrowing inequalities. Both arguments, of course, support equality only contingently.

resources. But these requirements are a supplement, and no substitute, for what egalitarian distributive justice, pure and simple, decrees.

Let me sum up this long introductory section. My discussion in this chapter sidesteps much of contemporary debate concerning justice in education, and in two significant ways. First, it eschews the limits of parental partiality (which it reserves for the next chapter), and second, it eschews the sufficiency versus equality debate. The remaining scope of the discussion is intentionally narrow: what is it that distributive justice in education requires us to equalize?

II. Equality of Opportunity in Basic Education

It would be useful to get some obvious objections to EOp in education out of the way. For one thing, it is compatible with a levelling down of educational achievement. Levelling down is generally problematic, but seems even more so with respect to education. This is so because education has not only instrumental value for the individual, but also intrinsic value, and instrumental value for third parties (say, society as a whole). This means that we care not only about the distribution of education but also about the absolute size of the educational achievements pie.[12] Still, we have said that our concern here is with what justice in education requires, and not with the broader issue of overall desirable rules of regulation in education. Given that our inquiry targets justice, it thus sidesteps the worry for levelling down. Another familiar objection to EOp in education is that it may be achieved by means of a lottery. Think of a stratified educational system as it currently exists in Britain, say; one consisting of private ('public') and state schools. Suppose, though, that, unlike contemporary Britain, placement in these schools is based on a lottery. (And suppose the state subsidizes the high fees of non-wealthy kids who win places at Eton and the like.)[13] EOp is thus obtained, but the outcome still seems unacceptable.

---

[12] Michael Walzer may think he is condemning EOp when he writes that 'the goal of the reading teacher is not to produce equal chances, but to achieve equal results'. [Michael Walzer, *Spheres of Justice: A Defence of Equality and Pluralism* (Oxford: Basic Books, 1983), p. 203.] But obviously, the goal of equal results would also be vulnerable to levelling down, which presumably Walzer would not endorse.

[13] Recall, similarly, Fishkin's idea of swapping babies around shortly after birth, thereby achieving EOp. James Fishkin, *Justice, Equal Opportunity and the Family* (New Haven, CN: Yale University Press, 1983), p. 57.

This, however, would be true of what we have termed *total* EOp, but untrue of *radical* EOp. Radical EOp (recall our discussion in the introductory chapter) neutralizes, as much as possible, the effect of luck on one's welfare. It would therefore not recommend EOp in education by means of lottery (in as much as it could be avoided).

Having gotten these two familiar (though somehow persisting) objections out of the way, let us inquire more closely into the application of EOp to education. As we have already seen in the introduction to this book, in identifying an ideal of EOp, in education, or in general, we may ask three different questions, regarding currency, subject matter, and scope. In inquiring after the currency, we ask, first, what types of obstacles this ideal is concerned with removing (or neutralizing). In inquiring, second, about the subject matter, we ask 'EOp for what?'. The third question, regarding scope,[14] need not detain us here. Suppose we simply talk of equality of opportunity between all the pupils in a given classroom. Now, most of what I have to say in this chapter concerns the first question, but let me first say something about the second one. Two prominent options are offered in the literature with regard to the question 'EOp for what in education?'. The obvious answer is of course educational achievements (measured in cognitive abilities, grades, certificates, or any other qualitative measure). But another option sometimes mentioned is equality in the fulfilment of the child's potential. According to this second interpretation, to achieve justice in education is to ensure that children realize an equal share of their potential.[15] I admit that I have always been puzzled by the allure that this second interpretation seems to exert. Even setting aside the obvious (empirical?) question of whether or not children (or adults for that matter) have a fixed potential, I find the normative implications of this view implausible. For justice in education to equalize a percentage of one's potential is much the same as for justice in health (see the next part of the book) to strive to equalize a certain percentage of individuals' innate capacity for health. Consider two 40-year-old heart patients. And suppose it is ascertained that with the best available care one individual

[14] See Peter Westen, 'The Concept of Equal Opportunity', *Ethics* 95 (1985), 837–50; Lesley E. Jacobs, *Pursuing Equal Opportunities: The Theory and Practice of Egalitarian Justice* (Cambridge: Cambridge University Press, 2004), esp. ch. 2.
[15] Debra Satz, for example, considers this as a serious interpretation of the ideal of EOp in education. See Satz, 'Equality, Adequacy, and Education for Citizenship', p. 631.

will live to 60 whereas the other will live to 80. Suppose there are only 32 QALY's (Quality Adjusted Life Years) at our disposal that we may allocate between them. Suppose further that that translates to the choice between (56, 56) (48, 64) [the numbers representing their life expectancy following the treatments]. In terms of percentage of capacity for health this would read as (0.93, 0.7) as compared with (0.8, 0.8). Medical intervention, on the principle of equal opportunity for equal fulfilment of potential would recommend the second policy. From a fairness perspective this is absurd. So in speaking of equality of opportunity in education we shall be speaking, from now on, about EOp for educational achievements, measured absolutely rather than relative to one's starting point, innate potential, or what have you.

We are left with the question of currency of EOp. What type of obstacles should EOp in education remove? Rawlsian (or meritocratic) EOp asserts that inequality in educational achievements is justified only when it reflects differences in merit, where merit is understood as the combination of the child's effort and her skills (say, in terms of IQ).[16] Differences owed to socio-economic background, in contrast, are rendered unjust on this reading. This meritocratic account (as proposed by Brighouse and Swift)[17] has already received some critical attention, much of which I do *not* share. One reason to think that this meritocratic ideal is wrong, it has been suggested, is that while meritocracy might be a suitable principle of justice for higher education or for jobs, it would be wrong to apply it to children. And the reason is that it is wrong to treat children's skills as fully developed. They are obviously not, and it is therefore wrong, or so says Elizabeth Anderson, to devise educational policy based on a snapshot of non-fully developed skills.[18] One, rather obvious, problem with this objection is that it is not clear that it is an objection to meritocracy in K–12, as

---

[16] For some scepticism with regard to IQ as a measurement of intelligence, see Paul Gomberg, *How to Make Opportunity Equal? Race and Contributive Justice* (Malden, MA: Blackwell, 2007), pp. 122–4.

[17] Adam Swift, *How Not to be a Hypocrite: School Choice for the Morally Perplexed Parent* (London and New York: Routledge, 2003) p. 29. 'Educational equality means at minimum, that the resources devoted to a child's education should not depend on the ability of their parents to pay for, or choose well among educational experiences.' Brighouse, *School Choice*, pp. 122–3. Brighouse explicitly says that this is only a minimum requirement, but does not go on to offer a more comprehensive account. Furthermore, he explicitly rejects the policy of equalizing achievement regardless of ability. (See *School Choice*, p. 129.)

[18] Anderson, 'Rethinking Equality of Opportunity', p. 101. See also Satz, 'Equality, Adequacy, and Education for Citizenship', p. 630.

opposed to meritocracy in general. It is undeniable that children's skills are far from fully developed. But when, exactly, may we say that an adult's level of skills is fully fixed: at 25, at 45, 65?[19] If the meritocratic ideal may be applied to adults but not to children, it seems, the distinguishing factor cannot be the contrast between fully developed as opposed to non-fully developed skills.

Critics of meritocratic EOp in education may drive at a slightly different point. Perhaps what distinguishes the appropriateness of applying meritocracy to adults but not to children is the thought that adults are responsible for their current level of skills (however much developed they are), whereas children are not. This strikes me as a more plausible suggestion. The problem here, however, is that even if the assumption (on which it relies) is true, it does little to help undermine meritocratic education. This is so for the simple reason that responsibility is for the most part irrelevant for meritocracy. It can sometimes be permissible to appoint individuals on the basis of features for which they are *not* responsible (tall individuals for the position of basketball players), and it may be impermissible to reject applicants on the basis of features for which they *are* responsible (a discrimination on religious grounds against a convert).[20] Indeed, no one would suggest that sports academies that select children based on some athletic tests are wrong because they are out of step with some meritocratic ideal. (They might be wrong, of course, for other reasons.) So the suggestion that children are not responsible for their skills, even if true, is neither here nor there. It certainly does not preclude the application of meritocracy to basic education. (Notice, I am not denying that the suggestion that children may not be responsible for their skills *may* have moral implications for the distribution of educational resources. I am only denying that the view that children are not responsible for those skills should prevent the adoption of a meritocratic ideal in education.) In as much as one accepts the meritocratic ideal (which I don't) then there is no reason to think it may not be applied to children (at least not for the reasons we have seen so far).[21]

---

[19] See also Chambers ('Each Outcome is Another Opportunity', p. 393) on this point.

[20] See also Cavanagh, *Against Equality of Opportunity*, p. 187.

[21] Equally unpersuasive is Anderson's claim that on contractarian grounds, only developed skills and not innate talents may be the basis of allocation ('Rethinking Equality of Opportunity', pp. 101–2). If the parties in the original position have an interest in the best possible surgeons, then it may well be justified to identify teenagers on the basis of IQ and motivation and invest resources in training them in a pre-med school. Another criticism of the meritocratic ideal which I don't find particularly persuasive is mounted by Jencks. He claims that it is prima facie incoherent to require the removal of social obstacles to a child's

III. Holding Children Responsible

Applying the meritocratic ideal to education is not false for the reasons outlined by its sufficientarian critics, but for a different, and much simpler reason. Namely, if inequalities in educational achievement arising from social factors are unjust then there is no reason to suppose that those arising from natural factors are not. Consider two pupils who have equal difficulty in reading, but where one's is attributed to some in-born disorder, whereas the other's is the product of a disorganized and neglectful home. Suppose it costs the same amount of resources to improve their reading. Is there any reason of justice to prioritize the latter over the former? This seems highly unlikely.[22] If one accepts that, then the problem with meritocratic EOp in education is not that it is too egalitarian but rather that it is not egalitarian enough. Since the allocation of talents is morally arbitrary, it is simply unjust to distribute educational resources in a way that favours the naturally talented.

The radical ideal of EOp to education, in contrast, says that EOp in education obtains when educational achievement varies with effort and effort alone.[23] In other words, inequalities in educational achievements are just only when correlating with inequalities in effort exercised by the children themselves. Let me say right away, though, that I am *not* proposing that educational systems should, in any substantial way, hold children responsible for their educational achievements. This would be a highly un-desirable way of regulating our educational systems. What I *do* hold is that this is precisely what justice requires.

Still, this approach raises, of course, a host of potential objections. We may divide these objections between those targeting the general

---

success, but not the natural ones. And the reason is that it is inconsistent to say that society is responsible for socio-economic inequalities but not to inequalities in IQ. The reason being that by allowing individuals with low IQ to marry and have children, the state is essentially responsible for the generation of these natural inequalities as well. (Jencks, 'Whom Must We Treat Equally for Educational Opportunity to Be Equal?' p. 523.) The argument, as it happens, would support the claim I advance in this chapter, but I don't find it particularly convincing, and so shall set it aside. For what it is worth, I would say this. Luck egalitarians, typically, are not concerned with whether *society* is responsible for a child's genes (Jencks's concern), but, rather, with the fact that the *child* is *not*.

[22] On this I am in agreement with Jencks, 'Whom Must We Treat Equally for Educational Opportunity to Be Equal?' pp. 523–4.

[23] Satz mentions this ideal but does not bother discussing it. 'Equality, Adequacy, and Education for Citizenship', p. 629, fn. 14.

implications of holding children responsible for the effort they display, and objections that centre on the specific educational implications of that principle. Let me begin with the latter type of objections. Radical EOp in education says that inequalities in educational achievements are not unjust so long as they track effort, and effort alone. But the question arises: what do we owe those children who display little effort? Embarrassingly, radical EOp has no qualms about these children graduating with very low educational skills. Indeed, the principle does not rule against having these students graduate with skills that fall below something we would deem essential for living in a democratic society.[24] One thing to note, in reply, is that it is not obvious why such a consequence, embarrassing as it is, would be bad only in democratic societies. It is an embarrassment for a theory to sanction the graduation of students with intolerably low skills in *any* society, whether democratic or not.[25] Similarly, we may observe that this objection applies not only to the radical account but also to the meritocratic one. If a child's level of talent is sufficiently low, meritocratic EOp will tolerate her graduating with correspondingly low educational achievements.[26] In fact, and as already noted, any truly egalitarian (as opposed to sufficientarian) account of justice in education may result in some (or even all, in the case of levelling down) children falling below some level of adequacy. Consequently, radical, as well as meritocratic, egalitarians have a similar response to this 'abandonment' objection. EOp, I have already said, does not purport to provide a comprehensive ethical account of how educational resources ought to be distributed. It is meant only as an account of *fairness* in education. It concerns itself only with the justice of the comparative holdings of educational resources by children. It is therefore compatible (and very plausibly, in need of supplementing) with a principle of adequacy, stating a threshold beneath which it is morally unacceptable (for reasons independent of fairness) for a child to graduate school.

The same sort of trade-off will be called for in order to deliver radical EOp from a related problem. Namely, some children are bad converters

---

[24] See Anderson, 'Fair Opportunity in Education'; Satz, 'Equality, Adequacy, and Education for Citizenship'; and also Amy Gutmann, *Democratic Education* (Princeton, NJ: Princeton University Press, 1987).

[25] Something which Anderson's and Satz's 'democratic' and 'civic' equality, respectively, do not guarantee.

[26] See Satz, 'Equality, Adequacy, and Education for Citizenship', p. 630.

of educational resources into educational achievements. Some students will always fall short in their achievements, no matter how many resources we throw at them. Radical EOp in education may thus seem hopeless.[27] Admittedly, meritocratic EOp, in contrast, may escape this 'bottomless pit' problem, because it strives to equalize outcomes between children of equal talent. Still, the objection is not peculiar to radical EOp alone. An ideal of equality of outcome (of educational achievements), for example, would be similarly vulnerable to this bottomless pit objection. But in any case, this objection is no embarrassment to the radical egalitarian. The rules of regulation that it supports would call for some trade-off between the requirements of fairness and those of efficiency. Bottomless pits do not embarrass an account of fairness.

Let us, then, turn to the perhaps more substantial problem afflicting radical EOp in education. It is simply wrong, many would say, to hold children responsible for the level of effort they exert with regards to their studies.[28] It might be useful to break this worry down into two, related, concerns. First, is it right, in principle, to hold children responsible? And second, is it right to hold children responsible for something (their effort at school, say) which we suspect to be the product of (unequal and potentially unjust) socio-economic background? Let me deal with these in turn.

We might think, first, that it is wrong to hold children responsible for anything, let alone their educational effort, for the simple reason that it is wrong to treat them as full autonomous agents. This concern can be broken into two distinct ones. One claim is that children simply do not control their actions, and the other is that regardless, it is unfair to allow one's long-term prospects to be determined by decisions made in childhood. Now, it is doubtful that these two very plausible claims generate the conclusion that it is always unjust to allow under eighteen year-olds to bear responsibility for their actions. To begin with, in criminal law, many democracies do hold children between ten and eighteen accountable.[29] We do not hold them *as* responsible

---

[27] Brighouse, *School Choice*, p. 131.

[28] Kenneth R. Howe, 'In Defence of Outcome-Based Conceptions of Equal Educational Opportunity', *Educational Theory* 39 (1989), 317–36; 'Equal Opportunity is Equal Education', *Educational Theory* 40 (1990), 227–30; 'Equality of Educational Opportunity and the Criterion of Equal Educational Worth'; Paul Gomberg, *How to Make Opportunity Equal?*, e.g. p. 25.

[29] A minimal age of criminal responsibility in western countries is not always set. The lowest age in a western country at which a child may be charged with a criminal offence is

for a particular infringement of the penal code as we would a person older than eighteen, and the penalties are correspondingly substantially lighter, but we do hold them responsible nevertheless. It is, of course, possible that we are wrong in doing so. But it does seem that most of us have no qualms holding individuals under eighteen responsible to some degree, if not with regard to distributive justice, at least with regard to retributive justice. Now, one might say that the rationale in under-eighteen incarceration is not actually punitive but reformative. And as such the point proves nothing. But it is not obvious, first, that the case is different with regard to adults. (That is, we may think that the end of the criminal system should be that of rehabilitation also when it comes to adults). And second, even if the ends of juvenile incarceration are not punitive, handing out such sentences still must rely on an assumption of responsibility. After all, we don't incarcerate all children, only those we think are responsible for criminal activity.

The same is true, more specifically, with regard to education. Upon reflection, we normally do not have qualms about holding children under eighteen responsible for their educational achievement. David Miller writes that 'a person who decides to leave school at sixteen cannot later complain that she was denied the opportunity to go to university, if by staying on at school she would have achieved that goal'.[30] Although I am not sure I agree with Miller that such a person had *no* complaint, it does seem to be the case that, at least sometimes, it is right to hold K–12 students responsible for their educational achievements. There is an obvious, although perhaps overlooked, reason why we do so. If adults have some

in North Carolina, where it is set at the age of 6. For federal crimes the age has been set at 11. Next in line are the United Kingdom (including England, Wales, and Northern Ireland), Australia, South Africa, and Switzerland where the minimal age is set at 10. In New Zealand, it varies from 10–14, depending on the crime (10 is the minimal age for the criminal offences of murder and manslaughter). Amnesty International, *Betraying the Young: Children in the US Justice System*, November 1998, <http://www.amnesty.org/en/library/asset/ AMR51/060/1998/en/fd7dc551-d9bc-11dd-af2b-b1f6023af0c5/amr510601998en.pdf>, Children and Young Persons Act 1963, <http://www.legislation.gov.uk/ukpga/1963/37>, Child Justice Act 75 of 2008, <www.info.gov.za/view/DownloadFileAction?id=108691>, Australian Institute of Criminology, The Age of Criminal Responsibility, No. 121 November 2000, <http://www.aic.gov.au/documents/0/0/A/%7B00A92691-0908-47BF-9311- 01AD743F01E1%7Dti181.pdf>, Children, Young Persons, and Their Families Act 1989, <http://www.legislation.govt.nz/act/public/1989/0024/latest/DLM153418. html?search=qs_act_murder+manslaughter+10+years_resel&p=1&sr=1>.

[30] David Miller, 'Liberalism, Equal Opportunities and Cultural Commitment', in David Held and Paul Kelly (eds), *Multiculturalism Reconsidered* (Cambridge: Polity Press, 2002), 45–61, p. 47. Cited in Chambers, 'Each Outcome is Another Opportunity', p. 394.

measure of free will, then it is hard to see why children should lack it *completely*. It is implausible, in other words, that children's entire actions in the classroom (and beyond) are pre-determined. And if children have some control over their actions, minute as that control might be, then, it is at least sometimes permissible to hold them responsible for them. (It might not be desirable, all things considered, to do so, but it is nevertheless not unfair.)

Let us turn, then, to the other worry mentioned. It hardly needs pointing out that educational motivation is another of those features that children acquire at home, and as such is surely tainted by social injustice. One need not hold a radical account of EOp in order to contend that, in as much as pupils' effort and motivation is determined by their socio-economic background, that factor must not affect educational achievements.[31] A Rawlsian, substantive ideal of EOp will equally condemn such an implication. To the extent that socio-economic background affects effort,[32] the question for the radical egalitarian is not whether we should neutralize it, but only how. Following John Roemer's practical guide to the egalitarian planner,[33] we may devise an equivalent guideline in educational policy.[34] We may, in other words, divide the student population into as fine-grained as we deem necessary categorization according to socio-economic background (e.g. children to parents of the 5th percentile income with one parent holding a menial job). And we may consequently identify a mean standard of behaviour for each of these groups of children. [After, of course, subtracting for poor performance due to natural causes (e.g. ADHD).] The measured conduct may refer to anything from hours spent on homework, to attentiveness and cooperativeness in the classroom. Consequently, a pupil may be held responsible for falling below the mean that is characteristic of her relevant reference group. If all this

[31] As Jencks says, any theory of justice in education which exonerates providers from affecting pupils' effort and motivation is 'morally suspect'. 'Whom Must We Treat Equally for Educational Opportunity to Be Equal?' p. 525.

[32] For some qualitative data on how socio-economic background affects individuals' choice to enrol in higher education see Kristin Voigt, 'Individual Choice and Unequal Participation in Higher Education', *Theory and Research in Education* 5 (2007), 87–112.

[33] John E. Roemer, 'A Pragmatic Theory of Responsibility for the Egalitarian Planner', *Philosophy and Public Affairs*, 22 (1993), 146–66.

[34] In fact, Roemer has already taken such a step in subsequent work. See John E. Roemer, *Equality of Opportunity* (Cambridge MA: Harvard University Press, 1998), p. 78. See also his various remarks about how to structure the education system in 'Jerry Cohen's Why Not Socialism: Some Thoughts', *The Journal of Ethics* 14 (2010), 255–62.

is sound, it follows that radical EOp will provide us with a different input than substantive EOp, even when applied to K–12 education. It stipulates that inequality in educational achievements is just when, and only when, it is the consequence of differential effort. To be just, educational achievements need not, and must not, track talent.

IV. Radical EOp in Education

We saw that it is possible both to impute some responsibility to children, and to control for the way in which unjust socio-economic background affects the level of effort that they exert. Moreover, I want to suggest in this final section that it is not only permissible to hold children responsible for their educational achievements but that doing so in fact makes for an attractive account of justice in education.

The point is this. It is sometimes claimed that egalitarians face a difficulty in identifying the correct moment from which EOp should be measured. If this is a real problem then, notice, it is primarily a problem for meritocratic accounts. If goods are to be allocated according to merit then any meritocratic account would entail a 'before' and an 'after'. That is, a 'before' period in which merit is formed, and an 'after' period in which goods are to be allocated according to one's particular level of merit.[35] But what is the exact moment that splits these 'before' and 'after' periods? Most writers conveniently place that moment of inception at the age of eighteen. Rawls, for example, speaks of the 'age of reason' as the correct initial moment,[36] and Arneson similarly talks about 'the onset of responsible adulthood'.[37] But this is of course arbitrary.[38] Setting the age of eighteen as

---

[35] David Miller, *Principles of Social Justice* (Cambridge, MA: Harvard University Press, 1999), p. 181.

[36] John Rawls, *Justice as Fairness: A Restatement* (Cambridge, MA: The Belknap Press of Harvard University Press, 2001), p. 44.

[37] Richard J. Arneson, 'Equality of Opportunity for Welfare Defended and Recanted', *Journal of Political Philosophy* 7 (1999), p. 488. Thomas Christiano similarly advocates equality 'during the preadult phase of life', and 'a kind of equality of opportunity for well-being at the onset of adulthood'. *The Constitution of Equality: Democratic Authority and its Limits* (Oxford: Oxford University Press, 2008), p. 45. Peter Vallentyne, for all the difficulty with his principle of 'equality in initial chances' wisely, I think, leaves open the question of the exact point at which initial chances should be measured. See his 'Brute Luck, Option Luck, and Equality of Initial Opportunities', *Ethics* 112 (2002), p. 540.

[38] Chambers, 'Each Outcome is Another Opportunity'.

the onset of responsible adulthood as a practical policy is *not* problematic, but setting it that way as a matter of a principle of justice is.[39] Whatever else its strengths or weaknesses, then, the account presented here bypasses this problem. In taking into account the effort that children make—children of *all* ages—it avoids the need to assume (and justify) any such arbitrary cut-off.

Still, there might be some lingering doubts about radical EOp in education, and in particular about the way it tracks effort at any given age. Here is a rather obvious objection that I haven't addressed yet. A personal anecdote may help illustrate it. I remember how appalled I was when told by a colleague about her four-year-old child being interviewed as part of the selection process to a Harvard-affiliated kindergarten. One thing that might explain such reaction is that we think that it is wrong for individuals' overall life chances to be affected by how they have conducted themselves at as early an age as that. This worry, notice, is different from the two objections to the meritocratic account that we have dismissed in the previous section. The point here is not that children's skills are not fully developed whereas adults' are; nor is it the claim that children are not responsible for their skills whereas adults are. The point, rather, is that however much children are responsible, at least to some extent, for their actions, it would still be wrong to allow their choices to affect the just distribution of educational resources and consequently their opportunities later on in life. What we need, instead, is some sort of moratorium to be imposed, say at eighteen. The reason being that it would be wrong to allow decisions made before the 'onset of responsible adulthood' (even if made during '*responsible* childhood') to affect an individual's life chances. It is not that she is not responsible for her actions, the claim goes, but rather that it would be wrong, for other moral considerations, to allow her to suffer the immaturity of her younger self.[40] It is hard to argue with this demand for essentially 'a fresh start'. But notice two points about this particular claim as an objection to radical EOp in education. First, if the appeal to fresh start is presented as a means to enhancing that person's autonomy, then there is

[39] Arneson in fact concedes this. 'Liberalism, Distributive Subjectivism and Equal Opportunity for Welfare', *Philosophy and Public Affairs* 19 (1990), p. 179.

[40] This is nicely illustrated in Michael Walzer's recounting of George Orwell's school days: 'Orwell was told that he would either do well on the exams or end up as a "little office-boy at forty pounds a year". His fate was to be decided, with no chance of *reprieve*, at the age of twelve.' *Spheres of Justice*, p. 213 (my emphasis).

no reason why this should stop at the age of eighteen. Adults, it hardly needs pointing out, are also prone to committing life-altering mistakes (gambling all your money away, having children with the wrong person). A concern with autonomy would thus recommend also imposing a moratorium on the consequences of one's choices later in life.[41] There is therefore no reason to restrict it to children and to basic education. Second, and more to the point here, this 'fresh start' argument does not undermine radical EOp as an account of *fairness* in education. For the claim is not that it would be unfair to allow decisions made early in life to stand (assuming they meet the requirement of personal responsibility), but rather that it would be bad for other moral reasons (autonomy, say). Radical EOp in education is thus compatible with an all things considered account that constrains it in the name of preserving an adequate measure of autonomy throughout a person's life.[42]

My response to the 'fresh start' claim, then, is that radical EOp in education may accept a moratorium on just educational achievements, by means of a trade-off with the value of autonomy. But cannot a moratorium also be a requirement of fairness? Here is one suggestion to that effect. There is something not entirely under one's control, and therefore unjust, about the way in which one's early decisions (whether as a child or as an adult) have repercussions that reverberate throughout one's life. Consider a variation on an example given by Clare Chambers in this context. Consider Jeremy who, compared to his friend Jason, misses admittance to Eton by a margin of a point. It seems unfair for this slight difference to have substantial implications for Jeremy and Jason's respective ability to be accepted to a good university, find a good job, and develop a successful career later on.[43] To fully appreciate the dilemma here, it would be useful, I think, to distinguish two slightly different scenarios. Suppose Jason and Jeremy have precisely equal qualifications for Eton, and thus a lottery is used to decide that it is Jason who is admitted. Following his Eton degree Jason then is admitted to Oxford whereas Jeremy enrols in Oxford Brookes, say. In this scenario, it is right to

---

[41] See Marc Fleurbaey, *Fairness, Responsibility, and Welfare* (Oxford: Oxford University Press, 2008), ch. 7.

[42] For trading off the requirements of luck egalitarian justice with those of autonomy, see Nicholas Barry, 'Reassessing Luck Egalitarianism', *The Journal of Politics* 70 (2008), 136–50.

[43] Chambers, 'Each Outcome is Another Opportunity'. For a similar argument see Patrick Tomlin, 'Choice, Chance, and Change: Luck Egalitarianism over Time', *Ethical Theory and Moral Practice* 16 (2013), pp. 393–407.

say that any subsequent disadvantage (compared to Jason) that Jeremy suffers (following his non-admittance to Eton) is not his fault. In fact, any resulting disadvantage is a matter of bad brute luck. Thus, it must be neutralized. Luck egalitarians would therefore have no difficulty justifying (what amounts to) a moratorium on the benefits that Jason has gained from his lucky admittance to Eton.[44]

The more difficult case obtains, of course, when Jason overtakes Jeremy into Eton on (effort-based) merit, albeit a minute one. Here it isn't chance, but rather choice and effort that propelled Jason past Jeremy. Still, to allow this negligible difference to result in huge gains and disadvantages later on in life seems wrong. I agree. But here, notice, we must look at the *extent* to which the initial gain leads to subsequent gains. It is Jeremy's fault, strictly speaking, for not getting into Eton. But the extent to which City employers automatically prefer Eton graduates over equally qualified other graduates is *not* his fault. It is thus a requirement of justice to minimize the extent to which Jeremy's initial loss may lead to subsequent disadvantages. Notice, further, that constraining the extent to which an Eton education leads to other advantages is not something that Jason (the one who graduated from Eton) can complain against. Jason has a claim to the Eton place he got, because he achieved it on effort. What he has *no* claim over is the extent to which that Eton education opens up doors for him later in life. (Of course, we are setting aside here legitimate expectations—suppose the policy in question was announced before he was admitted.) A luck egalitarian would thus move to constrain the extent to which a loss in one round, however justified, leads to disadvantage in access to the next round, as it were.[45] Something rather close to a moratorium, then, could be justified

---

[44] Cf. Elizabeth Anderson, 'How Should Egalitarians Cope with Market Risks?' *Theoretical Inquiries in Law* 9 (2008), p. 246. Anderson, we can now see, gets this point wrong when she says that non-desert-based luck egalitarianism must accept the eventual inequality between Jason and Jeremy as not unfair.

[45] Fleurbaey makes this general point with regard to stakes. There is no unfairness in, ex ante, constraining the stakes of the game. Furthermore, it is not unfair to use up some of those saved stakes for the purpose of reimbursing the winner. To illustrate, consider two versions of a game. In the first version, chips are divided equally between two participants who then proceed to win or lose them according to some stated rules. In the second version, two-thirds of the chips are distributed equally, and a third is reserved as a stock to be distributed to players who have lost all their chips. There is no reason to think the former version is fairer than the latter. (*Fairness, Responsibility, and Welfare*, p. 180.) I agree. This same logic operates in constraining the windfall from admittance to Eton.

on reasons of fairness rather than merely autonomy. Radical EOp in education thus endorses constraining the advantages that each stage (within basic education) confers on the next one.[46]

Conclusion

This chapter defended radical EOp in education. Let me, however, offer three qualifications in conclusion. First, I have stressed several times here that radical EOp is only meant as an account of fairness in education, and not as an account of all-things-considered rules of regulation. It follows that a defender of radical EOP in education need not oppose an arbitrary cut-off (say, eighteen) with regard to educational policy. My claim, rather, is that such a cut-off can only be justified on practical rather than principled grounds. Here is a second qualification. It is sometimes pointed out by luck egalitarians that it is no embarrassment for their theory if hard determinists are proved right, and free will is indeed impossible. Such a revelation would have rather straightforward implications for their theory. If no one can be held responsible for the level of effort that they exhibit, then it follows that no inequalities of outcome can ever be fair.[47] The same holds for EOp for basic education. If children are deemed to be entirely irresponsible for their educational effort then we must simply endorse the principle of equality of outcome. The luck egalitarian would have no qualms endorsing such a conclusion. Here is the third and final qualification. It is sometimes suggested that children with low innate talent stand to benefit from having more educational resources devoted to other, more talented children, since doing so would benefit the former

---

[46] Notice that in practice, this may amount to something akin to equality of outcome in education. See Howe, 'In Defence of Outcome-Based Conceptions of Equal Educational Opportunity'.

[47] In this I follow Cohen and Arneson. Cohen writes: 'The idea motivating equality of access to advantage does not even imply that there is such a thing as genuine choice. Instead, it implies that if there is no such thing, because, for example, 'hard determinism' is true, then all differential advantage is unjust.' G. A. Cohen, 'Equality of What? On Welfare, Goods, and Capabilities', in *On the Currency of Egalitarian Justice and Other Essays* (Princeton, NJ: Princeton University Press, 2011), p. 60. Arneson writes: 'The norm of equal opportunity for welfare is distinct from equality of welfare only if some version of soft determinism or indeterminism is correct. If hard determinism is true, the two interpretations of equality come to the same thing.' 'Liberalism, Distributive Subjectivism and Equal Opportunity for Welfare', *Philosophy and Public Affairs* 19 (1990), p. 179.

later on in life (e.g. having good doctors when in need for medical treatment). This is a familiar enough argument,[48] and we also noted its relevance in the previous part of the book. Notice, though, that to accord with radical EOp in education, diverting resources to the more talented should serve not merely to improve the position of the worse-off, but rather to narrow overall inequalities.

[48] Richard Arneson makes this prioritarian case in 'Against Rawlsian Equality of Opportunity', *Philosophical Studies* 93 (1999), 77–112.

7

If you're a Luck Egalitarian, How Come You Read Bedtime Stories to Your Children?

We each reach adulthood with a bundle of skills that is determined by a combination of both nature and nurture. Luck egalitarians and Rawlsians alike treat the unequal distribution of these skills and talents as morally arbitrary. But they differ in their strategy for dealing with it. That is, they disagree on what justice requires with regard to children's unequal skills. Luck egalitarians hold that for the sake of genuine equality of opportunity (EOp), justice requires neutralizing such inequalities (in as much as they are a matter of brute luck). According to the Rawlsian conception of EOp, in contrast, justice requires only that we mitigate these innate inequalities. 'Mitigating' innate inequalities means ensuring that they do not give rise, later in life, to undue inequalities in access to social and political advantages. We may correspondingly refer to these contrasting views as the neutralization and the mitigation approaches to inequality in innate skills. Here is a more formal understanding of the two contrasting approaches:

- *Neutralization Approach*—Justice requires eliminating (neutralizing), at the outset, all un-chosen disadvantages, whether social or natural
- *Mitigation Approach*—Justice (only) requires ensuring that disadvantages (whether chosen or not, whether natural or social) do not affect access to a set of designated primary goods, upon adulthood

Andrew Mason raises the following objection to the neutralization approach, and to luck egalitarianism more generally.[1] The luck egalitarian

---

[1] Andrew Mason, *Levelling the Playing Field: The Idea of Equality of Opportunity and its Place in Egalitarian Thought* (Oxford: Oxford University Press, 2006), pp. 99–109.

insistence on abolishing brute luck disadvantages, he writes, would imply a ban on parents bestowing any advantage on their children. The radical ideal arguably tells us to refrain from reading bedtime stories, practising the piano alongside them, shooting baskets with them in the backyard, and so forth. In as much as these activities confer on one's child an undue advantage that is not shared by other children—those whose parents cannot afford the time or resources to undertake those activities (or whose own talents and skills are below average and thus would not result in imparting an advantage)—the luck egalitarian would be forced to condemn them as unjust. Surely, Mason says, this implication of luck egalitarianism is absurd. This, in turn, indicates that the attempt to interpret the ideal of EOp along the radical luck egalitarian lines (namely, neutralizing *all* brute luck advantages) is misguided. 'My claim', he says, 'is that if the neutralization approach were the correct one, parents would have a reason of justice not to behave in any way whatsoever that advantages their child relative to others, yet this is highly implausible'.[2] Instead, Mason advances the mitigation approach, which, he claims, does not appear so counterintuitive in the face of the bedtime stories dilemma. Since mitigators are not committed to neutralizing natural or nurtured inequalities they are consequently not forced to advocate that parents prevent those from coming into being. Rather, mitigators advocate merely ensuring that these nurtured inequalities be prevented from turning into significant social or political inequalities later on in life. Thus, mitigators would not condemn bedtime story-telling as unjust but would, rather, insist that well-off parents contribute in taxes towards ameliorating natural and nurtured inequalities. These taxes would go, for example, toward funding the public education system, scholarships for deprived children, and so forth. (Note that luck egalitarians, also, would recommend all these measures, but crucially, as a complimentary, and not a substitute measure to that of neutralizing the passing on of advantageous skills.)

The luck egalitarian conception of EOp, I want to try and demonstrate in this chapter, is no less attractive than its Rawlsian rival, even when applied to the difficult case of parental partiality and familial intimacy. My argument proceeds as follows. In the first section I shall flesh out the two

---

[2] Mason, *Levelling the Playing Field*, p. 99. See also p. 134. More generally on the contrast between the mitigation and neutralization approach see his *Living Together as Equals: The Demands of Citizenship* (Oxford: Oxford University Press, 2012), ch. 5.

competing egalitarian approaches to inequalities in nurtured skills (and distributive justice more generally), and how they pan out with regard to the case of bedtime story-telling. In the second section I examine Mason's bedtime stories objection and offer some initial reasons to be sceptical about how damning it is for luck egalitarianism. Section III then harnesses the Swift/Brighouse account of the good of familial relationship to help square radical EOp with our intuitions concerning bedtime story-telling. In the concluding section, I turn to examine whether or not the mitigation approach (to inequalities in nurtured skills) is as immune from the bedtime reading objection as its proponents suggest.

I. The Rawlsian and Radical Approaches to Bedtime Story-Telling

Bedtime story-telling, and parental partiality more generally, possess a serious challenge to all egalitarians. Indeed, there has been much discussion, in recent years, about the proper limits that distributive justice places on parents' legitimate partiality towards their children.[3] The basic egalitarian intuition here seems to be that it is unfair for well-off parents to impart advantages to their children, thereby exacerbating socio-economic inequalities. Whereas the anti-egalitarian impact of bequeathing wealth has long been recognized and incorporated in egalitarian theory, the emphasis in recent years has shifted to how other, more intimate means of parental partiality may upset egalitarian justice.[4] In those discussions the example of bedtime story-telling crops up time and again. Adam Swift writes: 'Most evenings I read a bedtime story to my kids. I am showing a

---

[3] James Fishkin, *Justice, Equal Opportunity, and the Family* (New Haven, CN: Yale University Press, 1986); David Estlund, 'Liberalism, Equality, and Fraternity in Cohen's Critique of Rawls', *The Journal of Political Philosophy* 6 (1998), 99–112; Veronique Munoz-Darde, 'Is the Family to be Abolished Then?' *Proceedings of the Aristotelian Society* 99 (1999), 37–56; Adam Swift, *How Not To Be a Hypocrite: School Choice for the Morally Perplexed Parent* (London and New York: Routledge, 2003); Elizabeth Anderson, 'Rethinking Equality of Opportunity: Comment on Adam Swift's How Not to Be a Hypocrite', *Theory and Research in Education* 2 (2004), 99–110; Harry Brighouse and Adam Swift, 'Legitimate Parental Partiality', *Philosophy and Public Affairs* 37 (2008), 43–80.

[4] E.g. Anca Gheaus, 'How Much of What Matters Can We Redistribute? Love, Justice, and Luck', *Hypatia* 24 (2009), 63–83; Hugh Lazenby, 'One Kiss Too Many? Giving, Luck Egalitarianism, and Other-Affecting Choice', *The Journal of Political Philosophy* 18 (2010), 271–86.

special, partial interest in my children. I know that reading to them gives them advantages that will help them in the future, advantages not enjoyed by less fortunate others. It is unfair that they don't get what mine do. The playing field is not level; our bedtime stories tilt it in their favour.'[5] The concern for social justice here, it should be stressed, is a real one. The differential impact of parental care, sociologists have established in recent years,[6] may be as significant, in determining a person's opportunities in life, as the material resources that her parents bequeath her. Most of us, however, typically think that parents need not refrain from bedtime story-telling. As Swift puts it, 'bedtime stories are the right side of the line'.[7] There is a dilemma here,[8] then, for egalitarians in how to draw the line between just and unjust equality-upsetting parental care.

The difference in how Rawlsians and luck egalitarians treat advantage-bestowing bedtime story-telling corresponds, predictably, to general differences between their approach with regard to egalitarian justice, and EOp in particular. Luck egalitarians typically consider as unjust any disadvantage for which individuals are not responsible. This would include, among other things, inequalities in access to advantages that arise out of the unequal distribution of nurtured skills (through parental care). Importantly, *any* disadvantage brought by a lesser talent or trait would be considered by luck egalitarians to be an infringement of EOp. It follows that luck egalitarians hold that inequalities in endowed traits are in themselves unjust. Now, it might be objected that even on the luck egalitarian reading, natural or endowed inequalities are only unjust in so far as they harbour inequality in access to advantage so, strictly speaking, these inequalities cannot be unjust in and of themselves. But this does not follow. Recall our discussion in Chapter 1 and the distinction between inequality and difference. Differential natural traits cannot

---

[5] *How Not To Be a Hypocrite*, p. 9.

[6] Kenneth Arrow et al. *Meritocracy and Economic Inequality* (Princeton, NJ: Princeton University Press, 2000); Annette Lareau, *Unequal Childhoods* (Berkeley, CA: University of California Press, 2003); Richard Rothstein, *Class and Schools* (Washington, DC: Economic Policy Institute, 2003); Samuel Bowles, Herbert Gintis, and Melissa Osborne-Groves (eds), *Unequal Chances: Family Background and Economic Success* (Princeton, NJ: Princeton University Press, 2005).

[7] Swift, *How Not To Be a Hypocrite*, p. 9. See also Brighouse and Swift, 'Legitimate Parental Partiality'.

[8] Notice that this is merely a *dilemma*, for we have already set aside the third alleged horn of Fishkin's famous trilemma, namely meritocracy. See Fishkin, *Justice, Equal Opportunity, and the Family*, pp. 5–6.

count as inequalities unless, to begin with, they harbour *some* advantage. It follows that for all intents and purposes luck egalitarians see inequalities in endowed skills as themselves unjust. Consequently, we may say that luck egalitarians hold that justice requires neutralizing all inequalities in endowed skills. This implies either preventing advantageous skills from being generated in the first place, or neutralizing them as soon as they are created. (Note, again, that luck egalitarians hold that this is what *justice* requires. Whether or not they would recommend doing so all-things-considered, say, by crushing the fingers of the talented pianist, is yet another matter. We have touched already in the book on this distinction between justice and rules of regulation, and I shall therefore invoke it only fleetingly in this chapter.) The Rawlsian mitigation approach differs from the luck egalitarian one, and is arguably superior to it, because it does not require neutralizing all advantageous traits. Mitigators avoid this (potentially counterintuitive) requirement because they hold that innate inequalities (such as in skills) are unjust only when they affect one's access to social and political advantages.[9] We may say, then, that Rawlsians and luck egalitarians differ here with respect to how wide the currency of justice, and EOp in particular, is.

Let us summarize, then, the relevant differences between the Rawlsian mitigation and the luck egalitarian neutralization approach, before turning to how they map out with regard to the specific bedtime story dilemma. We may now observe three dimensions along which the approaches differ. First, while luck egalitarians seek to neutralize all luck-induced disadvantages, Rawlsians confine their concern only to social and political ones (recall our discussion in the introductory chapter). A second dimension concerns what is to be done about the disadvantages that are deemed unjust. While luck egalitarians seek to neutralize them completely, Rawlsians only seek to mitigate their effect (that is, only make sure they do not translate into advantages in primary goods later in life). And a third dimension that we may add, concerns the agent whose responsibility it is to rectify the disadvantage (whether to neutralize it or mitigate it), where responses may differ between institutions, on the one

---

[9] On an even stricter reading it could be said that differences in endowed skills could not even qualify as 'inequalities' to begin with (let alone *unjust* ones). See Lesley A. Jacobs, *Pursuing Equal Opportunities: The Theory and Practice of Egalitarian Justice* (Cambridge: Cambridge University Press, 2004), ch. 3. I shall examine that objection in the next chapter.

hand, and individuals themselves, on the other. Let us call these the *scope*, the *method*, and the *agent*, dimensions along which Rawlsian mitigators and luck egalitarian neutralizers may diverge.[10]

It is not so difficult to see how these differences in approach to innate inequalities map onto the justice of bedtime story-telling. In a sense, the luck egalitarian position here is quite simple and straightforward. In as much as bedtime reading results in giving one's child an advantage over other children, justice requires that parents refrain from doing so. (More accurately, luck egalitarians will permit story-telling only in so much as a parent is able to carry it out in a manner that is not equality-upsetting.) The prima facie injustice of parents imparting marketable skills and other advantages through the upbringing of their children (when doing so exacerbates overall inequality) is therefore not something the luck egalitarian can be equivocal about. Rawlsian mitigators,[11] we said, might arguably escape this consequence, for they do not condemn bedtime story-telling as unjust, but rather see only the advantages it bestows, later in life, as unjust. Rawlsians thus require mitigating the equality-upsetting impact of bedtime story-telling and not the cessation of this parental activity itself.

II. Addressing the Bedtime Story-Telling Objection

I have belaboured enough the difference between Rawlsian mitigation and luck egalitarian neutralization. Now let us turn to how these approaches map onto the specific issue of parental care, as exemplified by the bedtime story-telling example.

In addressing the bedtime story-telling objection to radical EOp it is important, first, to identify whether it is a pro tanto claim or an

[10]   I am grateful to Kasper Lippert-Rasmussen for helping me clarify this typology.

[11]   Mason, whom I take to be representative of the mitigation approach, is actually critical of Rawls on various points. Most importantly, he rejects Rawls's fair equality of opportunity (see *Levelling the Playing Field*, ch. 3), as well as being critical of Rawlsian methodology more generally (see his concluding remarks, p. 221). But it seems to me that it is nevertheless accurate to characterize him as belonging to the Rawlsian camp when it comes to his views on innate inequalities. This is where one of the essential fault-lines between luck egalitarians and Rawlsians lies, and Mason is decisively Rawlsian on this. Kok-Chor Tan is another philosopher whose position it is hard to categorize in this respect. Tan is manifestly luck egalitarian, albeit an 'institutionalist' one. That seems to place him, for our purposes, in the

all-things-considered one. The former would criticize luck egalitarianism for giving us a pro tanto reason to refrain from bedtime reading. The latter claim would criticize luck egalitarianism for sometimes recommending, all things considered, that parents refrain from bedtime reading (again, in as much as it upsets equality). Mason, it appears, is making the first of these claims.[12] But that claim is a non-starter. Suppose that parents have two different methods of reading bedtime stories to their children which are identical in every respect except that one ends up upsetting equality, while the other (somehow) doesn't. If Mason was right then it would have followed that parents have *absolutely no reason* to prefer the latter, equality-preserving, to the former.[13] But that seems false. Mason may argue (implausibly, in my view, but let it pass) that even under those circumstances parents do not have an *obligation* to choose the equality-preserving method. But to argue that they don't even have a *reason* to do so seems to me to be obviously false. If Mason were right, the following exchange should ring true. Suppose a parent approaches an egalitarian sage and explains: 'I like reading bedtime stories to my child, and she likewise enjoys it. I found that there are two different methods of doing so, both equal in every conceivable respect apart from the fact that one bestows on my child an advantage not enjoyed by other children, whereas the other method does not. Is there any reason for me, any reason whatsoever, to opt for the latter method?' The egalitarian sage thinks for a moment, reflects on the empirical evidence according to which the impact of intimate forms of parental partiality is at least as equality-upsetting as that of material bequests, and then replies: 'Nah, egalitarian justice is completely indifferent here. As far as I am concerned you may flip a coin to decide between the two'. This seems to me to be hopelessly wrong.[14] It follows, then, that luck egalitarianism

---

Rawlsian mitigation camp. For example, he writes: 'The institutional approach aims only to mitigate the effects of brute luck. Brute luck pertains to the background conditions within which people make choices, and background inequalities are the sorts of inequalities (one's natural abilities, social class, etc.) that institutions can address'. *Justice, Institutions, and Luck: The Site, Ground, and Scope of Equality* (Oxford: Oxford University Press, 2012), p. 77.

[12] *Levelling the Playing Field*, p. 100.

[13] This point was made first in Serena Olsaretti, 'Review of A. Mason's "Levelling the Playing Field: The Ideal of Equality of Opportunity and its Place in Egalitarian Thought"', *The Journal of Moral Philosophy* 6 (2009), p. 134.

[14] In his reply to me, Mason puts forward an interesting defence of his insistence on the pro tanto argument. It goes like this. Part of the disagreement between us, Mason says, comes down to differences in our method in theorizing about justice. Segall's method, he says, involves first establishing the requirements of justice, and then examining cases in which these requirements should be overruled. Part of the reasons why justice must be overruled,

cannot be false simply for giving us a pro tanto reason to refrain from bed-time reading.

Since Mason rests much of his critique of luck egalitarianism on the bedtime stories objection,[15] we ought to investigate also the more plausi-ble, all things considered, claim (even though he explicitly holds the pro tanto one).[16] So the objection I intend to investigate in the rest of the chap-ter is this: luck egalitarian equality of opportunity is implausible because it *may sometimes* recommend, all things considered, that parents refrain from bedtime stories. (I say 'sometimes' because I do not impute to Mason the implausible view that luck egalitarianism recommends that parents *always* refrain from bedtime story-telling, no matter what the cost is.)

Mason imputes to me, is when it makes unreasonable demands of the agent. In contrast, his (Mason's) method, he says, is to begin the other way: in constructing an ideal of justice we must weigh against each other the demands of impartiality with legitimate partial preroga-tives. We must not generate, in the first place, requirements of justice which individuals can-not meet. His method is superior, Mason says, in that legitimate partiality is already built-in to the concept of justice, rather than being traded-off against it from the outside. If Mason's method is sound then it would explain why we do not have even a pro tanto reason of justice to refrain from bedtime story-telling. The concern that permits it is one which is *internal* to justice. [See Andrew Mason, 'Putting Story-Telling to Bed: A Reply to Segall', *Critical Review of International Social and Political Philosophy (CRISPP)* 14 (2011), p. 85.] I cannot delve here, unfortunately, into a discussion of how to construct principles of justice, but I will say this. To defend his preferred method of identifying principles of justice, and consequently, to defend his view that there is no pro tanto reason to refrain from equality-upsetting personal prerogatives, Mason would have to provide much more by way of a defence. For example, and as he himself (commendably) admits, he would have to explain why fundamental prin-ciples of justice should already take into account factual matters such as what it is and what it is not reasonable to expect individuals to comply with. Second, Mason must show in what way his method is superior to the luck egalitarian approach. He himself mischaracterizes that approach. It is not that luck egalitarians look for principles of justice and then examine whether they are over-demanding or not. Over-demandingness has nothing to do with it. Rather, they search for what justice, pure and simple, requires, and then examine whether the requirements of justice clash with other moral values. To decide what is morally right all things considered, the value of justice must be weighed against the value in question. [See G. A. Cohen, *Rescuing Justice and Equality* (Cambridge, MA: Harvard University Press, 2008).] The view that luck egalitarians form principles of justice that even they recognize it would be unreasonable to expect individuals to follow is a caricature. The issue is not whether the requirements are reasonable or not, but rather whether there is another, weightier, value that justice clashes with.

[15] See for example, *Levelling the Playing Field*, p. 99. He seems to somewhat retract the significance of his bedtime reading objection in the later piece mentioned. 'I do not regard the case of bedtime stories as providing a refutation of either the neutralization approach in general or luck egalitarianism in particular, but I do suppose that it creates a difficulty for both.' Mason, 'Putting Story-Telling to Bed', p. 82.

[16] Personal communication.

Perhaps the first thing we ought to do in addressing the (revised) objection is to remind ourselves of the distinction between ideal and non-ideal theory.[17] It is one thing for a parent, certainly one who is already relatively worse-off, to try and help her child attain certain skills knowing that all other parents are acting likewise (thus, not wanting to leave her child far behind everyone else's).[18] It is quite another thing to try and give one's child an edge over most other children when one (and consequently, one's child) is already better-off than most others. (The same holds for giving one's child an edge given an ideal, equal, state of affairs.) We may therefore incorporate the distinction between ideal and non-ideal theory into our subsequent discussion by simply speaking of giving one's child an *undue* advantage. Undue advantage would thus refer either to already better-off parents seeking to entrench their advantage in a non-ideal setting, or to parents wanting to impart an advantage under an ideal situation of an equal starting point.

Now, Mason's case against luck egalitarian EOp in upbringing rests on demonstrating its allegedly unacceptable implications. But it is important to try and discern which attribute, exactly, of luck egalitarian EOp is responsible for generating such a judgement. Recalling the three dimensions mentioned in the previous section, it would be useful to know whether it is the scope, the method, or the agent (or perhaps all of the above) that generate the counterintuitive implication.

I want to begin by raising a doubt about whether the bedtime story-telling is an objection to the first and second dimensions, namely those of scope (i.e. whether justice is concerned with all inequalities or only with social and political ones), and method (whether justice requires neutralization of disadvantages or rather only mitigating them later in life). Think of a child prodigy who is so talented that bedtime reading will stimulate her to such achievements that will place her well above all other children. The advantage she will gain is so huge that no amount

---

[17] See Adam Swift, 'Justice, Luck, and the Family: The Intergenerational Transmission of Economic Advantage from a Normative Perspective', in Samuel Bowles, Herbert Gintis, and Melissa Osborne-Groves (eds), *Unequal Chances, Family Background and Economic Success* (Princeton, NJ: Princeton University Press, 2005), pp. 260–1.

[18] Such parents, as Swift rightly points out, may not only be permitted in doing so, but may actually be under obligation to do so. See his, 'The Value of Philosophy in Nonideal Circumstances', *Social Theory and Practice* 34 (2008), p. 378. See also Brighouse and Swift, 'Legitimate Parental Partiality', pp. 74–5.

of mitigation later on in life (by all the means of institutional measures endorsed by Mason) will restore equality between her and others. Under those circumstances, it is easy to see, even mitigators must be forced to recommend refraining from bedtime reading. It is doubtful, then, that mitigators may invoke the bedtime reading example as an objection to the scope and method of luck egalitarian EOp. They themselves, it now appears, are similarly indicted by it.[19]

Perhaps then the bedtime objection (properly understood) targets the dimension of agent (i.e. whether it is only institutions or also individuals whose responsibility it is to curb disadvantages). Now, one benefit of distinguishing the three different abovementioned dimensions is that we may see now that not all luck egalitarians are necessarily condemned by the bedtime stories objection. On a certain, *institutional*, version of luck egalitarianism the scope and method dimensions are severed from the agent dimension.[20] On that view, distributive justice requires that political and social *institutions* move to neutralize all brute luck inequalities; it does not instruct individuals how to act in their personal life, let alone telling parents how to raise their children. So on the one hand, one need not be a luck egalitarian in order to subject individual behaviour to considerations of justice,[21] and, on the other hand, some luck egalitarians explicitly limit their conception of justice to the basic structure of society.[22] This indicates that the neutralization approach and the view that justice is not restricted to institutions are two independent ideals. It is therefore possible for one to endorse the neutralization approach to natural inequalities *while*

---

[19] I am grateful to Kasper Lippert-Rasmussen for helping me with this observation.

[20] Kok-Chor Tan, 'A Defence of Luck Egalitarianism', *The Journal of Philosophy*, 105 (2008), pp. 671–73; *Justice, Institutions, and Luck*, esp. chs 2, 3. The possibility of such a position is overlooked by Mason (see *Levelling the Playing Field*, p. 102).

[21] Joseph Carens and Liam Murphy, who cannot be described as card-carrying luck egalitarians (although, admittedly, both may very well harbour luck egalitarian sympathies), both reject the limitation of justice to the basic structure of society. See Joseph H. Carens, 'Rights and Duties in an Egalitarian Society', *Political Theory* 14 (1986), 31–49; Liam B. Murphy, 'Institutions and the Demands of Justice', *Philosophy and Public Affairs* 27 (1998), 251–91.

[22] See again Tan, 'A Defence of Luck Egalitarianism'; *Justice, Institutions, and Luck*, esp. chs 2, 3. Thomas Nagel, who holds luck egalitarian views, also seems to excuse individuals from the requirements of distributive justice. [Thomas Nagel, *Equality and Partiality* (Oxford: Clarendon Press, 1991), chs 6, 9.] Also, nothing in Ronald Dworkin's work, it seems to me, commits him to the expansion of luck egalitarian justice beyond the basic structure of society. [A personal communication reported by Cohen (*Rescuing Justice and Equality*, p. 127) seems to corroborate that.]

endorsing the basic structure (or institutional) limitation to justice. And vice versa: it is perfectly plausible, at least prima facie, for one to endorse the mitigation approach yet be committed to applying it beyond the basic structure of society. This later observation may be of relevance for our present inquiry, because if one happens to be persuaded by the bedtime reading objection to the neutralization approach, and consequently adopts Mason's proposed alternative (the mitigation approach), she may still find herself committed to applying that latter principle beyond the basic structure, including, that is, to parental conduct.[23] [This may prove relevant later on in our inquiry, when I turn to further examine how the mitigation approach handles bedtime story-telling (in Section IV).]

Endorsing the institutional version of luck egalitarianism thus seems to rescue the neutralizing approach from the bedtime reading objection, for parental conduct would, if this line of response is valid, be exempt from the very rigorous demands of preventing nurtured inequalities from ever coming into being. The problem with this response, though, is that rather than rescuing the neutralization approach it may actually further implicate it. The emphasis on *neutralization through institutions* may simply license sending state officials to every home around bedtime in order to make sure that no one is reading stories to their children (or that no parent exceeds the officially prescribed length and quality of story-telling). This would, obviously, make the luck egalitarian approach to EOp appear even more oppressive and counterintuitive than it already is.

Separating the agent from the scope and method dimensions of luck egalitarianism may therefore not be entirely helpful in meeting the bedtime stories objection. In any case, it should be obvious by now that the strategy in question is not available to the kind of luck egalitarianism endorsed in this book. The Cohenite version I follow famously says that principles of justice are not restricted to (what Rawls called) the basic structure of society, but rather also inform the conduct of individuals (as well as society's ethos).[24] The latter would presumably include the conduct of individual parents toward their children.[25] My neutralization approach

[23] This is something that Mason does not dispute. (Personal communication.)

[24] Cohen, *Rescuing Justice and Equality*, ch. 3, cf. Thomas W. Pogge, 'On the Site of Distributive Justice: Reflections on Cohen and Murphy', *Philosophy and Public Affairs* 29 (2000), 137–69.

[25] Richard Arneson, another leading luck egalitarian, hints at the possibility. 'One might also question the assumption that the pursuit of EFO [equality of fair opportunity, SS]

is therefore not restricted to institutions, and thus my radical approach to EOp remains vulnerable to the bedtime reading objection.

III. The Value of Family Relations

Here, then, is a different response to the bedtime reading objection that I think might be helpful in defence of (not-merely-institutional) luck egalitarianism. It entails distinguishing kinds of parental activity that are constitutive of the family (or the family relationship), from ones that are not.[26] Adam Swift distinguishes constitutive partiality—that is, partiality that is constitutive of the parent–child relationship—from one that is not (what he brands as 'illegitimate favouritism').[27] As 'constitutive partiality' would count interactions refraining from which would deprive the child and the parent of something that is constitutive of their special relationship.[28] Based on this distinction we may say that although bedtime story-telling might bestow an undue advantage, it is nevertheless an activity that is morally permissible when at stake is allowing individuals (parents *and* children) to enjoy the value of familial relations. The value of familial relations (or familial relationship goods [henceforth FRG], as Brighouse and Swift term it) acts as a rather useful and informative criterion. It explains why bedtime reading ought to be permitted but why other interactions such as 'Take our Daughters and Sons to Work Day' ought not. While that latter activity may be enjoyable and meaningful for both parent and child, it is nevertheless one that potentially entrenches socially-stratified roles in society. Crucially, this is one type of FRG-producing activity that might

---

cannot proceed to a significant extent without invasive interference in family life.... if the members of a society were committed to the ideal of EFO, they would not find reasonable and cost-effective measures to achieve it to be onerous'. See his 'Equality of Opportunity', *Stanford Encyclopaedia of Philosophy* (2002).

[26] Brighouse and Swift, 'Legitimate Parental Partiality', esp. §3.

[27] Swift, 'Justice, Luck, and the Family', p. 270. See also David Miller, 'Equality of Opportunity and the Family', in D. Satz and R. Reich (eds), *Toward a Humanist Justice: The Political Philosophy of Susan Moller Okin* (Oxford: Oxford University Press, 2009), p. 22.

[28] We may otherwise refer to this as 'the principle that parents and children should be able to enjoy successful intimate relationship with one another'. Harry Brighouse and Adam Swift, 'Educational Equality versus Educational Adequacy: A Critique of Anderson and Satz', *Journal of Applied Philosophy* 26 (2009), p. 120. See also Colin M. Macleod, 'Liberal Equality and the Affective Family', in D. Archard and C. M. Macleod (eds), *The Moral and Political Status of Children* (Oxford: Oxford University Press, 2002), 212–30.

be dispensable. The same is not true for bedtime reading, Brighouse and Swift convincingly argue,[29] and for a number of reasons. Bedtime reading is unique because it takes place at a special time of the day for the child, it is repeated everyday and thus may form part of the routine of the relationship, it involves sharing a physical and intimate space, and it may involve input by both child (who may choose the book or story) and parent. The combination of all these aspects implies that bedtime reading is a unique source of FRG and one that cannot be replaced (by an activity that may be less equality-upsetting).

The distinction between FRG-generating activities and those that don't yields a principled position. It says that although parents have a (pro tanto) fairness-based reason to refrain from bedtime reading (that is, neutralize the potential undue advantage that they are otherwise about to bestow) there are nevertheless overriding moral considerations, considerations that luck egalitarians are happy to endorse, that recommend trumping the neutralization approach on those occasions. A well-off luck egalitarian parent might reason something along these lines: 'I realize that being well-off, educated, and steeped in leisure time, my bedtime reading for my child is likely to endow her with an undue advantage. As an egalitarian I recognize that this constitutes an injustice, and as such I regret it. But I also recognize that this quality time is constitutive of our special relationship that will be seriously undermined (in ways that cannot otherwise be substituted) if I were to refrain from reading to her at bedtime. In the balance between distributive justice and the good of familial relationship, on this particular instance, the latter seems to weigh more heavily.' This is a perfectly reasonable and coherent position to hold, I submit. Notice also that such a conscientious parent would truly regret the in-egalitarian consequences of her conduct. This is important, because it indicates that rather than there not being any concern of justice to begin with (as Mason argues)[30] it is actually the case that there *is* an injustice here, but one that is trumped by other moral considerations.

It might be suggested that it is wrong to speak about trading off the concern for distributive justice (or fairness) with that for FRG, since if FRG is such an important good then it itself ought to be subject to distributive justice.[31] But notice that the position taken here need not deny that FRG is

---

[29] Brighouse and Swift, 'Legitimate Parental Partiality', p. 57.
[30] *Levelling the Playing Field*, p. 100.
[31] I am grateful to Adam Swift for raising this objection.

a subject of distributive justice.[32] The point, rather, is that FRG is one type of good with regards to which our concern for absolute value is likely to outweigh the concern for its relative distribution. This gives us an extra reason to refrain from levelling down FRG, compared with levelling down the instrumental value of story-telling. Again, this is not to deny that even FRG may have a positional aspect. (We might plausibly speculate that the more a child is loved the more she is likely to become a happier adult, and thus might make a more attractive job candidate.) Rather, the point is that compared to other goods, and certainly compared to endowed skills, we should be less inclined toward levelling down when it comes to FRG. Hence our rules of regulation may allow FRG-producing activities even when these clash with a concern for just distributions.

In accounting for parental partiality that is constitutive of the family and that is indispensible in producing the good of familial relationship, the luck egalitarian, I believe, meets the bedtime reading objection to the neutralization approach. We can now also see that it is not so counterintuitive to expect parents to refrain from trying to give their child an edge over other children. It is not unreasonable to expect parents to refrain from certain quality-time activities when the harm they present for EOp is greater than their benefit in terms of FRG. If so, Mason's bedtime-reading objection ceases to seem all that embarrassing for luck egalitarians. It appears that the rather straightforward distinction between quality time pursued for the sake of constitutive familial goods and quality time that primarily bestows an advantage helps us avoid the bedtime reading objection (or what's left of it).

Whether or not such partial conduct would be justified all things considered depends, we said, on weighing the value of the activity for the familial relationship, on the one hand, and the extent to which it exacerbates inequality of opportunity, on the other. I do not presume to know how to undertake this balancing act, but let me nevertheless offer the following thought experiment. Suppose that when some parents tell their children bedtime stories this happens to bestow on the child, not an undue

---

[32] For some doubts about whether parental love can be a subject of luck egalitarian distributive justice see Gheaus, 'How Much of What Matters Can We Redistribute?' Gheaus's doubts, however, concern the issue of redistributing love itself (e.g. the fact that it is impossible to coerce individuals to love). But of course such difficulties preclude only redistribution in kind, not compensation.

advantage but rather, an undue *dis*advantage. Think of a parent who is hopelessly confused in matters of geography and in the stories he tells, the Himalayas are transported to America, the Nile is made to flow from Glasgow to the North Sea, and so forth. The child very much enjoys the stories and derives much intimate value from the interaction with the parent, but she is also, consequently, at the lowest rung of her geography class. As a result, she never makes it to the good high school she and her parents set their sights on. Should the parent nevertheless continue the bedtime story-telling (suppose that offering the parent some tutoring in geography is not an option)? If we think that he should, then we must think that the value of the interaction outweighs the disadvantage in this case; that the absolute benefit in terms of the FRG outweighs the relative harm in terms of EOp. And if we think *that* about imparting an undue *dis*advantage then we ought to have the exact same judgement with regard to imparting an undue advantage. The point can be generalized. Suppose some religious schools disadvantage their pupils (with respect to the rest of society). Ultra orthodox schools in Israel, for example, generally turn out students who cannot compete with other pupils for university places because they teach no or very little English and Maths. (It is beside the point for present purposes that these pupils and their parents rarely do seek out enrolment in secular higher education.) If one thinks that it is permissible for a parent to disadvantage her child by sending her to such a school then one must, on pain of consistency, also think that it could be permissible for parents to send their kids to religious schools if these *happened* to bestow an advantage. Things would have been very different if a parent enrolled her child in a religious school *because* that school offers an edge over other kids. It is the value which is at stake (bestowing an advantage as opposed to safeguarding some essential familial good), I submit, that explains why we feel one way about the said Ultra-orthodox parent but very differently about those Londoners who upon locating an elite religious school in their vicinity suddenly 'discover' their Catholic roots.[33]

I should stress that, as I said in Section I, when parents are justified in bestowing undue advantages (when this is excused by the impact of the activity on their FRG) this does not mean that the undue nurtured advantage should be allowed to translate into a social advantage later in life. On

---

[33] Swift, *How Not To Be a Hypocrite*, p. 2.

the luck egalitarian reading, parents who bestow an undue advantage through bedtime reading still commit an injustice, even if the activity is nevertheless excused (because of the importance of the activity for their relationship). The (moral) permission to engage in bedtime reading does not excuse such a parent from acting to mitigate the advantage that she unjustly brought about. She will be expected to mitigate it, for example, by lobbying and supporting a high income tax on parents like herself, taxes that could be used to fund educational activities for less fortunate children, and so forth. In short, even when luck egalitarians do allow an advantage-imparting activity (because it generates FRG) they would still advocate mitigating, as much as possible, the consequent advantage. To stress: on my account, it is *not* the case that lobbying and supporting egalitarian public policies *justifies* one's partial conduct as a parent at home.[34] On the luck egalitarian account,[35] one must *always* strive in one's role as a citizen and a market participant to reduce inequality.[36] Neutralizing advantages in the public sphere does not, then, give one an excuse to endow one's children with undue advantages at home. That kind of partiality is never made just, but it can be excused on independent grounds, such as the one offered here (the contribution of the activity to familial relations).

IV. Do Rawlsians Escape the Bedtime Stories Objection?

Andrew Mason employs the bedtime stories objection to attack the neutralization approach and in support of his favoured mitigation approach. Mitigators, we said, may agree with luck egalitarians in maintaining that natural and nurtured inequalities are unjust, but they do not accept that neutralizing is the right way to go about dealing with these unjust inequalities. In difference from the neutralization approach, we said, there is no presumption under the mitigation approach to nip the advantage in

---

[34] Cf. Avner de Shalit and Yehonathan Reshef, 'A Review of Andrew Mason's "Levelling the Playing Field": The Idea of Equality of Opportunity and its Place in Egalitarian Thought', *Philosophical Quarterly* 59 (2009), 756–60.

[35] See for example Cohen, *Rescuing Justice and Equality*, ch. 3.

[36] See also Harry Brighouse and Adam Swift, 'Equality, Priority, and Positional Goods', *Ethics* 116 (2006), § 8.

the bud, as it were, and prevent it from being bestowed and coming into being. The imperative is only to prevent an advantage that is bestowed by nature or nurture from being translated into a social or political advantage.[37] Thus, the mitigation approach would allow for spontaneous parental quality-time regardless of its equality-upsetting impact.[38] But it is not at all clear why Mason (or anyone else holding the mitigation approach) should think that the bedtime reading objection afflicts only the neutralization approach but leaves the mitigation approach unharmed. Recall what I said at the top of Section I about there being nothing in the mitigation approach in itself (unless some other requirement is slapped on from the outside) to restrict it only to the basic structure of society. If so, and absent further argument, this commits Mason to the view that any parent would be expected to pursue the mitigation approach also in her personal conduct.[39] Now, part of what that would involve is surely the attempt to try and mitigate potential bestowed advantages, that is, prevent advantages borne by nature or nurture from affecting people's access to advantage. Mason's mitigating parent would therefore be obligated to vote and lobby for policies that would prevent the very advantages that she was encouraged to bestow on her child from translating into any real social advantage. This is no doubt commendable. The question, however, is whether or not the combined set of conduct that Mason expects from parents is one that could be characterized as morally plausible, not to mention psychologically coherent. (This is true even more so if we take him to be making the claim that parents do not even have a pro tanto reason to refrain from bedtime story-telling.) For Mason, in effect, tells parents that it is not only permissible to read bedtime stories to their

---

[37] Mason's approach, I should mention, also differs from the neutralization approach with regard to the pattern of distribution it favours, where Mason opts for what he calls quasi-egalitarian patterns instead of the neutralization preference for strict equality, but this has been immaterial for my dispute with him in this chapter. In his reply to me, Mason claims that the issue of pattern and currency within his position cannot be pried apart, and therefore that I have misunderstood his position ('Putting Story-Telling to Bed', pp. 83–4). Perhaps I do, but I insist that the account of his position that I give here is the best sense I can make of it. To put this differently, the reader is invited to think of my portrayal of Mason's position as the egalitarian version of the mitigation approach (even if not Mason's own position).

[38] I should stress that the mitigation approach may place considerable limits on the inequalities that parental partiality may generate. (See for example Mason's 'educational access principle' in *Levelling the Playing Field*, pp. 138–41). My criticism, though, centred on what kinds of parental action this approach considers justified, independently of the *extent* of inequality that it may generate.

[39] Mason confirms this in personal communication.

children so long as they act, under their citizen's hat, to mitigate the advantages bestowed. Rather, we can now see that he must also instruct parents that there is absolutely nothing wrong in being *motivated* by a desire to bestow an undue advantage at home so long as they strive to mitigate it for those affected. That seems to me to invite conduct that is not only hypocritical but actually schizophrenic.[40] It does not seem coherent to, effectively, encourage parents to be motivated by the desire to bestow undue advantages at home and then to rush to annul them in one's capacity as a citizen. In that respect, the mitigation approach would generate a perplexed parent indeed.[41]

Conclusion

In contrast to the mitigation approach, the luck egalitarian approach appears much more coherent. It says that although parents are justified in interacting with their child in a way that might happen to bestow an advantage (when the primary objective is the good of their relationship) the parent still has an obligation to try and mitigate the advantage she happened to bestow. She ought to lobby to have in place political and social mechanisms that would mitigate the effects of the brute luck advantages that, even though they were unjust, she was permitted, all things considered, to bestow. In this, luck egalitarians offer what seems to me morally coherent and psychologically sound guidance.

---

[40] By 'schizophrenic' I do not mean that it is psychologically impossible for parents to be selfish at home and egalitarian in the political sphere. I only mean that it is a morally suspicious position for individuals to hold and follow. See also Cohen (*Rescuing Justice and Equality*, pp. 174–5) on a similar point. (See also Murphy, 'Institutions and the Demands of Justice', p. 280.) Cohen notes that this line of criticism against Rawlsianism has appeared already in T. Grey, 'The First Virtue', *Stanford Law Review* 25 (1973), p. 324. Finally, it is worth noting that even Samuel Scheffler, whose views should be much closer to Mason's than to mine, admits that 'if the distinction between individual and institutional norms is associated with the distinction between the personal and impersonal standpoints, the psychologically unified character of our reactive responses seems difficult to explain.' *Equality and Tradition: Questions of Value in Moral and Political Theory* (Oxford: Oxford University Press, 2010), p. 122.

[41] To borrow from the subtitle of Swift's book: *How Not To Be a Hypocrite: School Choice for the Morally Perplexed Parent*. I should stress that Mason's approach does not tell parents to rush as citizens to annul specifically the advantages bestowed on *their* children. He only instructs them to annul advantages bestowed on children, no matter whose they are. But that effectively amounts to the same thing when it comes to privileged bedtime story-tellers, and so (at least) with regard to these individuals, would generate conflicting directives. I am grateful to Andy Mason for correcting me on this.

PART IV
Health

8

Equality of Opportunity
for Health

It is hard to deny the centrality of equality of opportunity to justice in
hiring and upbringing. But equality of opportunity, it has long been recognized, is no less central to thinking about justice in health care. The
dominant theory in that field, Norman Daniels's, famously grounds the
provision of health care in John Rawls's 'fair equality of opportunity principle' (FEOp).[1] I begin this chapter by recounting some problems with
the way in which equality of opportunity figures in Daniels's account. In
Section II I shall present the luck egalitarian, radical, alternative. That
alternative, what we may call 'equality of opportunity for health', says that
inequalities in health (and not merely health care) are unjust when they
are un-chosen. I will then briefly discuss some initial reservations about
equality of opportunity for health, and then address in more detail two
(additional) particular objections to it. These objections concern (respectively) the claim that equality of opportunity can regulate only competitive goods and, as such, is unsuitable for regulating health (Section III),
and the claim that equality of opportunity (henceforth EOp) is restricted
to social rather than natural inequalities (Sections IV–V). I hope to dis-
prove these two objections, and more generally to present EOp for health
as a plausible and attractive account of justice in health.

Let me make one quick qualification. My proposed account of 'equality
of opportunity for health' is intended as a narrower, as it were, account of
justice in health than Daniels's. Thus, for reasons to be elaborated in the
next section, it is somewhat more modest in its ambitions compared to
Daniels's. It is only fair to stress this now, because some aspects of justice

---

[1] Norman Daniels, *Just Health Care* (Cambridge: Cambridge University Press, 1985); *Just Health: Meeting Health Needs Fairly* (Cambridge: Cambridge University Press, 2008).

in health and health care on which Daniels's theory fails, my proposed account is simply silent on. The playing field between the two accounts, I should admit, is not level.

I. Daniels's 'Fair Equality of Opportunity'

I want to begin by recalling the challenge that Daniels faced in offering a theory of justice in health care, and the way in which he met it. I then want to outline the shortcomings of his proposed solution. Next, I present the idea of EOp for health, and say how it differs from Daniels's. I shall then briefly present two potential problems with EOp for health, two problems which I have had occasion to address elsewhere.[2]

Central to Daniels's approach is the straightforward, yet important, observation that we need to be healthy in order to be able to pursue the life plans that we have each formed for ourselves. Health, and by derivation health care, is thus crucial for equality of opportunity to fulfil one's life plans. This insight led Daniels to resist locating the distribution of health care under what would appear to be the obvious default place, namely John Rawls's Difference Principle (DP), and instead to place it under the lexically prior FEOp. This has the happy result of justifying an egalitarian, rather than a prioritarian, distribution of health care. In this way, health care makes a modest but important contribution to equalizing individuals' opportunity to pursue their life plans. That is the essence of Daniels's linkage of health care with EOp. This approach, however, is vulnerable to at least three fundamental objections (which I shall merely sketch here).[3] The first objection shows that the theory has difficulty justifying *in kind* universal health care. Even worse, says the second objection, Daniels's principle fails to justify *universal* health care, more generally. And worse still, according to the third objection, the principle does not justify public provision of health care *at all*.

Think of a patient who needs, and is thereby entitled to, some expensive medical treatment, but who would much rather have the cash equivalent of that treatment. She might argue that she can use that amount of money to boost her opportunity-set in a far more effective way. A cancer patient

---

[2] *Health, Luck, and Justice* (Princeton, NJ: Princeton University Press, 2010).
[3] See, for more detail, *Health, Luck, and Justice*, ch. 2.

with a 50 per cent chance of survival may rather use the cash equivalent of her treatment to sail around the world one last time.[4] Similarly, a paraplegic violinist might prefer a Stradivarius to an expensive wheelchair.[5] A commitment to boosting opportunities to fulfil one's life plans appears not to justify *in-kind* medical coverage. This, it is plausible to think, is a weakness in a theory of justice in health care. In reply, one thing that the proponent of Daniels's principle might say is that it (the principle) does not speak of equal opportunity to fulfil each and every person's particular life plan, but rather speaks of a fixed range of plausible life plans (or life plans that it is reasonable for individuals in a particular society to entertain). Such an interpretation does indeed cohere with some other things that Daniels says, such as the relativity of that range of opportunities to one's particular talents (a controversial aspect of Daniels's general theory which is not the focus of my criticism here).[6] While this may indeed get around the problem of patients whose particular life plan would benefit less from a certain medical care than from its cash equivalent, it is hard to see how Daniels could justify such a limitation of his account. Recall that Daniels's account of justice justifies medical aid on the basis of its contribution to people's ability to pursue their life plans. Given that approach's typically liberal (i.e. neutral) premise, it is not at all clear why a theory grounded in this way should limit itself to some average of life plans rather than to what individuals actually require in order to fulfil their particular life plans.[7]

Here is the second problem. Daniels's justification for a universal system, I said, is premised on health care's impact on EOp (to pursue one's life plan). But *equality* of opportunity to pursue life plans does not justify *universal*

---

[4] See Lesley A. Jacobs, *Pursuing Equal Opportunities: The Theory and Practice of Egalitarian Justice* (Cambridge: Cambridge University Press, 2004), pp. 196–200; Segall, *Health, Luck, and Justice*, pp. 83–6.

[5] Ronald Dworkin, *Sovereign Virtue: The Theory and Practice of Egalitarian Justice* (Cambridge, MA: Harvard University Press, 2000), p. 61.

[6] See my 'Is Health Care (Still) Special?' *Journal of Political Philosophy* 15 (2007), 342–63.

[7] Another plausible response by Daniels is that health care should enable individuals not only to pursue the life plans they already have, but also to allow them to revise their plans. [Rawls similarly talks about 'the capacity to have, to *revise*, and rationally to pursue a conception of the good'. *Justice as Fairness* (Cambridge, MA, London: Harvard University Press, 2001), p. 19, emphasis added.] I concede that that *would* justify in-kind health care in many cases, but I still think it wouldn't justify it on those occasions when a patient *must* choose, for independent reasons, between her current life plan and the ability to revise it (such as perhaps in the Stradivarius case).

access to health care. Rather, it justifies providing superior treatment to those who otherwise suffer inferior opportunities, namely the poor (or more accurately, the worse-off). Daniels's fair opportunity account would thus justify selective treatment that prioritizes the poor—or perhaps even one that turns the rich away from ERs!—all in the name of EOp. (Daniels is aware of this problem, but, as I have shown elsewhere, the argument he employs in reply, mainly resorting to depicting health care as a special and isolated sphere, is inconsistent with other components of his theory.)[8]

Using the health care system to narrow the gap in opportunities in society (e.g. between the rich and the poor), we can see, leads to consequences that are counterintuitive from a Rawlsian perspective. But even if we did not think the just mentioned consequence to be counterintuitive, it is still doubtful that the health care system could be counted upon to have such an impact on EOp. This is the third abovementioned objection. We said that Daniels's fair opportunities account relies on the health care system to narrow inequalities in health. But it turns out that the health care system is *not* an effective means for such an end. If we believe the epidemiological literature of the past twenty years or so, differences in access to health care account for only about a fifth of inequalities in health. The other 80 per cent determining health disparities are owed to 'the social determinants of health'. These include factors such as income, education, housing, and autonomy in the work-place.[9] The ethical implications of these empirical findings cannot be exaggerated. Recall that the premiss of Daniels's thesis is that justice requires narrowing health inequalities because of the way in which health impacts individuals' opportunity to fulfil their life plans. But to narrow down health inequalities most effectively we ought to divert resources away from hospitals and onto the more significant determinants of health (equal distributions of income, education, housing, diet, jobs, and so forth). In fact, some critics of Daniels have gone as far as to suggest that a commitment to narrowing down health discrepancies would force us to shut down hospitals altogether.[10] We can see, therefore, that

[8] See my 'Is Health Care (Still) Special?'; 'Is Health (Really) Special: Health Policy between Rawlsian and Luck Egalitarian Justice', *The Journal of Applied Philosophy* 27 (2010), 344–58.

[9] See Michael Marmot and Richard G. Wilkinson, *Social Determinants of Health* (Oxford: Oxford University Press, 2006); Michael Marmot, *The Status Syndrome: How Social Standing Affects Our Health and Longevity* (New York: Times Books, 2004).

[10] Gopal Sreenivasan, 'Health Care and Equality of Opportunity', *Hastings Centre Report* 37 (2007), 31–41.

grounding the justification for the public provision of health care in its impact on EOp to pursue one's life plans proves multiply problematic.

II. Equality of Opportunity for Health

The radical alternative to Daniels's way of linking EOp and health says that individuals ought to have an equal opportunity to obtain the best health possible. This simple view, in effect, turns Daniels's principle on its head. Instead of speaking of health (care) as a means to EOp we here speak, instead, of EOp *for* health.[11] The principle could be formulated as follows:

EOp for Health: It is unfair for individuals to suffer worse health than others owing to factors that they did not control.

Notice how the principle follows from our general understanding of radical EOp as formulated in the introductory chapter ['unequal opportunities are unfair when (and only when) pursuant to prudent conduct and when resulting in unequal outcomes']. Notice also that this principle avoids the three problems that afflict Daniels's account. First, EOp for health focuses attention on, well, health. Whatever other opportunities the agent may want for herself in life, EOp for health requires that she has an equal opportunity to be as healthy as possible.[12] It therefore does not follow that she may convert her entitlement to good health into other opportunities (say, a trip around the world, or a Stradivarius).[13] Second, stipulating that all individuals, irrespective of social background (among other things), are entitled to the best health possible avoids the second problem, that

---

[11] The term is not new, of course. See for example John E. Roemer, *Equality of Opportunity* (Cambridge, MA: Harvard University Press, 1998), ch. 8. We may mention, in this context, another variant that turns Daniels's 'health care as a means to EOp' on its head, namely 'equality of opportunity for health care', a view held by John Harris ['Justice and Equal Opportunities in Health Care', *Bioethics* 13 (1999), 392–413]. For Harris, 'equal opportunity for health care' means, controversially, that individuals' access to health care should not be determined either by their age or by their likelihood to benefit from the treatment. More on the former of which, in a moment.

[12] Daniels famously treats health care as an isolated sphere. My account, for the purposes of this chapter, takes health itself to be such an isolated sphere. In that respect I follow John Roemer's 'equality of opportunity for health'. See his *Equality of Opportunity*, p. 52.

[13] Another difference between my account and Daniels's is that his account relies on the (quite plausible, I concede) assertion that health is a good that individuals want whatever else they might want in life. EOp for health, in contrast, does not even have to make that assumption. It guarantees to individuals the opportunity for health, *if they so choose*. In that sense, the principle proposed is less perfectionist than Daniels's.

of discriminating against the rich. EOp for health thus justifies *universal* care. Finally, the principle also avoids the third problem observed, the one concerning the social determinants of health. 'EOp for health' speaks of individuals' opportunity for *health*, without specifying whether it ought to be achieved by the means of clinical care (e.g. hospitals) or by other, non-clinical, means. Justice requires narrowing the gap in opportunities for health between individuals,[14] whichever resources it might take to do so.

This proposed approach, however, might face its own set of problems. Let me briefly (because I have dealt with them elsewhere)[15] mention two such potentially problematic implications. I said that EOp for health speaks of providing individuals with the opportunity to be as healthy as they themselves choose to be. But what if individuals choose to waste, as it were, their opportunity for health? What does EOp for health say about society's obligations towards those who have damaged their own health through smoking, lack of exercise, unbalanced diet, non-compliance with their doctors' orders, and so forth? A responsibility-sensitive principle (such as EOp for health) would have to prioritize the treatment of the prudent over the imprudent, and that may strike many people as counterintuitive.[16] I shall not attempt to respond to this worry here, but will only offer the following thought. EOp for health will favour the non-smoker over the smoker only when both individuals truly had an equal opportunity to quit smoking [as well as, obviously, an equal opportunity not to pick up the habit to begin with (recall our discussion in Chapter 3)].[17] Likewise, the principle of EOp for health would favour the conscientious jogger over the couch-potato only when both individuals truly did have an equal opportunity to exercise, namely, that they had equal access to safe parks in which to jog, equal availability of flexible working hours around which one might find time to

---

[14]   One way, of course, to narrow down inequalities in health is to level them down, something which does not seem very attractive. This, however, is a problem common to all egalitarian approaches to health [including Daniels's. See Frances Kamm, 'Health and Equality of Opportunity', *American Journal of Bioethics* 1 (2001), 17–19], and not just to the one proposed here.

[15]   See *Health, Luck, and Justice*, ch. 4.

[16]   We have touched already, in Ch. 3, on the tendency of opportunity-based theories of justice to abandon, as it were, the imprudent. See again, Marc Fleurbaey, 'Equal Opportunity or Equal Social Outcome', *Economics and Philosophy* 11 (1995), 25–55; Jonathan Wolff, 'Fairness, Respect, and the Egalitarian Ethos', *Philosophy and Public Affairs* 27 (1998), 97–122; Elizabeth Anderson, 'What is the Point of Equality?' *Ethics* 109 (1999), 287–337.

[17]   See John E. Roemer, 'A Pragmatic Theory of Responsibility for the Egalitarian Planner', *Philosophy and Public Affairs* 22 (1993), 146–66; *Equality of Opportunity*, ch. 8.

exercise, and so forth. Since our non-ideal world does not yet come close to levelling the playing field in that respect, it will very often be the case that 'EOp for health' will not, in fact, abandon many of the (so-called) imprudent.[18]

Here is the other potential problem with a principle that guarantees to all individuals equal opportunity for health. We do not normally[19] think that a 30 year-old and a 70 year-old should be accorded an equal chance of receiving a (scarce) heart transplant (say, by tossing a coin to decide this). It may be problematic, then, to speak of EOp for health, pure and simple. (This intuition is consistent, notice, with the position taken in Chapter 5 with regard to so-called 'age-discrimination' in hiring.) Of course, that particular problem may be averted if we adopt what is often referred to as a 'complete life view' of EOp. We may then say that over the course of their lives individuals should have an equal chance to lead a long and healthy life. Still, that would only seem to take care of differences of age. What about differences of sex? We know that even in the best social circumstances, men and women do not have an equal opportunity to live a long and healthy life.[20] The ideal of EOp for health would commit us to narrowing the gap in life expectancy between men and women, something that would strike many readers as counterintuitive.[21] Endorsing EOp for health thus entails defending it from this 'inequality between the sexes' objection. I shall not address this objection here,[22] but will just note that it might be the case that upon further reflection the widespread intuition regarding the acceptability of health inequalities between the sexes may turn out to be not all that founded.[23]

---

[18] For a similar conclusion see Eric Cavallero, 'Health, Luck and Moral Fallacies of the Second Best', *The Journal of Ethics* 15 (2011), 387–403.

[19] Cf. Harris, 'Justice and Equal Opportunities in Health Care'.

[20] It may be of interest to note, though, that the more developed a society is the narrower the gap in life expectancy between men and women becomes. See Christopher J. L. Murray, 'Rethinking DALYs', in Christopher J. L. Murray and Alan D. Lopez (eds), *The Global Burden of Disease* (Cambridge, MA: Harvard School of Public Health, World Health Organization, World Bank, 1996), p. 18.

[21] See for example, Amartya Sen, *The Idea of Justice* (Cambridge, MA: The Belknap Press of Harvard University Press, 2009), p. 296.

[22] I do so in *Health, Luck, and Justice*, pp. 105–10.

[23] Marc Fleurbaey objects that the priority to men, mandated by the principle of EOp for health, clashes with the more general luck egalitarian goal of EOp for welfare, for men are generally better-off, welfare-wise, than women are. ['Review of Shlomi Segall, "Health, Luck, and Justice"', *Utilitas* 22 (2010), p. 505.] Let me quickly say that I concede the point. In fact I have noted the very point myself in *Health, Luck, and Justice* (p. 95). My reply there was that EOp for health merely *assumes* (for the sake of argument) the sphere of health to be a separate one. But, I noted, the luck egalitarian will typically be concerned with welfare more generally, and thus in cases of conflict it is the latter that ought to take precedence.

If 'EOp for health' could be successfully defended from the two above-mentioned objections then it may present an attractive alternative to Daniels's Rawlsian approach. In fact, the view that individuals should have an equal opportunity for health, and that health ought not to depend on social *and* natural factors, I want to suggest in concluding this section, could be traced back to Rawls. Rawls, of course, had very little to say about health, let alone specifying some ideal of EOp for health. But he did hold that: 'There is no more reason to permit the distribution of income and wealth to be settled by the distribution of natural assets than by historical and social fortune'.[24] With a change of one letter, as it were, we could read Rawls to be speaking here about how the distribution of health should be determined neither by social factors, nor by natural ones. That, in a nutshell, is the very idea underlying EOp for health. EOp for health strives to neutralize inequalities in health that are due to both social factors (over which the individual had no control), and ones that are due to differences in natural assets, such as one's genetic makeup.

These are the merits and potential weaknesses of EOp for health as an alternative to Daniels's approach to justice in health. In the rest of this chapter I want to discuss two other specific objections to EOp for health. The first of these objections says that EOp is a principle that is suitable only for the distribution of *competitive* goods. If true, this would prove problematic in the present context if we think (as I concede I do) that neither health nor health care ought to be thought of as a competitive good (the way jobs or enrolment in university conventionally are). In other words, health, unlike jobs or medals, say, ought not to be a subject of a competition. That is the first challenge (with which I deal in the next section). The second objection to EOp for health is this. EOp for health purports to regulate inequalities in access to health. But 'inequalities', some say, can only refer to social inequalities. This is so because, the objection goes, there is no such thing as natural inequalities, only natural *differences*. If this is true, then the only obstacles which EOp for health would then be removing are social ones. And this, crucially, is a weakness in an account of justice in

---

[24] John Rawls, *A Theory of Justice* (Oxford: Clarendon Press, 1972), p. 74. Rawls reiterates this in *Political Liberalism*: 'What the theory of justice must regulate is the inequalities in the life prospects between citizens that arise from social starting positions, natural advantages, and historical contingencies'. (New York: Columbia University Press, 1996), p. 271.

health. For, if EOp for health removes only social obstacles, then there is nothing in it to justify treatment for ill health that is due to natural causes. And that, of course, would be counterintuitive. I shall address this objection in Sections IV–V.

III. Is Equality of Opportunity Necessarily Competitive?

The first claim we are investigating, then, says that EOp for health is faulty because the concept of equality of opportunity is necessarily competitive,[25] and health, we all agree, ought not to be treated as a competitive good.[26] That is, most of us would object to allocating health outcomes through some sort of competition.

Before trying to respond to this objection, it is worth pointing out that it is not one that is unique to health. EOp for health is, in a sense, a special case of the more general concept of 'equality of opportunity for welfare' (recall our discussion of the three distinguishing aspects of radical EOp in the introductory chapter).[27] Now, if there is one good that egalitarians agree ought *not* to be treated as a subject of competition, it is surely the good of welfare. We might say, then, that if EOp for health is in trouble, then at the very least it is in good company.[28] More importantly, perhaps, the present 'competitiveness objection' would also spell trouble for Daniels's account. Recall that Daniels justifies health care based on its contribution to equality of opportunity to pursue one's life plans. But are life plans a competitive good? This seems (at least) equally unlikely.[29] If we may quote from Robert Nozick:[30] '...life is not a race in which we all

---

[25] Matt Cavanagh, *Against Equality of Opportunity* (Oxford: Clarendon Press, 2002), p. 124; Paul Gomberg, *How to Make Opportunity Equal*, e.g. pp. 18–19, p. 27.

[26] Jacobs, *Pursuing Equal Opportunities*, ch. 3.

[27] Richard J. Arneson, 'Equality of Opportunity for Welfare', *Philosophical Studies* 56 (1989), 77–93.

[28] Admittedly, though, some of the things that John Roemer (who is often in accord with Arneson) says point to the fact that he actually has a competitive view of EOp. 'Thus there is, in the notion of equality of opportunity, a "before" and an "after": before the competition starts, opportunities must be equalized, by social intervention if need be, but after it begins, individuals are on their own'. *Equality of Opportunity*, p. 2.

[29] See also my 'Is Health Care (Still) Special?' §3.

[30] The affinity between luck egalitarianism and libertarianism is not accidental, I think. Recall the conclusion to Chapter 4.

compete for a prize which someone has established; there is no unified race, with some person judging swiftness'.[31] If the competitiveness thesis is correct, then it would follow that the core of Daniels's account, namely the pursuit of one's life plan, is also not a suitable subject of equality of opportunity.

None of this, of course, exonerates EOp for health. In addressing that objection, then, I concede that the distribution of health should not be a subject of competition, but, predictably, I dispute that EOp is necessarily competitive (or at least, competitive in a way that makes it unsuitable for regulating the distribution of health). To see this we need to recall one of the points made in the introductory chapter. It concerns the distinction between chance and choice. Often, when we speak of opportunities, we speak of them in terms of *chances*.[32] We may speak of the opportunity, as in the ageism example above, to receive this or that organ for transplantation. On those occasions we are speaking of opportunities as a matter of a zero-sum game, and these, of course, *are* competitive. But not all linguistic usages of 'opportunity' comport to that. Think, for example, of one's opportunity to gaze at a sunset on the beach. 'Opportunity' here signifies that one has the *choice* of whether or not she goes to the beach and watches the sun set. Opportunities, then, could be understood either as chances, which are a matter of a zero-sum game, *or*, alternatively, as what has been termed 'non-competitive opportunity'.[33] Here, 'opportunity for X' signifies the fact that the agent may take advantage, or use, X, *if she so chooses*. Opportunity in that sense of the word, it is obvious, is not necessarily competitive. We may refer to these two uses of opportunity, then, as 'chance' as opposed to 'choice'.[34]

As I noted in the introductory chapter, the distinction is not merely linguistic. Radical EOp is committed to neutralizing all un-chosen impediments (that is, both social *and* natural). In so doing, the radical conception effectively holds that EOp obtains when outcomes are a function of equal choice. EOP obtains when outcomes are affected by un-chosen features to

---

[31] *Anarchy, State, and Utopia* (Oxford: Blackwell, 1974), p. 235.

[32] 'An opportunity is a chance of getting a good if one seeks it.' Richard J. Arneson, 'Liberalism, Distributive Subjectivism and Equal Opportunity for Welfare', *Philosophy and Public Affairs* 19 (1990), p. 176. See also Cavanagh, *Against Equality of Opportunity*, p. 120.

[33] D. A. Lloyd Thomas, 'Competitive Equality of Opportunity', *Mind* 86 (1977), p. 391.

[34] For more on the distinction between opportunity as chance and opportunity as choice see S. J. D. Green, 'Competitive Equality of Opportunity: A Defence', *Ethics* 100 (1989), p. 10.

the exact same degree. Radical EOp thus replaces equality of chance with equality of choice. In this way, the radical account successfully explains why merely equalizing chances is unsatisfactory from a fairness perspective. A lottery (for jobs, university places, or organs) equalizes chances but still leaves outcomes vulnerable to differential luck. Equalizing chances is therefore insufficient on the radical reading. Instead, radical EOp places equal choice at the heart of EOp.

We can distinguish, then, competitive opportunities, understood as chances, from non-competitive ones, understood as choices. But the critic might persist that even opportunities of the latter sense are in a way competitive. Even a simple case such as one's opportunity to gaze upon the sunset on the beach is in some sense competitive. To enable one's opportunity to get to the beach to watch the sun set one requires various resources (means of transportation, time away from work, child-care). All of these *are* scarce resources, and as such they may potentially be competitive. It may therefore seem as if one's seemingly non-competitive opportunity to travel to the beach depends upon a series of opportunities which *are* competitive.[35] It is perhaps that observation that may explain why some people conceive of opportunities as necessarily competitive. But a moment's reflection reveals that to speak of opportunities as competitive in this sense is trivial. Any good that is the subject of distributive justice is for that matter scarce. In as much as the claim regarding the competitiveness of equality of opportunity refers to its ultimate reliance on the distribution of goods which are finite and scarce, then that claim is surely true but trivial. In that respect, Nozick's famous remark that to boost Smith's opportunity (in the name of EOp) without willing to trample on (what Nozick believes to be) Jones' rights is to believe in EOp by means of 'a magic wand'.[36] In one sense he is certainly correct: EOp cannot be achieved without the redistribution of scarce, competitive goods. Health is no exception. Its redistribution relies on the distribution of medical care, income, education, jobs, and so forth. These are all, to a lesser or greater extent, scarce goods. (They may not necessarily be a matter of a zero-sum game, but they are certainly finite.) In that respect EOp, including EOp for health is indeed competitive. But if that is what is meant by 'competitive' (as in relying on

---

[35] There is a good discussion of this in Green, 'Competitive Equality of Opportunity', pp. 12–13.

[36] *Anarchy, State, and Utopia*, p. 236.

a distribution of scarce resources) then we might find that other ethical approaches to health are also guilty of relying on a competitive view. Think of the view that health equity requires setting some threshold of decent healthy living,[37] or the view (such as Daniels's), that resources should be spent so that individuals would be restored to 'normal species functioning'. All these patterns of distributing health rely on a redistribution of scarce, competitive resources. If EOp for health applies a competitive approach to a non-competitive good (health), then so are all its conceivable alternatives. In a sense, that is precisely Nozick's point. Nozick's objection to equality of opportunity is consistent with his objection to distributive justice more generally. Both entail the redistribution of scarce goods (goods which Nozick, of course, believes already belong to people). And accordingly, if one does not find the concept of distributive justice to be objectionable in and of itself, then neither should she find EOp for non-competitive goods such as health to be objectionable (at least not for the reason invoked by the competitiveness objection).

As we have seen in Part II, EOp has traditionally been associated with meritocracy, as the idea of careers open to talent.[38] That is probably why it was thought to be a procedure that is suitable for the regulation and distribution of competitive goods alone. But fortunately, and as I have tried to illustrate throughout the book, we no longer need to think of EOp as restricted to a meritocratic distribution of jobs. The radical account of EOp as developed by Arneson, Cohen, and Roemer, and as hopefully further developed in this book, demonstrates this. This evolution in our understanding of EOp, we shall see now, is also instrumental in addressing the other objection to EOp for health; the one concerning natural inequalities.

IV. Equality of Opportunity: Natural or only Social?

EOp for health says that individuals' health should be, to an equal measure, as independent as possible of social background or natural endowment. It is the latter requirement, the fact that EOp for health does not

[37] Allen Buchanan, 'The Right to a Decent Minimum of Health Care', *Philosophy and Public Affairs* 13 (1984), 55–78.

[38] See for example, Lloyd Thomas, 'Competitive Equality of Opportunity', p. 397; Green, 'Competitive Equality of Opportunity: A Defence', p. 5.

accept natural inequalities, which triggers the objection with which we are concerned in this section. A formal presentation of the objection under consideration might help here:

1. To be attractive, any account of justice in health would have to regulate both social and natural obstacles to good health.
2. EOp for X regulates *inequalities* in access to X.
3. But there is no such phenomenon as 'natural inequalities'.
4. EOp for health thus can only remove social inequalities in access to health.
5. EOp for health thus cannot (on its own) justify treatment for ill health that is owed to natural factors.
6. Any account of justice in health (of which EOp for health is one) which cannot justify treatment for naturally-caused ill health is unattractive.
7. EOp for health is therefore unattractive.

In responding to this objection I shall concede premises (1) and (2), as well as the inference from (3) to (7), and restrict myself to contesting premiss (3).

EOp for health aspires to remove social and natural impediments to good health, and I concede that it would not be an attractive guide to justice in health if it didn't remove both. EOp for health is therefore forced to consider as unjust both inequalities in health that are owed to social factors (over which individuals have no control), and ones which are owed to natural factors. EOp for health is therefore committed to the view that differences in genetic propensity constitute unjust inequalities and as such warrant rectification. In that sense, the ideal depends on the view that there are natural inequalities. Notice that this objection afflicts EOp for health but *not* Daniels's account. As premiss (2) shows, EOp for X is concerned with equalizing obstacles to X. EOp for health thus implies identifying, and levelling, inequalities in access to health. If social impediments generate the only *inequalities* that affect the distribution of health, then EOp would level them and only them. This proves problematic in as much as there are natural factors that lie behind ill health (which there obviously are). Daniels's principle is not vulnerable to that problem. It says, recall, that justice requires bringing everyone's level of health up to normal species functioning. This is an attractive feature of Daniels's principle (or at least prima facie so). Namely, it does not concern itself with whether the causes of ill health are natural or social,[39] but seeks to bring each individual up to the highest level of health. It therefore does not hinge on the existence of natural *inequalities*.

In difference to Daniels, EOp for health considers differences in genetic propensity to constitute unjust *inequalities*. Interestingly, until recently this last sentence would have been rather incomprehensible, let alone convincing. But, with the hindsight of Arneson's, Cohen's, and Roemer's work on the impact of luck on justice, it no longer strikes us as bizarre to think of EOp as entailing this rather radical implication. It is worth recalling here, however, what we have said at the very beginning of this book, namely that before the late 1980s EOp was often objected to, by egalitarians, precisely on the grounds of its alleged complicity with these innate inequalities.[40] Pre-Arnesonian, as it were, equality of opportunity was considered a licence for allowing inequalities in natural talent to legitimize the resulting inequalities in income and welfare.[41] We may say as a bi-conclusion, then, that whatever one might think is wrong with the concept of radical EOp, and with its application to health, it *cannot* be (or be thought to be) some alleged complicity with *anti*-egalitarian consequences.

All this is worth bearing in mind when addressing the claim according to which the principle of EOp for health is counterintuitive because it presumes to regulate something that in fact does not exist, namely natural inequalities. The objection is based, it seems, on the following argument. When people speak of so-called natural inequalities, what they actually mean is natural *differences*; differences which are then transformed by social institutions into inequalities (that is, disadvantages and advantages).[42] The deaf, to take a standard example, are at a disadvantage compared to the hearing not because

---

[39] And whether or not there is, indeed, a sharp distinction between natural and social causes of ill health is yet another matter. One possible interpretation of the famous Whitehall study, for example, would suggest that there is a strong link between social determinants and basic human biology entailed in social hierarchies. I am grateful to an anonymous OUP referee for suggesting this.

[40] Lesley Jacobs offers a nice summary of these views. *Pursuing Equal Opportunities*, pp. 48–49.

[41] See again John Schaar, 'Equality of Opportunity and Beyond', in J. Roland Pennock and J. W. Chapman (eds), *Nomos IX: Equality* (New York: Atherton Press, 1967), p. 238; Rawls, *A Theory of Justice*, pp. 106–7.

[42] See Jacobs, *Pursuing Equal Opportunities*, ch. 3. Notice that I treat inequalities and disadvantages as one and the same here. But it is worth pointing out that a critic of luck egalitarianism might not insist on the impossibility of natural inequalities (she might admit the natural inequality between two individuals who have different blood pressure, say), but rather on the impossibility of natural disadvantages. (I am grateful to Dan Hausman for raising this objection.) I have already touched on this in Chapter 1, but it is worth pointing out

they suffer from some natural inferiority. Rather, deafness, which is a natural trait, is transformed into a (social) disadvantage when the deaf individual finds herself in a society that is designed by, and for, those who hear.[43] In this way, natural traits are transformed into social disadvantages, and thus give rise to inequality. There is therefore nothing natural, only social, about that inequality.[44] I object to nothing in this account and its description of how some natural traits are contingently translated into social disadvantages. What is true of deafness is true enough also of high cheekbones. It, also, is a natural trait that is translated into a social advantage because of a particular ideal of beauty that is prevalent in a given society at a given time. What I do object to is the view that the abovementioned institutional and social aspect of inequality exhausts the way in which deafness, high cheekbones, or blindness gives rise to disadvantage.

To see this, consider a society consisting of blind and sighted individuals. Suppose (not implausibly) that some of the blind prefer to gain sight and none of the sighted wish to become blind. (Of course, if any of the latter did wish to become blind that would be much cheaper and easier to bring about than would be the reverse, but leave that aside.) In as much as this is the case, we may say, using Dworkin's envy test (recall Chapter 1),[45] that the blind who wish to regain sight are at a disadvantage compared to the sighted. Of course, it could be the case that the preferences (both of the blind to regain sight and of the sighted to remain so) are biased by the fact that the particular social context in which they all live is one which is tailored for the interests of the sighted (again, not an implausible assumption). Suppose, then, that everything conceivable (short of say, blocking the sun or banning fire and electricity) has been done to reform society such that it does not favour the sighted.[46] And suppose further that

again that on my account inequalities only pertain to differences in *goods*. Thus, differences in blood pressure, in and of themselves, do not constitute an inequality, unless individuals have a reason to prefer one over the other.

[43] See Anita Silvers, 'Formal Justice', in *Disability, Difference, Discrimination: Perspectives on Justice in Bioethics and Public Policy*, ed. Anita Silvers, David Wasserman and Mary B. Mahowald (Lanham, MD: Rowman & Littlefield, 1998), 13–145.

[44] And consequently, any putative injustice here would be social, not natural. As Rawls writes: 'The natural distribution [of talents] is neither just nor unjust; nor is it unjust that persons are born into society at some particular position. These are simply natural facts. What is just and unjust is the way that institutions deal with these facts.' *A Theory of Justice*, p. 102.

[45] Dworkin, *Sovereign Virtue*, pp. 67–8.

[46] Think of something along the lines of Jose Saramago's dystopia, *Blindness*.

under those circumstances some of the blind still prefer to regain their sight while none of the sighted prefer to lose theirs.[47] Under these circumstances, we may say, there is an *inequality in preference-satisfaction* with regard to eyesight. Is this inequality natural or social? By this stage of the discussion, this may not be a particularly important question (once the crucial fact of inequality has been observed), but, for what it's worth, my view is that it is difficult to see what is 'social', as opposed to 'natural', about this particular instance of inequality.[48] It is, then, intelligible to speak of 'natural inequalities', and consequently, an ideal of EOp does regulate both social and natural inequalities in access to health.[49]

V. From Equality of Opportunity to Affirmative Action

The objection to speaking of 'natural inequalities' (including speaking of them as the subject of EOp) proves unsustainable. But there might be a different, more tactical, reasoning underlying this objection. The objection might be motivated by the thought that speaking of inequalities as natural is in some sense 'morally complacent'. Some have employed this phrase in their critique against framing the debate on IQ differences between the races in the USA in terms of 'natural inequalities'.[50] Doing so is thought to

---

[47] Or suppose, to complete the picture that the blind were given full mandate to use society's resources either to redesign social institutions so that they are more accommodating to the blind or use these resources to regain sight through some medical procedure, and that they have chosen the latter.

[48] The critic might still insist that the fact that discerning this particular inequality (in sight-preferences) depends on a comparison (or envy) makes it 'social' (Jacobs, *Pursuing Equal Opportunities*, p. 58). But that comparison (of the blind to the sighted) does not make the inequality (in preference-satisfaction concerning sight) any more 'social' than it is, well, 'human'. Inequality, in any normative sense, is based on comparisons between (human) individuals. [Something Jacobs is well aware of. See *Pursuing Equal Opportunities*, p. 59, fn. 34.] There seems therefore nothing social, as distinct from human, about the very act of comparison.

[49] Notice that another inequality not captured by the 'social inequalities' account concerns pain. Consider Smith who suffers from chronic migraines and Jones who does not. It is hard to deny that there is an inequality between them with regard to pain. And yet it is difficult to see what is 'social', as opposed to 'natural', about this inequality. I am grateful to Tami Harel for pointing this out to me.

[50] Jacobs quotes Claude Fischer (et al.) who use this term to criticize the thesis of the famous *Bell Curve* [Richard J. Herrnstein and Charles A. Murray, *The Bell Curve: Intelligence and Culture Structure in American Life* (New York: The Free Press, 1994)], regarding natural inequalities in IQ. See Jacobs, *Pursuing Equal Opportunities*, p. 65.

be morally complacent because such statements seem to legitimize something (race) which is essentially a social construct, and what is worse, one which results from unjust institutions.

Notice, though, that even if speaking of natural inequalities in IQ between the races is repugnant in some way, this is less obviously the case with regard to health. There seems nothing 'complacent' about taking notice of the natural inequality in life expectancy between those suffering from a degenerative illness and those who don't, say. There is nothing problematic, then, about targeting natural inequalities as such. Perhaps, then, there is something problematic about the act of targeting natural inequalities when these overlap with some salient group membership (as opposed to an ad hoc one). (Recall our discussion of discrimination and salient groups in Chapter 5.) A case in point would be gender. Still, few people think there is something problematic about gynaecology, say, as a branch of medicine. To take an even more controversial issue, there does not seem anything 'morally complacent' about addressing the natural inequality in life expectancy between men and women (if anything, quite the contrary). So neither mere natural inequalities, nor natural inequalities that overlap with some salient group membership, are as such repugnant. The problem, if there is one, must lie elsewhere. Perhaps it is this. It is generally (although not universally) thought that women and men form distinct biological categories. Targeting health inequalities between other social groups, whether based on socio-economic lines (the poor) or racial lines (blacks) is different in that respect. Such a practice may carry the message that races and classes form distinct biological categories, which is of course controversial and potentially repugnant.

We should have a clearer view of the objection in question now. EOp for health can be problematic, the critic may say, in as much as it leads to targeting the health needs of groups that we otherwise resist viewing as forming a biological category. Think, for example, of the debate concerning the approval, in 2005, by the Food and Drug Administration (FDA) of the first ever drug (BiDil) specifically targeted at a racial group (African-Americans). The decision was based on research (itself questionable, but set that aside for a moment) suggesting that heart patients who are black benefit significantly more from this particular drug than do white patients. The case is interesting for all sorts of reasons (indeed, I shall revisit it in the next chapter), but it is particularly interesting in the present context for the following reason. Given that in the USA blacks have a (significantly) lower life expectancy compared to whites,[51] research into drugs specifically aimed at African-Americans can help curb over-all inequalities in health. The FDA's action, in other words, seems to fol-low directly from the ideal of EOp for health. (Daniels's approach, notice, would not prohibit such measures, but neither would it require taking them.)[52] Since the approval of BiDil has raised serious concerns, these in turn may reflect unfavourably on EOp for health. In particular, the FDA's decision provoked a worry about turning what is essentially a social con-struct (race) into a medical category, potentially adding further to the stigma suffered in the USA by people of colour.[53] Does this case show that it is wrong to speak of natural inequalities in health? And, in turn, is EOp for health wrong for recommending such a policy? My answer is: not nec-essarily, and I want, in the rest of this section, to try and explain why.

I said that the data on which the FDA based its decision to approve BiDil was suspect. Now, suppose a significant correlation was indeed discovered between benefiting from the use of BiDil and being African-American. Still, correlation does not imply causation. It could be the case that race is operating here as a proxy for something else, such as income, education, diet, levels of physical exercise, or other such factors that would explain why black patients responded better than whites to the drug.[54] If that is the case, then perhaps the FDA was wrong to approve a drug designated for African Americans rather than what it should have done, which is to insist on finding out what the exact causal mechanism was. If it did the latter, BiDil could have been marketed for what it truly was, namely as a drug for 'heart patients who have a carbohydrate rich diet', or 'patients who do not

---

[51] For 2009, life expectancy for White American males was 76.2, and 70.9 for black males. Kenneth D. Kochanek, Jiaquan Xu, Sherry L. Murphy, Arialdi M. Miniño, and Hsiang-Ching Kung, 'Deaths: Preliminary Data for 2009', *National Vital Statistics Report* 59 (2011), 1–68.

[52] Daniels's approach, recall, calls for bringing everyone together up to perfect health (normal species functioning). Its focus, as far as I understand it, is on individuals rather than groups. EOp for health, in contrast, focuses on groups because it targets individuals who are ex ante worse-off. Given that life expectancy is for the most part a group-attribute, it follows that, in practice at least, targeting ex ante worse-off individuals translates into identifying *groups* that suffer low life expectancy. Hence, the endorsement by EOp for health of affirma-tive action in general, and such measures as BiDil in particular.

[53] See Jonathan Kahn, 'How a Drug Becomes "Ethnic": Law, Commerce, and the Production of Racial Categories in Medicine', *Yale Journal of Health Policy, Law, and Ethics* 4 (2004), 1–46. Cited by Deborah Hellman, *When is Discrimination Wrong?* (Cambridge, MA and London: Harvard University Press, 2008), p. 184.

[54] Hellman, *When is Discrimination Wrong?* p. 65.

have time to exercise', or even 'heart patients whose income falls below so and so'. (Of course, these options may be stigmatizing in their own right, and carry the risk of having the drug dubbed as one for 'the poor, fat, and lazy'.) And if that is the case then it also follows that the inequality which the drug was helping to correct was not a natural, but a social one.

Suppose, however, that 'black' is not a proxy here for something else. Suppose that BiDil is genuinely more effective for African-Americans due to some mysterious genetic factor.[55] Would then the FDA's decision to market it as such be the correct one? And, more to the point for us here, would such a decision reflect badly on 'EOp for health', given its insistence on curbing natural inequalities in health? With Deborah Hellman (who discusses this issue in the more general context of discrimination), I answer the first question in the affirmative. 'If the social category 'African-American' is helpful in predicting who will likely benefit from the drug and no other substitute can be found (such as diet or income), perhaps the use of this classification does not—after all—demean blacks.'[56] In other words, the use of racial categories would not only be medically warranted in this case, it would also not be morally suspect.[57] If certain ethnic or racial groups do have some unique biological attributes (which is, to be sure, a big 'if'), then offering members of such groups, on occasion, separate medical treatment would not be troublesome.

Moreover, I want to end by saying that developing drugs which are specifically targeted at such disadvantaged minority groups is a desirable policy precisely because it could be seen as a sort of 'affirmative action in health'. (I speak here only of medical research and not of health care

---

[55] More recent research has hypothesized that BiDil's increased effectiveness for African-Americans stems from the fact that people of that ethnic group are known to have lower levels of nitric oxide (NO) in their blood. Nitric oxide is a gas molecule in the air (and in the human blood) known to decrease the chances and severity of heart failure. Since the primary component of BiDil (Isosorbide dinitrate) has the effect of increasing the levels of nitric oxide, and the secondary (Hydralazine HCl) increases its effectiveness, it was hypothesized that a combination of both will have more effect on African-Americans. See Anne L. Taylor et al, 'Combination of Isosorbide Dinitrate and Hydralazine in Blacks with Heart Failure', *New England Journal of Medicine* 351 (2004), 2049–57.

[56] Hellman, *When is Discrimination Wrong?* p. 67.

[57] More generally on the permissibility of using racial categories in combating racism and other instances of inequalities, see Elizabeth Anderson, *The Imperative of Integration* (Princeton, NJ, and Oxford: Princeton University Press, 2010), ch. 8. Cf. Carl Cohen, 'Why Race Preference is Wrong and Bad', in his and James P. Sterba, *Affirmative Action and Racial Preference: A Debate* (New York: Oxford University Press, 2003), 3–188.

more generally.) Because blacks are typically worse-off health-wise (and otherwise), prioritizing their treatment becomes a requirement of EOp for health. This ties in nicely with a more general intuition we might have here. We may recall that historically, racial categories in medical research have been used to demean and disadvantage blacks (e.g. the infamous Tuskegee experiment). At the very least, we may say, the medical establishment has been less than attentive to the medical (and other) needs of racial minorities. In the ideal scenario we have been sketching here, the approval of BiDil could be seen as a corrective step.[58] So, rather than pointing out some weakness in the ideal of EOp for health, the case of 'drugs for blacks', we can see now, actually points out a potential advantage. Just as pursuing substantive (as opposed to merely formal) equality of opportunity in education has given us the ideal (and practice) of affirmative action, so the ideal of radical EOp for health allows us to start thinking in terms of affirmative action in health. It allows us to correct for persistent inequalities in health, whether owed to nature or to nurture (society).

Conclusion

Equality of opportunity for health can be an attractive alternative to traditional, Rawlsian, thinking of justice in health. It says that all inequalities in health are unjust unless chosen. My aim in this chapter has been to sketch the way in which this account might improve on the currently dominant approach, namely Norman Daniels's 'health care *as a means to* (fair) equality of opportunity' account. I have attempted to address here only two potential objections to EOp for health: the charge that EOp only regulates competitive goods, something which health is manifestly not; and the claim that EOp for health cannot rectify ill health that derives from natural factors (because it relies on the allegedly false concept of 'natural inequalities'). Both objections, I hope to have shown, are unpersuasive. If so, EOp for health, as well as its derivative ideal of affirmative action in health, might be a useful way of thinking of justice in health. The next (and last) chapter is devoted to exploring further the ideal of affirmative action in health.

---

[58] Another such measure, perhaps, is the recent project of genetic research known as the African Diaspora Biobank conducted at Howard University. See <www.genomecenter.howard.edu>.

9

Affirmative Action in Health

The ideal of equality of opportunity, as we just saw, has long been considered central to justice in health. Rawlsians, such as Norman Daniels, speak of health care as a means to (fair) equality of opportunity,[1] whereas luck egalitarians have suggested the (diametrically opposed) ideal of equality of opportunity *for* health.[2] Now, egalitarians (Rawlsians and luck egalitarians alike), as we saw in the Introduction, hold that to achieve substantive (rather than merely formal) equality of opportunity we must often practise affirmative action.[3] And yet, health equity and affirmative action have never (to my knowledge) been linked. My purpose in this final chapter, then, is to try and elucidate what 'affirmative action in health' might look like. I want to do so by constructing and juxtaposing Rawlsian and luck egalitarian accounts of affirmative action in health. The former I glean from Daniels's most recent work. He says there that we have a good reason to prioritize the medical needs of those whose ill health is the product of unjust social circumstances. I want to contrast Daniels's account of affirmative action in health with an alternative which speaks of prioritizing the needs of members of groups who ex ante face worse health prospects (African-Americans, say, and, somewhat more controversially, men).

The discussion to follow is premised on a number of assumptions for which I shall not argue. It assumes, of course, that health (and not just

---

[1] Norman Daniels, *Just Health Care* (Cambridge: Cambridge University Press, 1985).

[2] Julian LeGrande, 'Equity, Health, and Health Care,' *Social Justice Research* 1 (1987), 257–74; *Equity and Choice: An Essay in Economics and Applied Philosophy* (London: Harper Collins, 1991), ch. 7; John E. Roemer, *Equality of Opportunity* (Cambridge, MA: Harvard University Press, 1998), ch. 8; Shlomi Segall, *Health, Luck, and Justice* (Princeton NJ: Princeton University Press, 2010), ch. 7.

[3] Although, as I noted earlier, Rawls himself was rather sceptical with regard to affirmative action. He saw it as an acceptable interim remedial measure, but as incompatible with long-term application of his 'fair equality of opportunity'. See Robert S. Taylor, 'Rawlsian Affirmative Action', *Ethics* 119 (2009), 476–506.

health care) is a subject of justice,[4] and that health inequalities could be unjust.[5] In addition, the discussion also assumes that we may discuss health inequalities in isolation from other inequalities. Let me quickly qualify this last premiss. Health inequalities are not, obviously, the only morally significant inequalities. Nor are they necessarily more unjust than other inequalities (e.g. in income). (Although I do think that is not far off the mark, as health does seem to underwrite much of our welfare.)[6] Rather, the point of my assumption is to try and isolate the discussion of health inequalities for analytical, rather than practical purposes.

Section I presents Daniels's position, which amounts to what is often called the (left) liberal (or substantive) approach to affirmative action. Assessing that liberal approach as it applies to health entails examining the grounds underlying affirmative action. These normally divide between backward-looking and forward-looking considerations (recall our discussion in Chapter 5).[7] The rest of Section I assesses whether backward-looking considerations may ground a liberal approach to affirmative action in health. Concluding that they cannot, I turn, in Section II, to examine and rebut forward-looking justifications. Section III then presents and defends an alternative to liberal affirmative action in health, one, predictably, derived from the radical account of equality of opportunity.

I. Liberal Affirmative Action in Health

According to Daniels, all health inequalities are bad from a moral perspective. However, health inequalities that result from an unjust distribution of socially controllable factors affecting health are not merely bad but also unjust. We have a duty to reduce *all* health inequalities, but we have an 'extra reason', Daniels says, to reduce health inequalities when they are *inequities*, that is, when they are owed to an unjust distribution of the social determinants of health.[8] The principle yields concrete policy recommendations.

---

[4] See my *Health, Luck, and Justice*, ch. 6.

[5] See *Health, Luck, and Justice*, ch. 7.

[6] See also Amartya Sen, 'Why Health Equity?' *Health Economics* 11 (2002), 659–66.

[7] Although I concede to George Sher that not all arguments for affirmative action divide neatly into forward- and backward-looking. See his 'Diversity', *Philosophy and Public Affairs* 28 (1999), 85–104; *Approximate Justice: Studies in Non-Ideal Theory* (Lanham, MA: Rowman & Littlefield, 1997), ch. 6.

[8] 'There is considerable force to the claim that we should increase the priority we grant to those whose health is worse if this is a result of racist or sexist policy or individual acts of racism or sexism.' *Just Health: Meeting Health Needs Fairly* (Cambridge: Cambridge University

Suppose we are faced with two equally needy patients, where one's neediness is the result of natural factors whereas the other's ill health is due to racism or (unjust) poverty. It follows from Daniels's principle that we must assign priority to the latter patient. Admittedly, he acknowledges that this reason might be outweighed by other considerations.[9] Daniels in fact goes as far as to say that some people may plausibly think that we ought to give *no* priority to the patient who is a victim of racism. He thus concludes that whether or not the victim of racism ought to be given priority over the patient whose illness is no one's fault is something over which there might be reasonable disagreement,[10] and that, consequently, this ought to be subject to a deliberative decision mechanism.

Contra Daniels, I want to claim that there is *no* room for reasonable disagreement over the case in question, and that it would be wrong (because unjust) to give priority to the patient who is the victim of racism (call her Rachel) over the patient who is the victim of ordinary bad luck (call her Lucy).[11] One way of teasing this out, I suggest, is to try and frame the issue in the second-person perspective introduced in Chapter 1. In other words, we should try and imagine how things would look from Lucy's perspective once we have automatically[12] passed over her in favour of Rachel (on account of the particular social circumstances that have led to Rachel's illness). To examine the case in its pure form, we must assume, of course,

---

Press, 2008), p. 304. In a later piece he writes: 'we now owe remedy to the worse off for two weighty reasons of justice, not one. This fact of extra reasons might translate into giving them more priority than they would otherwise have had.' 'Reducing Health Disparities: No Simple Matter', in Eyal, Nir, Hurst, Samia A., Firhtjof Norheim, Ole and Wikler, Daniel (eds), *Inequalities in Health: Concepts, Measures, and Ethics* (Oxford: Oxford University Press, 2013), p. 7.

[9] He says: 'Although we may give additional priority to meeting a group's health needs if they are the result of unjust social practices, we cannot give their needs complete priority.' *Just Health*, p. 305.

[10] 'Reasonable people will continue to disagree about how much additional priority to grant. Some of this disagreement may be the result of the original disagreement about how to make the trade-offs in the morally neutral distributive problems. But some of it may be the result of disagreement about how much weight to give to the underlying fact of injustice, be it race or gender based.' *Just Health*, pp. 305–6.

[11] Interestingly, this is a position that Daniels seemed to endorse in the past. In a much earlier piece he wrote that Rawlsian fair equality of opportunity requires the elimination of both social impediments as well as 'other biological or social accidents', 'Merit and Meritocracy', *Philosophy and Public Affairs* 7 (1978), p. 217.

[12] As I said, Daniels allows that prioritizing Rachel over Lucy is not automatic. Since he talks about 'non-absolute priority' it follows that we may adopt here something like a weighted lottery.

that Lucy was not directly complicit in the racist or otherwise unjust social practice that has led to Rachel's disadvantaged health status. And we must also assume, note, that Lucy did not benefit in any way from Rachel's disadvantage.[13] Under those circumstances, Lucy may plausibly say that it is *not her fault* that Rachel was a victim of racism. Moreover, now that she is placed behind Rachel in priority for medical treatment, Lucy wishes that she herself had been the victim of racism! (That is, she would prefer it to simply being the victim of bad old luck in the natural lottery of genes.) Giving priority to Rachel over Lucy thus seems arbitrary and unjust.[14] We might even say (to use Daniels's deliberative terminology)[15] that there is nothing reasonable we could say to Lucy to convince her that she was not discriminated against.

Notice that what I have just said obtains solely for the allocation of medical treatments, and not to any other form of compensation we can think of. This is important, because I do not want to deny that Rachel did suffer a more grave injustice, overall, compared to Lucy. Her ill health is, most likely, accompanied by the harm entailed in being the victim of racism. Moreover, a preference for Rachel may represent a blow to the racists who have imposed that harm on her. All these, I want to say, are weighty considerations in responding to the case, but all can (and should) be accommodated by means other than medical care. As far as access to medical care is concerned, it remains doubtful that being a victim of social injustice ought to give one an advantage over those suffering natural bad luck.[16]

Now, one thing that could be said in support of Daniels's position, and in favour of giving priority to Rachel (the victim of social injustice), is, indeed, to invoke affirmative action. We often do assign priority to those who were the victims of social injustice, so the claim goes, and crucially,

---

[13] Daniels makes a similar assumption. *Just Health*, p. 304.

[14] Rawlsians sometime say that addressing natural and not merely social inequalities places over-demanding burdens on those who are naturally gifted. [See for example, Christian Schemmel, 'Distributive and Relational Equality', *Politics, Philosophy, & Economics* 11 (2012), p. 132.] This might provide one reason to think that Rachel should be preferred to Lucy. But even if we thought the rationale was generally appealing (which I don't), it is hard to see why we ought to apply it in this case. Tossing a coin between Lucy and Rachel does not seem to over-burden members of society relative to simply prioritizing Rachel.

[15] See Norman Daniels and James Sabin, 'Limits to Health Care: Fair Procedures, Democratic Deliberation, and the Legitimacy Problem for Insurers', *Philosophy and Public Affairs* 26 (1997), 303–50.

[16] I am grateful to Zofia Stemplowska for pressing me on this point.

over and above equally suitable individuals who did not suffer such injustices. Just think of standard cases of affirmative action where among equally qualified candidates we opt for the one who belongs to a group that has suffered some historical injustice. Recall, for example, the landmark Bakke case (1978) in which a medical school (as it happens) practised quotas for African-Americans, in the name of affirmative action. The court, admittedly, ruled in favour of Bakke (on rather technical grounds), but nevertheless established that, in principle, majority candidates have no legitimate complaint against the policy of affirmative action even when they are equally qualified compared to the candidate that was ultimately chosen.[17] The practice of affirmative action is, of course, not beyond dispute but it is certainly not prima facie implausible. And that, crucially, is all that Daniels needs to show here. (Since, as we saw, his claim is that the priority of those suffering a social disadvantage over those suffering a natural one is something that ought to be subject to deliberation, because reasonable people may disagree over how much priority needs to be accorded.) If we think it is right (as the US Supreme Court evidently did) to allow for priority to be given to the minority candidate who was no more qualified than Bakke, then at the very least, one might say, it is not implausible to assign Rachel (the victim of racism) priority over Lucy (the victim of brute luck). If we ask, then, what affirmative action in health could possibly mean, the (reconstructed) Rawlsian answer would be: of two equally needy patients give priority to the one who suffered from social injustice.

I do not think, however, that we ought to give priority to Rachel, and I further doubt that we may derive such priority from any parallel one might draw from affirmative action in higher education. To see this it would be useful to recall the various potential rationales for affirmative action. These conventionally divide between backward-looking and forward-looking considerations. A typical *backward*-looking argument for affirmative action says that it compensates the minority candidate for some past disadvantages (whether suffered by him personally or by the group to which he belongs).[18] (This

<hr/>

[17] See Ronald Dworkin, *A Matter of Principle* (Cambridge, MA, and London: Harvard University Press, 1985), ch. 14.

[18] Notice that I speak of 'disadvantage' rather than 'injustice' because backward-looking justifications need not rely on a past injustice. They may, for example, strive to correct the outcome of a just lottery. Suppose that at time T we had to distribute an indivisible good A between groups X and Y, and X won the fair lottery. This gives us a reason, at time T+1 to award group Y with some good B. This can be seen as a measure of affirmative action,

rationale for affirmative action is not beyond controversy, of course, but we are setting such reservations aside for the sake of argument.) On this rationale, the minority candidate would have been even more qualified than the (currently) equally qualified majority candidate, had it not been for the past racism, say. Among other things, this argument clearly shows why affirmative action does not, in fact, discriminate against the white (majority) candidate. This rationale, however, does not apply easily to the case before us. It is *not* the case that Rachel would have been more deserving of the treatment (or of priority for the treatment) than Lucy had it not been for the social injustice. If anything, it is quite the opposite. If it wasn't for the racial injustice, Rachel would have been healthier, and as such, would have deserved *lower* priority for the treatment. There seems, then, to be an asymmetry between merit (an arguably determining factor in higher education) and need (a determining factor in the allocation of health care). Merit and need, in other words, pull in opposite directions.

It could be objected, though, that I haven't interpreted the case before us correctly. One might say, instead, that what is at stake here is not the entitlement to the medical *care*, but the entitlement to the health *status* in question. If it wasn't for the social injustice, Rachel would indeed have had better health, but that is precisely why she has a stronger claim to that level of health. That is why she ought to be given priority in the competition for the scarce medical care. It is, therefore, not a question of need but indeed one of merit, owing to the imperative of restoring one to the position one would have occupied in the absence of social injustice. This revised claim also reveals a nice symmetry with affirmative action in employment and higher education. On this interpretation, affirmative action (in office) does not, in fact, undermine meritocracy (i.e. the appointment of the best qualified) because it rewards those who *would have been* the most qualified if it was not for the systematic past discrimination against members of this group. Similarly, we might say that affirmative action in health restores individuals' health prospects to what they would have been if it wasn't for the social injustice. Affirmative action thus operates here as a restorative device.

---

based on backward-looking considerations, and one which need not necessarily correct for an injustice. I am grateful to Dan Hausman for pointing this out to me. [Although I still want to register that, in my view, the outcome of the lottery *would be* unfair (recall my discussion of total EOp).]

Notice, then, that what affirmative action accomplishes here is the removal of (arbitrary) social obstacles to individuals' ability to enjoy the fruits of their innate good health. This, again, is in parallel with meritocracy in employment and education. Meritocrats (including left-liberals such as Rawls) strive to level the playing field between equally talented individuals in the pursuit of jobs and university places for which their talents qualify them. The point of affirmative action on this reading, then, is to correct the distortion brought on by social injustice. Equally, then, a proponent of Daniels's approach might say, the point of affirmative action in health is to level the playing field, as it were, between individuals who possess equal genetic makeup, in their pursuit of a long and healthy life. But once such a parallel is drawn, the problematic implications become easy to spot. To begin with, while meritocracy in employment is certainly not implausible, neither is it beyond doubt, as we have seen in Chapter 4. One might say (as David Miller does) that the talented deserve the better jobs for which they are qualified.[19] And alternatively, one might say (as Rawls did)[20] that, while not itself a requirement of justice, it would *not be unjust* to assign the good jobs to the talented. Yet, however persuasive these claims are (and my view, recall Chapter 4, is that, ultimately, they are not), both lose force when applied to health. It is one thing (for critics of EOp in health) to claim that justice *does not require* equalizing health between the genetically lucky and unlucky. But it is quite another matter to hold that the genetically endowed *deserve* better health, compared to the genetically worse-off. It is hard to see a reason why there would be such a requirement of justice. To put this differently, one may claim (falsely, as the previous chapter sought to show, but leave that aside) that it is permissible to allow the genetically endowed to enjoy their better health. But it is a different matter altogether to claim that health policy should be structured in such a way as to *ensure* that the genetically endowed can enjoy their better innate health. It is not obvious why the winner of the natural lottery (in genes) deserves to have her natural advantage reinforced by institutional means.

One reason invoked by Rawls in defence of his 'careers open to talent' which might be relevant here is that levelling the playing field only

[19] David Miller, *Principles of Social Justice* (Cambridge, MA: Harvard University Press, 1999), chs. 7, 8.
[20] John Rawls, *A Theory of Justice* (Oxford: Clarendon Press, 1972), p. 84.

between equally talented individuals is likely to benefit society as a whole. (Notice, by the way, that with this reply we are edging to the realm of forward-looking considerations.) It is useful, from society's point of view, to allocate competitive positions of employment and higher education to the best talented. But the case is far less clear when applied to health. There might be a utilitarian case for allocating scarce medical care to those who are genetically superior, since it may produce more overall life-years. But this is not the case in our example: ex hypothesi, Lucy and Rachel will derive equal benefit from the treatment. There does not, therefore, seem to be any social value in prioritizing the naturally-gifted in this case.

II. Forward-Looking Considerations for Affirmative Action

Let us, then, turn to examine forward-looking considerations, and assess whether they may support Rawlsian affirmative action in health. Affirmative action in higher education and employment is sometimes said to be motivated by the social value entailed in boosting the representation of some historically excluded groups.[21] We commonly think that there are substantial benefits to having academic faculty, say, proportionally drawn from both genders and from the various ethnic and racial groups that make up society. (This is the case, notice, whether or not any of these groups were themselves subject to past injustices.) Consider how well (or poorly) this rationale applies to health. There is certainly social disvalue in the fact that different ethnic groups enjoy unequal levels of healthy life expectancy.[22] And quite apart from the egalitarian imperative of narrowing down these inequalities, there does, admittedly, seem to be some instrumental value in achieving greater racial equality in life expectancy. But this, notice, does not yet mean that there is social benefit to having the group of 'treated patients' (or even 'cured patients') made up of all strands of society. One potential benefit of having the group of 'treated patients' mirror the

---

[21] Elizabeth Anderson has a good discussion of this in *The Imperative of Integration* (Princeton, NJ, and Oxford: Princeton University Press, 2010), ch. 7.

[22] Just to give one example, in Belgium, Walloon males have a life expectancy that is lower than Flemish males. Life expectancy at 15 was 73.9 for Flemish males, as opposed to 71.6 for Walloon males. T. Van Oyen, J. Tafforeau, and M. Roelands, 'Regional Inequities in Health Expectancy in Belgium', *Social Science and Medicine* 43 (11) (1996), 1673–8.

makeup of society as a whole is that it allows medical staff the opportunity to interact with diverse patients, each representing different cultures and sensibilities, thus adding to the professional training of doctors and nurses. But note that this instrumental rationale does not give us a reason to draw patients *proportionately* from all segments of society, but only to have significant numbers of them so as to allow contact with medical staff.

A related forward-looking consideration for affirmative action often invoked in the literature is the 'role-model' effect.[23] Having more women and members of ethnic minorities as academic faculty, medical doctors, and CEOs sends an important message to young members of these groups that they may, and should, strive for these positions. But again this does not seem to be true in the case of health. While higher education and jobs carry some prestige, health typically does not. Individuals do not normally gain social status merely by being healthy. This fact explains why this forward-looking consideration for affirmative action does not apply to health. Now, it might be said that contrary to my assertion, health does carry some prestige. This is manifested, for example, in the case of bad teeth, which often carry a social stigma. But notice that whatever stigma bad teeth may have hinges on the particular medical condition and not on the *level* of health that it may manifest. This is further evidenced in the fact that some medical conditions carry prestige rather than stigma, such as broken legs around college winter break. It is the particular condition, not the level of health that tracks the stigma (or prestige). In that respect, health is different from goods such as income or employment, where (at least some of) the prestige resides in the quantity of the good the person controls. So while certain medical conditions (bad teeth, mental illness) do obviously carry negative stigma, a low level of health, in and of itself, does not. (Health of the lowest level, namely death, often brings prestige rather than shame to the person in question.)

<hr />

[23] Dworkin, *A Matter of Principle*, p. 295. George Sher says that the 'role model' argument is in fact a backward-looking argument for affirmative action, for it is worrisome that individuals prefer against seeking high office only to the extent that such disadvantageous preferences are shaped by oppression and discrimination in the past. (See George Sher, 'Diversity', pp. 95–6.) While I agree with the observation, I think it merely makes the role model argument a mix of backward- and forward-looking consideration. For the argument would not have worked if past oppression led only to static disadvantage, without also endangering future enrolment in high office and academia. (The latter point explains, I think, why we don't normally think that American Jews, say, despite their past discrimination in academia, should benefit from affirmative action.)

Forward-looking considerations do not easily map on in the case of health. To see the point more fully, consider cases where there are reasons to think that affirmative action (and anti-discrimination legislation more generally) may effectively narrow one type of inequality but, at the same time, exacerbate another. It is often noted, for example, that affirmative action benefits women and minorities at the cost of widening socio-economic gaps. The reason for this is that it is often those who are already privileged and well-connected who are in a position to take advantage of the opportunities introduced by affirmative action.[24] But despite recognizing that affirmative action may well widen socio-economic gaps, we normally still think it is right to pursue it. And one reason that may explain why we feel that way is that we think of the long-term benefits of smashing the glass ceiling that might be restricting the employment of women and members of ethnic minorities. We also often think that hiring more women and people of colour will not only reduce gender- and racial-inequality here and now, but would also trickle down (because of the role-model effect) and, in the long term, increase opportunities for women and blacks (say) of *all* socio-economic classes. It is largely for this reason that proponents of affirmative action are not deterred by its short-term effect of widening socio-economic inequalities. This rationale, however, does *not* seem to obtain in the case of health. Health, as I said, carries no prestige,[25] and having more of it is unlikely to have any role-model effect on those lacking it. Having more faculty members that are black is different, in that sense, from extending African-American life expectancy from 65 to 67. The ambitions and life-plans of young African-Americans may well be affected by the perception of more visible black individuals on University faculty; their ambitions and prospective life-plans are unlikely to change dramatically upon learning of the added two years to their life expectancy. Affirmative action in health cannot therefore be motivated by a consideration for breaking down some glass ceiling in the health gains of disadvantaged groups. To put this differently, we find it repugnant that life expectancy in some neighbourhoods of Glasgow is twelve years or so

[24] James S. Fishkin, *Justice, Equal Opportunity, and the Family* (New Haven, CN and London: Yale University Press, 1983), p. 130; Alan H. Goldman, 'Affirmative Action', *Philosophy and Public Affairs* 5 (1976), p. 191.

[25] See also Avishai Margalit, *The Decent Society* (Cambridge, MA, and London: Harvard University Press, 1996), pp. 241–2.

shorter than in the more affluent neighbourhoods of that city. And we do think that narrowing down that gap is valuable in itself (even while recognizing that this value may not always trump other values such as that of aggregate health, thus potentially resisting levelling down). But, crucially, we do not normally think that narrowing that gap will serve the end of smashing some imagined glass ceiling in some group's life expectancy. Narrowing inequalities in health between salient groups has an intrinsic value, but little or no instrumental value, it seems.

In considering backward-looking considerations (in the previous section) we witnessed the disanalogy between merit and need. In reviewing forward looking considerations, we now see the disanalogy between the expressive value in affirmative action in employment, compared with the absence of any such value in health. This disanalogy has some concrete implications, some of which may prove controversial. Suppose we are forced to choose between policy X which would benefit middle class black men and policy Y which would benefit poor white men. Measure X is likely, then, to decrease racial inequality in health, but increase class inequality, whereas measure Y will achieve the exact opposite effect. Which should we prefer? If we were discussing employment, we would probably opt for policy X (the one narrowing racial inequalities). The reason is that that policy has the additional expressive effect, and as such it is more likely, in the long term, to reduce overall inequalities (that is, both racial and class-based), precisely because of the role-model effect. In the case of health, I think, the choice is made easier, in a way, by the absence of such expressive value. In the absence of glass ceilings to break, we should simply find out which measure benefits those who are worse-off (which, in this example, may well be policy Y).

III. Radical Affirmative Action in Health

The liberal ideal of affirmative action does not seem very suitable to health. Consider, then, the alternative account. Recall that one thing that distinguishes radical from substantive EOp is that the former 'treats the inequality that arises out of native difference as a further source of injustice'.[26]

---

[26] G. A. Cohen, *Why Not Socialism?* (Princeton, NJ: Princeton University Press, 2009), p. 17.

Applied to health, radical affirmative action would strive to assign priority to those whose need is caused by an ex ante worse-off health prospect, whether generated by social or natural factors. We know, for example, that being poor, black, male, and so forth entails worse health prospects. Radical affirmative action in health directs us, then, to improve the health prospects of members of these groups. I should quickly qualify this, though. This ideal of affirmative action is meant to inform health policy rather than medical care narrowly understood. The suggestion here is not to practise affirmative action at the bed-side. For rather obvious reasons, it might not be such a good idea for doctors and nurses to prioritize patients on the basis of anything but their medical condition, let alone on the basis of race, sex, and socio-economic status. My suggestion escapes, I hope, this undesirable effect by focusing on the way in which health policy is set up rather than the way in which health care is delivered. (In any case, in this respect Daniels's account and mine rise and fall together.)

Notice also that the contrast between Daniels's account and mine applies not only domestically but also globally. Whichever account we adopt is something that has potential implications for aid policy in developing countries. Luck egalitarians commonly think that individuals ought to have equal opportunities, including opportunities for health, no matter where they happen to be born.[27] This has potential implications for priority-setting in global health policy. Suppose health-aid institutions (say, the WHO) are forced to decide between two countries, Colonia and Independensia. The former's low health status is a legacy of its colonial past, where its resources have been ransacked and its civil society undermined by the colonial power. Independensia, in contrast, had no colonial past, but rather has suffered a series of droughts (none of them owed to human agency), which has left its population malnourished and stunted. Assuming life expectancy is equally low in both countries, Daniels's principle would give priority to Colonia. But we may similarly anticipate the reaction on the part of the citizens of Independensia to such hypothetical WHO policy, possibly expressing regret over never having a colonial power rule over them. If all this is convincing, then, contra Daniels, it seems that countries whose disadvantaged life expectancy is owed to natural factors deserve the exact same priority as countries

[27] Simon Caney, 'Cosmopolitan Justice and Equalizing Opportunities', *Metaphilosophy* 32 (2001), 113–34.

whose low health is owed to unjust international practices.[28] Looked at from the perspectives of such developing nations, I suggest, it does not matter whether one's short life expectancy is owed to a ruinous colonial past or to some unfortunate act of nature.

Now, it might be suggested that some of the general objections to liberal affirmative action are true also of radical affirmative action in health. A common objection to affirmative action, we saw in Chapter 5, says that its direct beneficiaries have often not themselves suffered any disadvantage. Critics, thus, often point out that it is mostly middle-class blacks, for example, who benefit from practising affirmative action in higher education. And it is, furthermore, doubtful that these individuals are more deserving than some other poor white candidates. The ideal of radical affirmative action in health that I have defended can be said to suffer from the same objection. A health policy that prioritizes blacks as a rule may end up benefiting some such patients who happen to be healthier than some more deserving white patients. This might motivate an objection, say, to public sponsorship of BiDil (the drug for a heart condition that is said to be particularly effective for African-Americans). Of course, one thing to note is that this objection also afflicts the other account of affirmative action in health. Recall that Daniels's account prioritizes medical needs that are the product of unjust social practices, which he proposes to do by targeting socially disadvantaged groups. It is implausible, and Daniels indeed does not recommend doing so, to identify *individuals* who have suffered some social injustice. So that proposal, as indeed any account of affirmative action, is likely to be vulnerable to the objection that it would sometimes benefit well off members of worse off groups. But there is something else we should note. While affirmative action targets groups (or individuals qua members of groups), it is, to be sure, individuals as such that it is ultimately concerned with. That was true for affirmative action in employment and higher education, and is, moreover, also the case with regard to health (moreover so because of the absence of the

[28] Both would count as 'circumstance' or 'bad brute luck' and as such equally deserve to be neutralized. For a luck-egalitarian-informed approach to international aid which emphasizes the contrast between circumstance and choice, see Humberto G. Llavador and John E. Roemer, 'An Equal-Opportunity Approach to the Allocation of International Aid', *Journal of Development Economics* 64 (2001), 147–71. Roemer applies the same model to health aid in *Distributing Health: The Allocation of Resources by an International Agency* (Washington, DC: World Institute for Development Economics Research of the United Nations University, 1989).

abovementioned expressive value in breaking glass ceilings). The reason behind health policy targeting groups rather than individuals is a practical rather than a principled one. The currency of health inequalities is healthy life expectancy. And so long as (technically speaking) this is an attribute of groups rather than individuals, affirmative action in health could target individuals qua members of groups and not individuals as such. Notice, though, that with the advent of medical research, we are likely to be able to have an increasingly refined account of healthy life expectancy. This fact, we can see, casts a more favourable light on the radical account than it does on Daniels's, because radical affirmative action is not restricted to salient groups who have suffered some social injustice. An account whose concern is social *as well as* natural sources of ill health may therefore appeal to a snapshot of groups that is as refined and specific as can be. Returning to the example of BiDil, we may identify not only African-Americans but 'African-Americans with an income below $40k a year' as the worse-off, health-wise, group in society. And if, crucially, we can devise health measures that would target such a specific group, the radical account of affirmative action in health would endorse it.

Conclusion

Endorsing the ideal of equality of opportunity in the sphere of health gives rise to the practice of affirmative action. I have contrasted, in this chapter, two accounts of affirmative action in health. The first, Norman Daniels's liberal affirmative action, sought to prioritize patients whose medical condition is the result of social injustice. The other, radical, account sought to prioritize the needs of all patients who ex ante face worse-off health prospects, whether owed to social *or* natural factors. I hope to have shown that radical affirmative action in health is the more defensible and attractive of the two ideals.

References

Ackerman, Bruce, 1980. *Social Justice in the Liberal State*. New Haven: Yale University Press.

Alexander, Larry, 1992. What Makes Wrongful Discrimination Wrong? Biases, Preferences, Stereotypes, and Proxies. *University of Pennsylvania Law Review*, 141, 149–219.

Amnesty International, *Betraying the Young: Children in the US Justice System*, November 1998, <http://www.amnesty.org/en/library/asset/AMR51/060/1998/en/fd7dc551-d9bc-11dd-af2b-b1f6023af0c5/amr510601998en.pdf>.

Anderson, Elizabeth, 1999. What is the Point of Equality? *Ethics*, 109, 287–337.

Anderson, Elizabeth, 2004. Rethinking Equality of Opportunity: Comment on Adam Swift's How Not to Be a Hypocrite. *Theory and Research in Education*, 2, 99–110.

Anderson, Elizabeth, 2007. Fair Opportunity in Education: A Democratic Equality Perspective. *Ethics* 117, 595–622.

Anderson, Elizabeth, 2008. How Should Egalitarians Cope with Market Risks? *Theoretical Inquiries in Law*, 9, 239–70.

Anderson, Elizabeth, 2010. The Fundamental Disagreement between Luck Egalitarians and Relational Egalitarians. *Canadian Journal of Philosophy*, 36, 1–23.

Anderson, Elizabeth, 2010. *The Imperative of Integration*. Princeton, NJ: Princeton University Press.

Arneson, Richard J., 1989. Equality and Equality of Opportunity for Welfare. *Philosophical Studies*, 56, 77–93.

Arneson, Richard J., 1990. Liberalism, Distributive Subjectivism, and Equal Opportunity for Welfare. *Philosophy and Public Affairs* 19, 158–94.

Arneson, Richard J., 1997. Equality and Equal Opportunity for Welfare: A Postscript. In Pojman, Louis P., and Westmoreland, Robert (eds), *Equality: Selected Reading*. New York and Oxford: Oxford University Press, 229–41.

Arneson, Richard J., 1999. Against Rawlsian Equality of Opportunity. *Philosophical Studies*, 93, 77–112.

Arneson, Richard J., 1999. Egalitarianism and Responsibility. *The Journal of Ethics*, 3, 225–47.

Arneson, Richard J., 1999. Equality of Opportunity for Welfare Defended and Recanted. *Journal of Political Philosophy*, 7, 488–97.

Arneson, Richard J., 2000. Luck Egalitarianism and Prioritarianism. *Ethics*, 110, 339–49.

Arneson, Richard J., 2001. Luck and Equality. *Proceedings of the Aristotelian Society*, Supplement, 75, 73–90.

Arneson, Richard J., 2002. Equality of Opportunity. *The Stanford Encyclopaedia of Philosophy*. <http://plato.stanford.edu/entries/equal-opportunity>.

Arneson, Richard J., 2006. What is Wrongful Discrimination? *San Diego Law Review*, 43, 775–807.

Arneson, Richard J., 2007. Desert and Equality. In Holtug, Nils, and Lippert-Rasmussen, Kasper (eds), *Egalitarianism: New Essays on the Nature and Value of Equality*. Oxford: Oxford University Press, 262–93.

Arneson, Richard J., 2008. Justice is not Equality. *Ratio*, 21, 371–91.

Arrow, Kenneth, Bowles, Samuel, and Durlauf, Steven (eds), 2000. *Meritocracy and Economic Inequality*. Princeton, NJ: Princeton University Press.

Australian Institute of Criminology, *The Age of Criminal Responsibility*, No. 121 November 2000, <http://www.aic.gov.au/documents/0/0/A/%7B00A92691-0 908-47BF-9311-01AD743F01E1%7Dti181.pdf>.

Barry, Nicholas, 2008. Reassessing Luck Egalitarianism. *The Journal of Politics*, 70, 136–50.

Berlin, Isaiah, 1956. Equality. *Proceedings of the Aristotelian Society*, 56, 301–26.

Bou-Habib, Paul, 2011. Racial Profiling and Background Injustice. *The Journal of Ethics*, 15, 33–46.

Bowles, Samuel, Gintis, Herbert, and Osborne-Groves, Melissa (eds), 2005. *Unequal Chances: Family Background and Economic Success*. Princeton, NJ: Princeton University Press.

Brighouse, Harry, 2000. *School Choice and Social Justice*. Oxford: Oxford University Press.

Brighouse, Harry, and Swift, Adam, 2006. Equality, Priority, and Positional Goods. *Ethics*, 116, 471–97.

Brighouse, Harry, and Swift, Adam, 2006. Parents' Rights and the Value of the Family. *Ethics*, 117, 80–108.

Brighouse, Harry, and Swift, Adam, 2008. Legitimate Parental Partiality. *Philosophy and Public Affairs*, 37, 43–80.

Brighouse, Harry, and Swift, Adam, 2009. Educational Equality versus Educational Adequacy: A Critique of Anderson and Satz. *Journal of Applied Philosophy*, 26, 117–28.

Broome, John, 1984. Selecting People Randomly. *Ethics*, 95, 38–55.

Broome, John, 1990. Fairness. *Proceedings of the Aristotelian Society*, 91, 87–101.

Buchanan, Allen, 1984. The Right to a Decent Minimum of Health Care. *Philosophy and Public Affairs*, 13, 55–78.

Cake, Helen M., 1972. Palmer vs. Thompson: Everybody Out of the Pool! *Hastings Law Journal*, 23, 889–912.

Caney, Simon, 2001. Cosmopolitan Justice and Equalizing Opportunities. *Metaphilosophy*, 32, 113–34.

Cappelen, Alexander W., 2005. Responsibility and International Distributive Justice. In Follesdal, Andreas, and Pogge, Thomas (eds), *Real World Justice: Grounds, Principles, Human Rights, and Social Institutions*. Dordrecht: Springer, 215–28.

Cappelen, Alexander W., and Norheim, Ole F., 2005. Responsibility in Health Care: A Liberal Egalitarian Approach. *Journal of Medical Ethics*, 31, 476–80.

Cappelen, Alexander W., and Tungodden, Bertil, 2006. A Liberal Egalitarian Paradox. *Economics and Philosophy*, 22, 393–408.

Cappelen, Alexander W., and Tungodden, Bertil, 2006. Relocating the Responsibility Cut: Should More Responsibility Imply Less Redistribution? *Politics, Philosophy, & Economics*, 5, 353–62.

Carens, Joseph H., 1981. *Equality, Moral Incentives, and the Market*. Chicago: University of Chicago Press.

Carens, Joseph H., 1986. Rights and Duties in an Egalitarian Society. *Political Theory*, 14, 31–49.

Carter, Ian, 2011. Respect and the Basis of Equality. *Ethics*, 121, 538–71.

Casal, Paula, 2007. Why Sufficiency is Not Enough. *Ethics*, 117, 296–326.

Cavallero, Eric, 2011. Health, Luck, and Moral Fallacies of the Second Best. *The Journal of Ethics*, 15, 387–403.

Cavanagh, Matt, 2002. *Against Equality of Opportunity*. Oxford: Oxford University Press.

Chambers, Clare, 2009. Each Outcome is Another Opportunity: Problems with the Moment of Equal Opportunity. *Politics, Philosophy, & Economics*, 8, 374–400.

Child Justice Act 75 of 2008, <www.info.gov.za/view/DownloadFileAction?id=108691>.

Children and Young Persons Act 1963, <http://www.legislation.gov.uk/ukpga/1963/37>.

Children, Young Persons, and Their Families Act 1989, <http://www.legisla-tion.govt.nz/act/public/1989/0024/latest/DLM153418.html?search=qs_act_murder+manslaughter+10+years_resel&p=1&sr=1>.

Christiano, Thomas, 1999. Comment on Elizabeth Anderson's 'What Is the Point of Equality?' <http://www.brown.edu/Departments/Philosophy/bears/9904chri.html>.

Christiano, Thomas, 2007. A Foundation for Egalitarianism. In Holtug, Nils, and Lippert-Rasmussen, Kasper (eds), *Egalitarianism: New Essays on the Nature and Value of Equality*. Oxford: Oxford University Press, 41–82.

Christiano, Thomas, 2008. *The Constitution of Equality: Democratic Authority and its Limits*. Oxford: Oxford University Press.

Clayton, Matthew, 2012. Equality, Justice, and Legitimacy in Selection. *The Journal of Moral Philosophy*, 9, 8–30.

Cohen, Carl, and Sterba, James P., 2003. *Affirmative Action and Racial Preference: A Debate*. New York: Oxford University Press.

Cohen, Gerald A., 1989. On the Currency of Egalitarian Justice. *Ethics*, 99, 906–44.

Cohen, Gerald A., 1992. Incentives, Inequality, and Community. *The Tanner Lectures on Human Values*, 13, 263–329.

Cohen, Gerald A., 2001. Why Not Socialism? In Broadbent, Edward (ed.), *Democratic Equality: What Went Wrong?* Toronto: University of Toronto Press, 58–78.

Cohen, Gerald A., 2006. Casting the First Stone: Who Can and Who Can't Condemn the Terrorists. *Royal Institute of Philosophy Supplement*, 58, 113–36.

Cohen, Gerald A., 2006. Luck and Equality: A Reply to Hurley. *Philosophy and Phenomenological Research*, 72, 439–46.

Cohen, Gerald A., 2008. *Rescuing Justice and Equality*. Cambridge, MA: Harvard University Press.

Cohen, Gerald A., 2009. *Why Not Socialism?* Princeton, NJ and Oxford: Princeton University Press.

Cohen, Gerald A., 2011. *On the Currency of Egalitarian Justice, and Other Essays in Political Philosophy*. Princeton, NJ and Oxford: Princeton University Press.

Crisp, Roger, 2003. Equality, Priority, and Compassion. *Ethics*, 113, 745–63.

Daniels, Norman, 1978. Merit and Meritocracy. *Philosophy and Public Affairs* 7, 206–23.

Daniels, Norman, 1985. *Just Health Care*. Cambridge: Cambridge University Press.

Daniels, Norman, 2008. *Just Health: Meeting Health Needs Fairly*. Cambridge: Cambridge University Press.

Daniels, Norman, 2013. Reducing Health Disparities: No Simple Matter. In Eyal, Nir, Hurst, Samia A., Norheim, Ole Frithjof, and Wikler, Daniel (eds), *Inequalities in Health: Concepts, Measures, and Ethics*. Oxford: Oxford University Press.

Daniels, Norman, and Sabin, James, 1997. Limits to Health Care: Fair Procedures, Democratic Deliberation, and the Legitimacy Problem for Insurers. *Philosophy and Public Affairs*, 26, 303–50.

de-Shalit, Avner, and Reshef, Yonathan, 2009. A Review of Andrew Mason's 'Levelling the Playing Field: The Idea of Equality of Opportunity and its Place in Egalitarian Thought'. *Philosophical Quarterly*, 59, 756–60.

de-Shalit, Avner, and Wolff, Jonathan, 2011. The Apparent Asymmetry of Responsibility. In Knight, Carl, and Stemplowska, Zofia (eds), *Responsibility and Distributive Justice*. Oxford: Oxford University Press, 216–29.

Dworkin, Ronald, 1985. *A Matter of Principle.* Cambridge, MA and London: Harvard University Press.

Dworkin, Ronald, 2000. *Sovereign Virtue: The Theory and Practice of Equality.* Cambridge, MA: Harvard University Press.

Dworkin, Ronald, 2011. *Justice for Hedgehogs.* Cambridge, MA and London: The Belknap Press of Harvard University Press.

Estlund, David, 1998. Liberalism, Equality and Fraternity in Cohen's Critique of Rawls. *The Journal of Political Philosophy,* 6, 99–112.

Eyal, Nir, 2003. *Distributing Respect.* Oxford: Oxford University DPhil Thesis.

Eyal, Nir, 2005. A Review of S. L. Hurley's 'Justice, Luck, and Knowledge'. *Economics and Philosophy,* 21, 164–71.

Eyal, Nir, 2007. Egalitarian Justice and Innocent Choice. *Journal of Ethics and Social Philosophy,* 2, 1–18.

Fishkin, James, 1983. *Justice, Equal Opportunity, and the Family.* New Haven, CN: Yale University Press.

Fiss, Owen M., 1976. Groups and the Equal Protection Clause. *Philosophy and Public Affairs,* 5, 107–77.

Fleurbaey, Marc, 1995. Equal Opportunity or Equal Social Outcome. *Economics and Philosophy,* 11, 25–55.

Fleurbaey, Marc, 2001. Egalitarian Opportunities. *Law and Philosophy,* 20, 499–530.

Fleurbaey, Marc, 2008. *Fairness, Responsibility, and Welfare.* Oxford: Oxford University Press.

Fleurbaey, Marc, 2010. Review of Shlomi Segall's 'Health, Luck, and Justice'. *Utilitas,* 22, 503–6.

Frankfurt, Harry, 1987. Equality as a Moral Ideal. *Ethics,* 98, 21–43.

Frankfurt, Harry, 1997. Equality and Respect. *Social Research,* 64, 3–15.

Frankfurt, Harry, 1997. Equality as a Moral Ideal. In Louis P. Pojman, and Robert Westermoreland (eds), *Equality: Selected Readings.* New York and Oxford: Oxford University Press, 261–73.

Gardner, John, 1989. Liberals and Unlawful Discrimination. *Oxford Journal of Legal Studies,* 9, 1–22.

Gheaus, Anca, 2009. How Much of What Matters Can We Redistribute: Love, Justice, and Luck. *Hypatia,* 24, 63–83.

Goldman, Alan H. 1976. Affirmative Action. *Philosophy and Public Affairs* 5, 178–95.

Gomberg, Paul, 2007. *How to Make Opportunity Equal? Race and Contributive Justice.* Malden, MA: Blackwell.

Goodin, Robert E., 1988. *Reasons for Welfare: The Political Theory of the Welfare State.* Princeton, NJ: Princeton University Press.

Goodwin, Barbara, 2005. *Justice by Lottery.* Exeter: Imprints Academic.

Green, Simon J. D., 1989. Competitive Equality of Opportunity: A Defence. *Ethics,* 100, 5–32.

Grey, Thomas C., 1973. The First Virtue. *Stanford Law Review,* 25, 286–327.

Guttman, Amy, 1987, *Democratic Education.* Princeton, NJ: Princeton University Press.

Harris, John, 1999. Justice and Equal Opportunities in Health Care. *Bioethics,* 13, 392–413.

Hausman, Daniel M. 2011. Review of Shlomi Segall, 'Health, Luck, and Justice'. *Economics and Philosophy,* 22, 190–7.

Hausman, Daniel M., and Waldren Matt, 2011. Egalitarianism Reconsidered. *The Journal of Moral Philosophy,* 8, 567–86.

Hellman, Deborah, 2008. *When is Discrimination Wrong?* Cambridge, MA: Harvard University Press.

Hernstein, Richard J., and Murray, Charles A., 1994. *The Bell Curve: Intelligence and Culture Structure in American Life.* New York: The Free Press.

Holmes, Elisa, 2005. Anti-Discrimination Rights without Equality. *The Modern Law Review,* 68, 175–94.

Holtug, Nils, and Lippert-Rasmussen, Kasper, 2007. An Introduction to Contemporary Egalitarianism. In their, *Egalitarianism: New Essays on the Nature and Value of Equality.* Oxford: Oxford University Press.

Howard University website. National Human Genome Center, <http://www.genomecenter.howard.edu/>.

Howe, Kenneth R., 1989. In Defence of Outcome-Based Conceptions of Equal Educational Opportunity. *Educational Theory,* 39, 317–36.

Howe, Kenneth R., 1990. Equal Opportunity is Equal Education. *Educational Theory,* 40, 227–30.

Howe, Kenneth R., 1993. Equality of Educational Opportunity and the Criterion of Equal Educational Worth. *Studies in Philosophy and Education,* 11, 329–37.

Hurka, Thomas, 2003. Desert: Individualistic and Holistic. In Olsaretti, Serena (ed.), *Desert and Justice.* Oxford: Oxford University Press, 45–68.

Hurley, Susan L., 2004. *Justice, Luck and Knowledge.* Cambridge, MA: Harvard University Press.

Jacobs, Lesley A., 2004. *Pursuing Equal Opportunities: The Theory and Practice of Egalitarian Justice.* Cambridge: Cambridge University Press.

Jencks, Christopher, 1988. Whom Must We Treat Equally for Educational Opportunity to Be Equal? *Ethics,* 98, 518–25.

Kahn, Jonathan, 2004. How a Drug Becomes 'Ethnic': Law, Commerce, and the Production of Racial Categories in Medicine'. *Yale Journal of Health Policy, Law, and Ethics,* 4, 1–46.

Kamm, Frances M., 2001. Health and Equality of Opportunity. *American Journal of Bioethics,* 1, 17–19.

Kelman, Mark, 2001. Market Discrimination and Groups. *Stanford Law Review,* 53, 833–96.

Knight, Carl, 2011. Inequality, Avoidability, and Healthcare: On Shlomi Segall 'Health, Luck, and Justice'. *Iyyun: The Jerusalem Philosophical Quarterly,* 60, 74–7.

Kochanek, Kenneth D., Xu, Jiaquan, Murphy, Sherry L., Miniño, Arialdi M., and Kung, Hsiang-Ching, 2011. Deaths: Preliminary Data for 2009. *National Vital Statistics Report,* 59, 1–68.

Kymlicka, Will, 2002. *Contemporary Political Philosophy.* Oxford: Oxford University Press.

Lake, Christopher, 2001. *Equality and Responsibility.* Oxford: Oxford University Press.

Lareau, Annette, 2003. *Unequal Childhoods.* Berkeley, CA: University of California Press.

Lazenby, Hugh, 2010. One Kiss Too Many? Giving, Luck Egalitarianism, and Other-Affecting Choice. *The Journal of Political Philosophy,* 18, 271–86.

LeGrande, Julian, 1987. Equity, Health, and Health Care. *Social Justice Research,* 1, 257–74.

LeGrande, Julian, 1991. *Equity and Choice: An Essay in Economics and Applied Philosophy.* London: Harper Collins.

LeGrande, Julian, 2013. Responsibility, Health, and Health Care. In Eyal, Nir, Hurst, Samia A., Norheim, Ole F., and Wikler, Daniel (eds), *Inequalities in Health: Concepts, Measures, and Ethics.* Oxford: Oxford University Press.

Lippert-Rasmussen, Kasper, 1999. Arneson on Equality of Opportunity for Welfare. *Journal of Political Philosophy,* 7, 478–87.

Lippert-Rasmussen, Kasper, 2001. Egalitarianism, Option Luck, and Responsibility. *Ethics,* 111, 548–79.

Lippert-Rasmussen, Kasper, 2005. Hurley on Egalitarianism and the Luck-Neutralizing Aim. *Politics, Philosophy, and Economics,* 4, 249–65.

Lippert-Rasmussen, Kasper, 2006. Private Discrimination: a Prioritarian, Desert-Based Account. *San Diego Law Review,* 43, 817–56.

Lippert-Rasmussen, Kasper, 2006. The Badness of Discrimination. *Ethical Theory and Moral Practice,* 9, 167–85.

Lippert-Rasmussen, Kasper, 2007. Nothing Personal: On Statistic Discrimination. *The Journal of Political Philosophy,* 15, 385–403.

Lippert-Rasmussen, Kasper, 2009. Reaction Qualifications Revisited. *Social Theory and Practice,* 35, 413–39.

Lippert-Rasmussen, Kasper, 2011. 'We are All Different': Statistical Discrimination and the Right to be Treated as an Individual. *The Journal of Ethics,* 15, 47–59.

Lippert-Rasmussen, Kasper, 2012. Intentions and Discrimination in Hiring. *Journal of Moral Philosophy,* 9, 55–74.

Llavador, Humberto G. and Roemer, John E., 2001. An Equal-Opportunity Approach to the Allocation of International Aid. *Journal of Development Economics*, 64, 147–71.

Lloyd Thomas, David A., 1997. Competitive Equality of Opportunity. *Mind*, 86, 388–404.

Macleod, Colin M., 2002. Liberal Equality and the Affective Family. In David Archard, and Colin M. Macleod (eds), *The Moral and Political Status of Children*. Oxford: Oxford University Press, 210–30.

Macleod, Colin, 2010. Justice, Educational Equality, and Sufficiency. *Canadian Journal of Philosophy*, 36, 151–75.

Margalit, Avishai, 1996. *The Decent Society*. Princeton, NJ: Princeton University Press.

Marmot, Michael, 2004. *The Status Syndrome: How Social Standing Affects Our Health and Longevity*. New York: Times Books.

Marmot, Michael, and Wilkinson, Richard G., 2006. *Social Determinants of Health*. Oxford: Oxford University Press.

Mason, Andrew, 2001. Equality of Opportunity: Old and New. *Ethics*, 111, 760–81.

Mason, Andrew, 2006. *Levelling the Playing Field: The Idea of Equality of Opportunity and its Place in Egalitarian Thought*. Oxford: Oxford University Press.

Mason, Andrew, 2011. Putting Story-Telling to Bed: A Reply to Segall. *Critical Review of International Social and Political Philosophy (CRISPP)*, 14, 82–5.

Mason, Andrew, 2012. *Living Together as Equals: The Demands of Citizenship*. Oxford: Oxford University Press.

Mill, John Stuart, 1869 (1975). On the Subjection of Women. In *Three Essays*. Oxford and New York: Oxford University Press.

Miller, David, 1982. Arguments for Equality. *Midwest Studies in Philosophy*, 7, 73–87.

Miller, David, 1998. Equality and Justice. In Mason, Andrew (ed.), *Ideals of Equality*. Oxford: Blackwell, 21–36.

Miller, David, 1999. *Principles of Social Justice*. Cambridge, MA: Harvard University Press.

Miller, David, 2002. Liberalism, Equal Opportunities and Cultural Commitment. In Held, David, and Kelly, Paul (eds), *Multiculturalism Reconsidered*. Cambridge: Polity Press.

Miller, David, 2009. Equality of Opportunity and the Family. In Satz, Debra, and Reich, Rob (eds), *Toward a Humanist Justice: The Political Philosophy of Susan Moller Okin*. Oxford: Oxford University Press, 93–112.

Moreau, Sophia, 2010. Discrimination as Negligence. *Canadian Journal of Philosophy*, 36, 123–49.

Moreau, Sophia, 2010. What is Discrimination? *Philosophy and Public Affairs,* 38, 143–79.

Munoz-Darde, Veronique, 1999. Is the Family to be Abolished Then? *Proceedings of the Aristotelian Society,* 99, 37–56.

Murphy, Liam, 1998. Institutions and the Demands of Justice. *Philosophy and Public Affairs,* 27, 251–91.

Murphy, Liam, and Nagel, Thomas, 2002. *The Myth of Ownership: Taxes and Justice.* Oxford: Oxford University Press.

Murray, Christopher J. L., 1996. Rethinking DALYs. In Murray, Christopher J. L., and Lopez, Alan D. (eds), *The Global Burden of Disease.* Cambridge, MA: Harvard School of Public Health, World Health Organization, World Bank, 1–98.

Nagel, Thomas, 1973. Equal Treatment and Compensatory Discrimination, *Philosophy and Public Affairs,* 2, 348–63.

Nagel, Thomas, 1979. *Mortal Questions.* Cambridge: Cambridge University Press.

Nagel, Thomas, 1991. *Equality and Partiality.* Oxford: Clarendon Press.

Nagel, Thomas, 2005. The Problem with Global Justice. *Philosophy and Public Affairs,* 33, 113–47.

Norman, Richard, 1998. The Social Basis of Equality. In Mason, Andrew (ed.), *Ideals of Equality.* Oxford: Blackwell, 37–51.

Nozick, Robert, 1974. *Anarchy, State, and Utopia.* Oxford: Blackwell.

O'Brian, William E., 2010. Equality in Law and Philosophy. *Inquiry,* 53, 266.

O'Neill, Martin, 2008. What Should Egalitarians Believe? *Philosophy and Public Affairs,* 36, 119–56.

Olsaretti, Serena, 2009. Responsibility and the Consequences of Choice. *Proceedings of the Aristotelian Society,* 109, 165–88.

Olsaretti, Serena, 2009. Review of A. Mason's 'Levelling the Playing Field: The Ideal of Equality of Opportunity and its Place in Egalitarian Thought'. *The Journal of Moral Philosophy,* 6, 133–6.

Olson, Kristi A., 2012. Review of Jennifer Prah Ruger's 'Health and Social Justice' and Shlomi Segall's 'Health, Luck, and Justice'. *Perspectives on Politics,* 491.

Otsuka, Michael, 2002. Luck, Insurance, and Equality. *Ethics,* 113, 40–54.

Otsuka, Michael, 2004. Equality, Ambition, and Insurance. *Proceedings of the Aristotelian Society,* 78, 166.

Parfit, Derek, 1995. Equality or Priority? *The Lindley Lectures.* Lawrence, Kansas: Lawrence University of Kansas Press.

Parfit, Derek, 1997. Equality and Priority. *Ratio,* 10, 214.

Peters, Christopher, 1997. Equality Revisited. *Harvard Law Review,* 110, 1201–64.

Pogge, Thomas W., 2000. On the Site of Distributive Justice: Reflections on Cohen and Murphy. *Philosophy and Public Affairs,* 29, 137–69.

Radcliffe Richards, Janet, 1997. Equality of Opportunity. *Ratio,* 10, 253–79.

Rawls, John, 1971. *A Theory of Justice*. Oxford: Clarendon Press.

Rawls, John, 1996. *Political Liberalism*. New York: Columbia University Press.

Rawls, John, 1999. Social Unity and Primary Goods. In his *Collected Papers*. Cambridge, MA: Harvard University Press.

Rawls, John, 2001. *Justice as Fairness: A Restatement*. Cambridge, MA: The Belknap Press of Harvard University Press.

Raz, Joseph, 1986. *The Morality of Freedom*. Oxford: Oxford University Press.

Ripstein, Arthur, 1999. *Equality, Responsibility, and the Law*. Cambridge: Cambridge University Press.

Risse, Mathias, and Zeckhauser, Richard, 2004. Racial Profiling. *Philosophy and Public Affairs*, 32, 131–70.

Roemer, John E., 1989. *Distributing Health: The Allocation of Resources by an International Agency*. Washington, DC: World Institute for Development Economics Research of the United Nations University.

Roemer, John E., 1993. A Pragmatic Theory of Responsibility for the Egalitarian Planner. *Philosophy and Public Affairs*, 22, 146–66.

Roemer, John E., 1998. *Equality of Opportunity*. Cambridge, MA; London, England: Harvard University Press.

Roemer, John E., 2003. Defending Equality of Opportunity. *The Monist*, 86, 272–9.

Roemer, John E., 2010. Jerry Cohen's Why Not Socialism: Some Thoughts. *The Journal of Ethics*, 14, 255–62.

Rothstein, Richard, 2003. *Class and Schools*. Washington, DC: Economic Policy Institute.

Sandbu, Martin E., 2004. On Dworkin's Brute-Luck-Option-Luck Distinction and the Consistency of Brute-Luck Egalitarianism. *Politics, Philosophy, & Economics*, 3, 283–312.

Satz, Debra, 2007. Equality, Adequacy, and Education for Citizenship. *Ethics*, 117, 623–48.

Scanlon, Thomas S., 2003. *The Difficulty of Tolerance: Essays in Political Philosophy*. Cambridge: Cambridge University Press.

Schaar, John, 1967. Equality of Opportunity and Beyond. In Pennock, J. Roland, and Chapman, J. W. (eds), *Nomos IX: Equality*. New York: Atherton Press, 230–1.

Schauer, Frederick, 2003. *Profiles, Probabilities, and Stereotypes*. Cambridge, MA, and London: The Belknap Press of Harvard University Press.

Scheffler, Samuel, 2003. What is Egalitarianism? *Philosophy and Public Affairs*, 31, 5–39.

Scheffler, Samuel, 2010. *Equality and Tradition: Questions of Value in Moral and Political Theory*. Oxford: Oxford University Press.

Schemmel, Christian, 2012. Distributive and Relational Equality. *Politics, Philosophy, & Economics*, 11, 123–48.

Schemmel, Christian, 2012. Luck Egalitarianism as Democratic Reciprocity? A Response to Tan. *The Journal of Philosophy*, 109, 435–48.

Segall, Shlomi, 2007. In Solidarity with the Imprudent: A Defense of Luck Egalitarianism. *Social Theory and Practice*, 33, 177–98.

Segall, Shlomi, 2007. Is Health Care (Still) Special? *Journal of Political Philosophy*, 15, 342–63.

Segall, Shlomi, 2010. *Health, Luck, and Justice*. Princeton, NJ: Princeton University Press.

Segall, Shlomi, 2010. Is Health (Really) Special: Health Policy between Rawlsian and Luck Egalitarian Justice. *The Journal of Applied Philosophy*, 27, 344–58.

Segall, Shlomi, 2012. Health, Luck, and Justice Revisited. *Ethical Perspectives*, 19, 325–34.

Sen, Amartya, 1992. *Inequality Reexamined*. Oxford: Clarendon Press.

Sen, Amartya, 2002. Why Health Equity? *Health Economics*, 11, 659–66.

Sen, Amartya, 2009. *The Idea of Justice*. Cambridge, MA: The Belknap Press of Harvard University Press.

Sher, George, 1988. Qualification, Fairness, and Desert. In Norman E. Bowie (ed.), *Equal Opportunity*. Boulder, CO: Westview, 113–27.

Sher, George, 1997. *Approximate Justice: Studies in Non-Ideal Theory*. Lanham, MD: Rowman and Littlefield.

Sher, George, 1999. Diversity. *Philosophy and Public Affairs*, 28, 85–104.

Shiffrin, Seana Valentine, 2000. Paternalism, the Unconscionability Doctrine, and Accommodation. *Philosophy and Public Affairs*, 29, 239.

Shiffrin, Seana Valentine, 2004. Race, Labor, and the Fair Equality of Opportunity Principle. *Fordham Law Review*, 72, 1643–75.

Shin, Patrick, 2009. The Substantive Principle of Equal Treatment. *Legal Theory*, 15, 149–72.

Silvers, Anita, 1998. Formal Justice. In Anita Silvers, David Wasserman, and Mary B. Mahowald (eds), *Disability, Difference, Discrimination: Perspectives on Justice in Bioethics and Public Policy*. Lanham, MD: Rowman & Littlefield, 13–145.

Singer, Peter, 1993. *Practical Ethics*, 2nd edition. Cambridge: Cambridge University Press.

Sreenivasan, Gopal, 2007. Health Care and Equality of Opportunity. *Hastings Centre Report*, 37, 31–41.

Stemplowska, Zofia, 2009. Making Justice Sensitive to Responsibility. *Political Studies*, 57, 237–59.

Stemplowska, Zofia, 2011. Responsibility and Respect: Reconciling Two Egalitarian Visions. In Knight, Carl, and Stemplowska, Zofia (eds), *Responsibility and Distributive Justice*. Oxford: Oxford University Press, 115–35.

Stemplowska, Zofia, 2012. Luck Egalitarianism. In Gaus, Gerald, and D'Agostino, Fred (eds), *The Routledge Companion to Social and Political Philosophy*. Abingdon: Routledge, 389–400.

Stone, Peter, 2011. *The Luck of the Draw: The Role of Lotteries in Decision-Making.* New York: Oxford University Press.

Streitmatter, Janice L., 1999. *For Girls Only: Making a Case for Single-Sex Schooling.* Albany, NY: State University of New York Press.

Sunstein, Cass, 1994. The Anticaste Principle. *Michigan Law Review*, 92, 2410–55.

Surtees, Robert, and Blau, Nenad, 2000. The Neurochemistry of Phenylketonuria. *European Journal of Pediatrics*, 169, S109–S113.

Swift, Adam, 2003. *How Not To Be a Hypocrite: School Choice for the Morally Perplexed Parent.* London and New York: Routledge.

Swift, Adam, 2005. Justice, Luck, and the Family: The Intergenerational Transmission of Economic Advantage from a Normative Perspective. *In* Bowles, Samuel, Gintis, Herbert, and Osborne-Groves, Melissa (eds), *Unequal Chances: Family Background and Economic Success.* Princeton, NJ: Princeton University Press, 256–76.

Swift, Adam, 2008. The Value of Philosophy in Nonideal Circumstances. *Social Theory and Practice*, 34, 363–87.

Synnott, Marcia, 1982. The Half Opened Door: Researching Administration Discrimination at Harvard, Yale, and Princeton. *The American Archivist*, 45 (2), 186.

Tan, Kok-Chor, 2008. A Defence of Luck Egalitarianism. *The Journal of Philosophy*, 105, 665–90.

Tan, Kok-Chor, 2012. *Justice, Institutions, and Luck: The Site, Ground, and Scope of Equality.* Oxford: Oxford University Press.

Taylor, Anne L. et al., 2004. Combination of Isosorbide Dinitrate and Hydralazine in Blacks with Heart Failure. *New England Journal of Medicine*, 351, 2049–57.

Taylor, Robert S., 2009. Rawlsian Affirmative Action. *Ethics*, 119, 476–506.

Temkin, Larry, 2003. Egalitarianism Defended. *Ethics*, 113, 764–82.

Temkin, Larry, 2011. Justice, Equality, Fairness, Desert, Rights, Free Will, Responsibility, and Luck. In Carl Knight, and Zofia Stemplowska (eds), *Responsibility and Distributive Justice.* Oxford: Oxford University Press, 51–77.

Tomlin, Patrick, 2013. Choice, Chance, and Change: Luck Egalitarianism over Time. *Ethical Theory and Moral Practice*, 16, 393–407.

Tooley, James, 1995. *Disestablishing the School.* Aldershot: Avebury Press.

U.S. Equal Employment Opportunity Commission website. Pregnancy Discrimination, <http://www.eeoc.gov/laws/types/pregnancy.cfm>.

Vallentyne, Peter, 2002. Brute Luck, Option Luck, and Equality of Initial Opportunities. *Ethics*, 112, 529–57.

Vallentyne, Peter, 2003. Brute Luck Equality and Desert. In Serena Olsaretti (ed.), *Desert and Justice.* Oxford: Oxford University Press, 169–85.

Vallentyne, Peter, 2006. Hurley on Justice and Responsibility. *Philosophy and Phenomenological Research*, 72, 433–8.

Vallentyne, Peter, 2007. Of Mice and Men: Equality and Animals. In Holtug, Nils, and Lippert-Rasmussen, Kasper (eds), *Egalitarianism: New Essays on the Nature and Value of Equality*. Oxford: Clarendon Press, 211–38.

Van Oyen, T., Tafforeau, J., and Roelands, M., 1996. Regional Inequities in Health Expectancy in Belgium. *Social Science and Medicine*, 43 (11), 1673–8.

Van Parijs, Philippe. Talking to Stanley: What Do We Need for Global Justice to Make Sense, Keynote speech at the Annual Conference of the Association for Legal and Social Philosophy, Trinity College, Dublin 29 June 2006, <http://www.uclouvain.be/cps/ucl/doc/etes/documents/Van_Parijs_-_Oxford_1.pdf>.

Voigt, Kristin, 2007. Individual Choice and Unequal Participation in Higher Education. *Theory and Research in Education*, 5, 87–112.

Walzer, Michael, 1983. *Spheres of Justice: A Defence of Equality and Pluralism*. Oxford: Basic Books.

Wertheimer, Alan, 1983. Jobs, Qualifications, and Preferences. *Ethics*, 94, 99–112.

Westen, Peter, 1982. The Empty Idea of Equality. *Harvard Law Review*, 95, 537–96.

Westen, Peter, 1985. The Concept of Equal Opportunity. *Ethics*, 95, 837–50.

WHO Health Report 2011. <http://www.who.int/whosis/whostat/2011/en/index.html>.

Wilson, John, 1991. Does Equality (of Opportunity) Make Sense in Education? *Journal of Philosophy of Education*, 25, 28.

Wolff, Jonathan, 1998. Fairness, Respect, and the Egalitarian Ethos. *Philosophy and Public Affairs*, 27, 97–122.

Wolff, Jonathan, and de Shalit, Avner, 2007. *Disadvantage*. Oxford: Oxford University Press.

Index

Printed and bound by CPI Group (UK) Ltd, Croydon, CR0 4YY